By the same Author

TIGERLAND

Tiger!

The Story of the Indian Tiger

KAILASH SANKHALA

SIMON AND SCHUSTER

NEW YORK

Library of Congress Cataloging in Publication Data

Sankhala, Kailash, date.
Tiger!

Includes index.
1. Tigers.   I. Title.
QL737.C23S25   599'.74428   77-11116
ISBN 0-671-22595-2

Contents

Illustrations

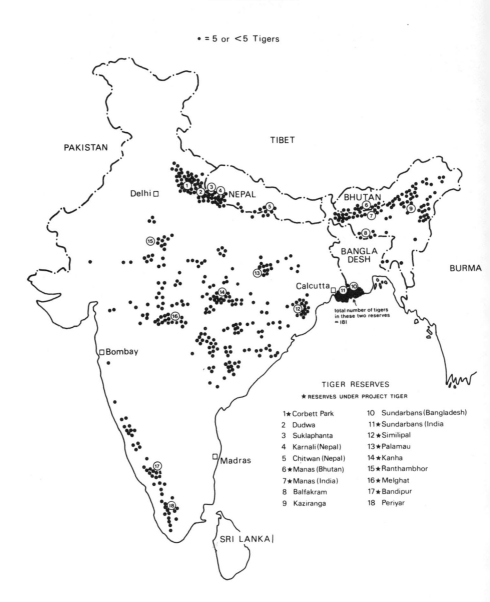

INDIA

DISTRIBUTION OF TIGERS

(1972 official census)

• = 5 or <5 Tigers

PAKISTAN

TIBET

Delhi □   NEPAL

BHUTAN

BANGLA
DESH

BURMA

Calcutta □

total number of tigers
in these two reserves
= 181

□ Bombay

TIGER RESERVES

★ RESERVES UNDER PROJECT TIGER

1 ★	Corbett Park	10	Sundarbans (Bangladesh)
2	Dudwa	11 ★	Sundarbans (India
3	Suklaphanta	12 ★	Similipal
4	Karnali (Nepal)	13 ★	Palamau
5	Chitwan (Nepal)	14 ★	Kanha
6 ★	Manas (Bhutan)	15 ★	Ranthambhor
7 ★	Manas (India)	16 ★	Melghat
8	Balfakram	17 ★	Bandipur
9	Kaziranga	18	Periyar

□ Madras

SRI LANKA

A map of India, showing the distribution of tigers and the various tiger reserves. For a detailed analysis see page 176 and following.

Acknowledgments

The Jawaharlal Nehru Memorial Fund provided me with the time and resources to pursue my study of the tiger. I am grateful to Dr Karan Singh, its Secretary, for giving me the opportunity to fulfil my ambition of undertaking such a study. His subsequent encouragement and guidance as Chairman of Project Tiger have been in valuable.

A photo-naturalist, especially if he stays for long – and he generally does – can be a nuisance; but wherever I went for my field studies I received the active co-operation of my forester colleagues. I am particularly thankful to Bharat Singh, O. P. Mathur, J. P. Kapur, Fateh Singh, Y. D. Singh of Rajasthan and H. S. Panwar, Field Director of Kanha, for tolerating my presence.

In my search for tigers in prehistory and history I depended largely on the goodwill of Munish Joshi of the Archaeological Survey of India and Dr Shivram Murty, K. N. Dixit, Dr Brahm Dutta and O. P. Sharma of the National Museum who opened their "restricted treasures" to me. The co-operation of the officers of the Oriental Research Institute, Jodhpur, Baksh Oriental public library, Patna, and the Khuda of the India Intenational Centre enabled me to pursue my studies of the tiger through the ages. Dr H. K. Khan helped me to search for fossil cats. Discussions with M. Krishnan, the noted naturalist-writer, always enriched me and he read the first draft of this book.

Bahadur Singh of Bundi, Bhim Singh of Kotah and Martend Singh of Rewa permitted me to have free access to their hunting diaries.

I have drawn heavily on the resources of Delhi Zoo, which was almost like my own laboratory for conducting experiments under controlled conditions. I am grateful to the Keepers and Rangers, and to O. P. Bhatnagar, Mohan Singh and J. H. Desai, Joint Director, in particular. Kashinath, a living legend in Indian pictorials, and A. R. Tak, doyen of professional photography, guided me in planning my photographic documentation. Champalal and Brahm Deo traced drawings from my photographs, and Chandra Mohan helped me to prepare the manuscript. I am thankful to all of them.

I was kept informed of the latest literature on the subject by Dr Gustav Krik of West Germany, Dr Theodore H. Reed, Director of the National Zoological Park at Washington DC, William G. Conway, Director of New York Zoological Park, and Professor Malcolm Coe of Oxford University. Dr M. L. Roonwal, Scientist Emeritus, guided me throughout the project. Dr Bernhard Grzimek solved my problem of long lenses and a bigger format camera by lending his equipment. I am indebted to them all.

I shall not forget the advice and help of the late S. S. Negi and Dr R. N. Misra of the Wildlife Preservation Society of India, of N. N. Sen, and of my friends A. K. Roy, Sohan and Kalyan Singh with whom I spent days discussing my plan of study. Valuable suggestions were made by S. K. Seth, Inspector General of Forests, and the whole script read by Sir Hugh Elliot, who suggested several important changes.

I would like to thank many more individuals, especially the Field Directors of the Reserves; omission of their names owing to lack of space in no way underestimates their help and my gratitude to them. I would also particularly like to thank Mrs Sonia Cole, for all her work on my typescript, and Miss Jane Scott, who is responsible for designing the book. My wife Suraj assumed my responsibilities by staying at home during my long absences on field studies, and I thank her and my son Pradeep who read my drafts and helped in field photography.

In my crusade to save the tiger the greatest encouragement came from the late Miss Padmaja Naidu. Unfortunately the work was not completed in time for her to see the results.

Above all I am grateful to the late Sir William Collins for his valuable advice in shaping the book. Together with Lady Collins he shared many excursions into tigerland with me. I received his letter planning a visit to the Tiger Reserve at Kanha and the sad news of his death on the same day; I wish he had lived to see the book published.

In great respect and admiration I dedicate this book to Miss Naidu and to Billy Collins.

Introduction

This book might be called the autobiography of a tiger addict, but I have tried to keep my personal story down to a minimum as the hero is the tiger, not myself, and it is his biography that I wish to write. However, my whole life has been closely bound up with his and any new contributions I have been able to make about him are based on my own observations.

It is impossible to study the tiger in isolation – or for that matter any wild animal – without distorting the picture. The tiger is part of the land of India, intimately connected with his terrain and his neighbours, and therefore they too must come into the story. The outstanding riches of India's wildlife, which compare very favourably with the more publicized fauna of Africa, are perhaps not sufficiently realized. Part I of this book, therefore, is concerned not only with tigers but also with their land and its inhabitants.

The tiger's attributes – what one might call the essential "tigerness" of tigers – have made him into nature's most efficient predator. In the first three chapters I describe what I have learnt about his methods of hunting, attack and killing, as well as the more intimate aspects of tiger family life. The tiger is closely linked with his habitat and of course with his prey; but he also has close ties with his co-predators and camp followers, the scavengers who profit by his kills and clean up the environment after he has finished his meals. Tigerland and the animals that live in it are the subject of the next three chapters. All the inhabitants of this closely interwoven system live in harmony and balance with one notable exception: modern man.

The second part of the book concerns man's relationship with and attitudes towards the tiger. In the past these attitudes oscillated between worship and persecution, as outlined in chapter 7. The myths that grew up about tigers included often unjustified accusations of man-eating, forming a ready excuse to kill and plunder. Until recent times man's lust for hunting was limited by the weapons at his disposal, but within the last century the dice have been loaded so heavily against the tiger that it seemed he was doomed to extinction. My life has been dedicated to preventing this from happening, and in fact most of Part II is an account of one man's relationship with the tiger: my own.

My years in the Indian Forest Service provided wonderful opportunities to study tigers and tiger country, but many details of, for example, birth and growth are impossible to obtain in the wild. As Director of Delhi Zoo 1965–70 – and with a tiger in my own home! – I was able to conduct experiments and compile careful records of such matters. During this time also I followed the fortunes and genetic history of the fabulous white tigers of Rewa, many of which we bred in Delhi Zoo. These events are recorded in chapters 8–10.

In order to convince people that the situation of wild tigers was desperately urgent I set out on the task of making a one-man count of them in their far-flung habitats all over India (chapter 11). The Indian Government then stepped in and conducted a formal census, and the figures we arrived at were not very different: only about 2000 wild tigers left, compared with some 30,000 within my own lifetime.

There are innumerable reasons for this disastrous decline, notably man's destruction of the habitat for forest produce and to obtain more grazing lands for his cattle. With the population pressure as it is today this can be understood, even condoned; but what cannot be forgiven is man's greed for trophies and skins. The tiger has always suffered because of his glorious skin, and my personal investigations into this trade (chapter 12) revealed truly alarming figures. Tourism is said to be an "industry without smoke", yet in the 1950s and early 1960s it consumed more than 3000 tigers for the sake of trophies. The ban on shooting was not imposed until 1970, and it was only just in time.

The shock caused by the figures revealed in the census and those obtained by my investigations into the skin trade created a favourable climate of public opinion for the launching of Project Tiger (chapter 13). In 1972 this experiment in wildlife ecology was given the blessing of the Prime Minister, and was supported by conservationists all over the world. The tiger cannot be preserved in isolation and if he is to survive the whole habitat must also be preserved in certain selected areas. This is what we have done, and are still doing in our tiger reserves. I am proud to have served as Project Tiger's first executive director and happy beyond description to see my life's ambition to save the tiger fulfilled.

In this book I hope to show that the tiger must be preserved not only for its intrinsic beauty but also so that man himself may live in harmony with the whole of nature in my homeland of India. My entire life has been a tiger project, and the birth of Project Tiger was its culmination. To see how my personal project came about it is necessary to give some account of my background.

My home State of Rajasthan in northern India derives its name from *Registhan*, "land of sand", and indeed 50% of it is part of the Thar desert. It is famed for its wildlife and for tiger hunting or *shikar*, and its hunting registers record all the well-known names of the British Raj, from George V to Queen Elizabeth and Prince Philip.

I was born at Jodhpur on the fringe of the desert where the first rains are greeted with feasting and ceremonial drenching. My people came from still further west, almost from the heart of the desert of Jaisalmer where the phenomenon of water falling from the sky has to be explained to children. Just when they left Jaisalmer is not known, but their exodus must have been in a year of exceptional drought, and they settled in the first depression which had even a trickle of water. This village, Chopsani, six miles from Jodhpur, featured in the history of the two world wars as the school of the gallant soldiers of the Jodhpur Risala.

My father was a forest ranger, and his area in the Aravali Hills was famous for sloth bears and leopards. In many of the villages it was not safe to be out after sunset as the paths were virtually taken over by leopards on the prowl looking for goats and dogs. We children had strict instructions to return home before dark to avoid encounters with wild boars or hyenas. Jodhpur was once the finest region for antelopes and often we would see a herd of blackbuck* on the way to school. The richness of the blackbuck population, which lingers even today in some pockets (Dholi Sanctuary, near Jodhpur, for instance) was partly due to religious protection by the Vishnoi community, but the main protection for all wildlife in those days was by princely decree; only the Maharaja and members of his family could shoot. Instances are on record where the Maharaja pardoned a crime of murder but exiled those who shot leopards or tigers without permission. Even in cases of defence of property people would wait for the shikar officers rather than take the law into their own hands: benefit of the doubt was always given to the animals.

My father lost his father at the age of six, and was brought up by my grandmother, who earned a precarious living on our small farm. Although totally uneducated herself, she respected education and somehow managed to send her son to school. Afterwards my father trained in surveying and engineering, eventually becoming sub-overseer with a construction company which was building the Maharaja of Jodhpur's palace. Then the State Department needed a field surveyor, and to do this work my father was appointed Forest Ranger – even though he had had no training in forestry. My mother augmented the family income by keeping dairy animals, and I still begrudge her affection for the calves and our occasional neglect when it came to sharing the milk.

Foresters' sons do not settle down well. Partly this is due to living in primitive conditions with no educational facilities, or with frequent changes of village schools. The lack of playmates and social life make such children shy, which is not helpful when it comes to competing in life. My father earned less than Rs 60 a month (about £4) and it was not possible for his four children to board out, so my mother stayed at Jodhpur for our schooling while my father lived mostly by himself in the forests. I was the only one of the family who could go on to college.

Having failed to become an engineer himself, my father very much wanted

* For specific names see chapters 4–6.

me to succeed as one, for the profession had much prestige and was well paid. In order to study engineering at college I had to offer mathematics; I attended two lectures on trigonometry but failed to understand it so, without my father's knowledge, I changed to biology. By the time he came to know about this it was too late for the decision to be changed.

Biology I liked. My interest was in plants, especially the desert plants. Early in my college career an offer came to join an expedition to cross the Thar desert in May, the hottest month. The idea was to study the ecology in the worst period. I joined as botanist and photographer, and although the leader of the expedition was a fraud and the project collapsed I learned in that short time to love the desert. At first sight animal life appears to be non-existent, but late in the evening the desert comes to life. Hedgehogs, hares, rats and insects become active and their predators – foxes, both red and silver, and snakes – look for an easy meal. Even a small group of chinkara gazelles crossed the sand dunes with the same ease as they negotiate rocky hills and ravines. Already I had identified what was to become India's first and only Desert National Park; I had to wait until 1970 to initiate the idea, and I pursued it for another seven years, so my ultimate success in establishing it was particularly satisfying.

On my return to college I prepared an 8 mm film on vegetation types which I submitted as part of the course leading to a Master's degree. Although it gained me no credit at college it put me at the head of the queue for selection to the Forest Service. By that time the princely States had merged and appointments to the Forest Service, previously given to the chosen few, were extended to everyone. Overnight I became a potential forester. My father, whose interest in wildlife and plants had by then led him to become Director of Jodhpur Zoo, at last had a sparkle in his eye: his son was settled, and in his own old profession.

I joined the Indian Forest College at Dehra Dun and two years passed uneventfully measuring heights and diameters at "breast height" (which seemed to me a curious word to use in forestry, since neither trees nor foresters have breasts). During my training period all that I learned about wildlife management was how to protect trees from animals and whether seven strands of wire, a deep trench or an electric fence would best hold back elephants or deer from plantations. But this training reinforced my love of outdoor life and gave me a clear understanding of forest ecology and the different habitats of India's wildlife.

At one time I was tempted to switch to history..In medieval times Rajasthan was divided into small principalities which were always fighting among themselves, and each one built forts for its defence. I became fascinated by these ruins. Overgrown with grasses and creepers, their wells filled with debris, these fortresses are now the haunt of tigers, leopards, hyenas and jackals; but they have witnessed forgotten events of history, feuds and atrocities and human sufferings. They seem to echo to the galloping hooves of horses, the rattle of swords, the cries of dying soldiers, and the melancholy wails of women ready to jump into the fire to save their honour rather than fall into the hands of the invaders. I was sorely tempted to try to unearth the hidden romance of these places, but Bora, my senior colleague, advised me not to be diverted from my chosen field. His advice was sound. A lifetime is insufficient to study the natural history of the living, which must surely be of more interest and importance than the history of the dead.

I have never regretted my time in the Forest Service, with its fine century-old tradition of conservation. This training, augmented at intervals by short courses on ecology and park administration both in India and the USA, made me a purist. The unlimited opportunities of studying nature under the sun and the stars I got only as a forester. And above all I was able to live with tigers in the wild for days and nights on end, often in full knowledge of each other's presence but probably even more often in ignorance of it.

My first posting was to Bundi, once a tiny princely State. In Colonel William Rice's book *Hunting in Rajputana* (1857) he mentions that there were more tigers in Bundi than in any other area where he shot, so I reported for duty on 1 April 1953 with even more than the usual enthusiasm of a young forester. In those days the maharajas, though without power, were still VIPs, and protocol demanded that I should pay my respects. I duly turned up at the Maharaja's palace in a loading truck and was conducted through his trophy room where tigers, tigresses and even unborn cubs were displayed along with antelopes' and deers' heads. The shikar registers were meticulously kept, recording details of all the specimens shot. Seven tigers were killed annually on average in that tiny State, extending little over 2000 square miles, with less than a quarter of its area under forest.

After my practical training was over I was posted to take charge of Khairwara, a small forest in the south-west of Udaipur. By that time I was married and my wife and baby son came with me. From the medieval city of Udaipur we proceeded by bus. The conductor used to collect a tax from each passenger to hand over to the bow-and-arrow man who was supposed to protect us from bandits. When I told the conductor of my destination he looked at me curiously; later I learned that in the princely days Khairwara was a place of punishment and the people still regarded it as such. Our journey of fifty miles took eight hours.

Khairwara is a small village with only a handful of people but it has a fine church. It was once the British cantonment of the Mewar Bhil Corps, and in the cemetery I saw the names of British soldiers who had died far from home. Although the place was named after the acacia forests of Khair there are no forests now. Hill after hill has been devastated, and wildlife is practically non-existent as the Bhils had wiped out even the pigeons. There were still a few leopards then, living mostly on goats and dogs; I was astonished at their powers of adaptation, living in a devastated land on tit-bits from the villages. Certainly there were no tigers.

After four months I was placed in charge of a forest division of Bharatpur, a place which shaped me and my future career. The division extended over four civil districts and the finest wildlife areas had been passionately preserved by the ex-maharajas. There was no timber to fell and my main job was to collect revenue from whatever existed in the forest – firewood, grass, honey, wax, dry leaves, flowers, fruits, even cow dung – and to issue permits freely for shooting tigers, leopards and game birds. The licence fee was less than the price of a drink.

I knew little about the population of the game I was authorizing people to kill, and I became painfully aware of this when a man came to get a permit to shoot four tigers after he had already killed two. There were no regulations to stop me from signing the death sentence, but I decided to visit his camp. There I found every comfort, as well as a full armoury of heavy-bore weapons. There were two jeeps with blinding spotlights and a van to carry the carcasses, and two tiger skins were stretched out for drying. A couple with American accents were basking in the sun, but the applicant for the permit was a landowner with rights of revenue collection in Gwalior State who had become a shikar operator. Taking advantage of the absence of rules on commercial shikar I refused the permit. I felt guilty at having issued permits for the other two tigers, but I had the consolation of knowing that I had saved the lives of four more.

Bharatpur is famous for its fort; thought to be invincible, it fell eventually to the British in 1826 after a three-weeks' siege. Thereafter in the great Ghana marshes close by the epitaphs of thousands of ducks are testimony to the visits of all the Governor Generals. On 6 February 1937 Lord Linlithgow shot over 2000 birds in a single day. I am proud to say that I managed to get Bharatpur declared a Bird Sanctuary, but the success was only partial: the Maharaja had exclusive rights, and he was jealous in their exercise. As late as 1965 when I took Sir Peter Scott to the Sanctuary the Maharaja turned up and opened fire to underline his privilege. Sir Peter was pained. We did not have to wait long: the Maharaja's rights vanished with the passing of an amendment to the Indian Constitution in 1972. Today Bharatpur is a paradise for bird watchers, a feast for photographers, and a research station for ornithologists.

It was here that I made my own first attempts at wildlife photography, having been inspired by F. W. Champion, author of *With a Camera in Tigerland* and like me a member of the Indian Forest Service. By riding on a water buffalo or swimming through the leech-infested waters, holding my old box camera high with one hand, I was able to approach the colonies; but all I could·photograph were nests with eggs or helpless chicks in the absence of their parents.

My father-in-law, appreciating that the distance between the nests and me was too great with such a camera, then gave me an old 35 mm Edixa miniature with a biotar lens but with its view-finder yellowed by age. The labour of creeping close to my quarry was still arduous and a telephoto lens was far beyond my means. But at last I found one in a junk shop, its surface scratched as if rubbed with sandpaper. It was a 12-inch tele-lens from some obsolete camera, and I took advantage of the dealer's ignorance and bought it for less than a pound. In spite of its not having a pre-set aperture I managed to get some good pictures, but my failures were many: animals, I found, did not wait for me to set apertures and I discovered that one has to surpass even the patience of the tiger to stalk a good picture. Trying to capture the wide spectrum of colours in the habitat proved to be just as challenging, but I gained immense satisfaction in trying to portray tigerland in all its splendour.*

A condition of admission to the Indian Forest College is that every trainee is assured of a job so I had no worries on that score, but I was never promotion-orientated and it was always far more important to me to do the work I enjoyed. Photography became a passion and, as an alcoholic runs to the first pub with any money he has in his pocket, I would rush to the nearest shop for a film or a filter. I was fortunate in that my in-laws ran a chain of photographic studios and the facilities for free developing and printing gave me the opportunity to learn wildlife photography in the most extravagant way. Even so, my addiction severely disturbed the household budget, and here I must pay tribute to my wife's forbearance. We were married just before I entered the Forest Service, having been betrothed when she was only twelve years old. We both believe that marriages are made in heaven, and we did not know each other at all before our engagement was fixed. She says the only difference it made to her was that she got some new clothes, and she wondered why!

As I have already mentioned, my father had been Director of Jodhpur Zoo – where tiger cubs were like my half-brothers and sisters – and in due course I followed in his footsteps in the same profession. Next I became Director of Delhi Zoo, where for five years I spent many days and nights in the tiger house, munching my food near courting and mating tigers, watching tigresses in labour and giving birth. Then in 1970 I was awarded the coveted Jawaharlal Nehru Fellowship which enabled me to jump with both feet into the field of wildlife, and I exchanged vigils in the tiger house for malarial waterholes and malodorous kills.

For the next two years I travelled round the country to see with my own eyes the land where tigers live and how they use it. I walked through each

* Tracings made from my photographs are used throughout the book to illustrate important aspects of the tiger and his life-style: facial designs and expressions; the sequence of action in a kill, the leap, grip and carrying of the prey; walk and movements, courtship and mating, birth and growth, and so on. Other sketches show some of the animals that share the tiger's habitat. Such visual aids reduce dependence on words and will, I hope, make what I have tried to convey easier to understand.

major habitat from the evergreen forests of Assam and the deltaic swamps of the
Sundarbans to the dry scrublands of Rajasthan, from the foothills of the
Himalayas to the central plateau and the Western Ghats, often repeating my
visits in different seasons. I covered tracts in Nepal and in the forests of Bhutan,
where I had the responsibility of setting up its Tiger Reserve as a joint venture
of the Indian Government and the Royal Government of Bhutan. Ideally I
would have wished to make a detailed study of the ecology in each of the
tiger's habitat types, but clearly this was beyond the capacity of any single
person. However, my two-years' walkabout did enable me to obtain first-
hand information that could not have been collected in any other way.

    The field stations for my main areas of study were at Sariska and Ranthambhor
in Rajasthan. To supplement my work there I needed a somewhat different
habitat and I chose Kanha National Park in Madhya Pradesh. George Schaller
had worked there in 1964–5, and my own work in 1971 proved helpful in
taking a second look at his observations and adding new ones. I found that the
information he had collected was mostly from one family of conditioned tigers,
which had been provided with baits for more than one-and-a-half years. The
group included only one male and was confined to a small area of 10–15 sq km.
Vital aspects such as reproduction and the behaviour of a tigress and her infant
cubs had not been studied in depth. Schaller's work was valuable in being the
first ever to be fully recorded in the field, but it was insufficient to justify wider
application. At that time the real facts about tigers' distribution, numbers and
the conditions under which they were surviving in other parts of the country
were not known.

    When I first decided to study tigers the large number of books written about
them – over 200 since 1828 – tended to damp my enthusiasm, particularly after
the publication of *The Man-Eaters of Kumaon* by Jim Corbett (1944). F. W.
Champion's book *With a Camera in Tigerland* (1927) and R. I. Pocock's *Tigers*
(1930) made every effort to present the facts correctly (the former worked in the
field and the latter in the museum). *The Book of the Tiger* by R. G. Burton when
published in 1933 was considered to be the last word on the tiger, but it contained much unverified information and some which was highly subjective. A
closer look at other books revealed that most of them related to how to place a
bullet in a tiger's heart and how to measure a dead tiger. Stories recollected and
reconstructed long after the event were invariably exaggerated and told far
more about the hunter than the tiger. Thus my resolution to study tigers was
not shaken for long by the number of words already written about them.

    I shall never forget the first tigress I ever saw in the wild: she enchanted me:
it was love at first sight. As apprentice trainees in the Forest Service we were
supposed to spend at least 20 nights out of every month in the field. There
is a tradition that a forester does not take the same route home, and one day I
took a short cut back to camp by crossing a stream by means of boulders.

Suddenly I saw something running, then I realized there were two animals, somewhat larger than dogs. They had stripes. The whole thing happened so quickly that it hardly registered in my mind, but a few steps further on I saw a half-eaten carcass and it dawned on me that they must have been tiger cubs.

I decided to climb a tree and wait for them to return to their kill. For an hour nothing happened and then, as the light began to fade, I heard quick steps on the dry leaves behind me. I turned my head and saw a sleek golden body with black vertical stripes, obviously the mother of the two cubs. Her movement created an optical illusion, causing her to appear strangely elongated. At the speed she was moving I expected her to be on the kill within a moment, but after a couple of minutes when nothing happened I looked back cautiously, moving my head in slow motion. She was right under my tree, hardly six feet below me, yet apparently she had not picked up my scent. My first wild tigress at such close quarters made my heart beat faster and a nervous movement produced a metallic sound from my belt. She looked up, jumped, and was off. Within a few days I heard she had been shot by a maharaja, who also captured the cubs.

During my period of training in the Forest Service I had to listen to gossip round the camp fire: how a certain officer got promotion for shooting a tiger during his first year of service; how someone was awarded an OBE for arranging a successful hunt for the British Governor; how another was summarily dismissed by a maharaja for failing to produce a tiger for his gun. The last lecture I had attended included a mock tiger beat. The instructor was the top brass of the Forest Service, the Inspector General of Forests, the late Mr M. D. Chaturvedi, who had been a celebrated tiger hunter in his day. "Shoot your first tiger in your first year," he told us, and eventually I steeled myself to obey. With a borrowed Express rifle and antiquated black powder ammunition I sat up one night over a buffalo killed by a tiger.

When I got up on the *machan* in an acacia tree the last rays of the sun were still lighting up the valley. In an hour it was dark and the temple bells of a distant village announced that the gods were ready to go to bed. Within minutes of the fading of the bells I heard sounds of a tug-of-war and the heaving of a carcass, then the animal settled down to eat. My companion, an experienced shikari and Forest Guard, pressed my arm to get ready. I levelled the "cannon" and as he switched on his torch I fired. With a deep-throated "Oonooh" the animal jumped into the bush. Peacocks called and langurs whooped, then after a time there was silence. The smoke of the black powder persisted over the *machan* as I flashed my torch over the buffalo carcass. It was not there. A moan came from the bushes; evidently the tiger had been hit. A thousand thoughts flashed through my mind: the tiger cubs which used to come to our house, the mock beat at the Forest College. Was it courage, or cold-blooded murder in the dark? The picture of the tigress's beauty haunted me, and with every groan from the bushes my feelings of guilt increased. Not surprisingly I did not sleep, and when the crows called and sunlight lit the valley once more I found it difficult to wear a brave smile when I saw the tiger dead, his legs up and his eyes open. He seemed to look in my eyes and ask the reason for his death. "Is this sport, when all the rules are in your favour?" I could not even bluff myself that he was a man-eater or even a cattle-lifter. Humbled in guilt I touched his body to beg his pardon. Even today the scene is as fresh as it was that morning, and the open eyes of that tiger have haunted me all my life.

I never repeated that murder, and to overcome my guilt I have dedicated my life to the cause of tiger preservation. The first thing I did was to get the area of Sariska Sanctuary extended to include the Madhogarh forests where I shot the tiger so that no other should die in the same way. For the past 20 years no licensed gun has been fired in the Sariska valley and this is reflected in the behaviour of the animals. I derive immense pleasure in watching them at the waterhole and my heart gladdens when I hear a roar. In the next two chapters I describe some of the information I have gleaned, and the rewards I have had by quietly watching these magnificent animals.

Part One

CHAPTER I

The mighty predator

The tiger is the spirit of the Indian jungle. Even his distant roar, or an alarm call from some animal announcing his presence, charges the whole atmosphere.

Acute sensitivity, secretiveness and the ability to surprise, untiring perseverance, agility in attack, tenacity to follow and hold, and strength to overpower are the qualities necessary in a successful predator. The tiger possesses them all in extraordinary measure. A set of powerful canine teeth combined with strong jaw muscles make up dental equipment with tremendous crushing power, and sharp claws with a strong gripping mechanism in the forearm complete his armoury. This formidable predator can bring down animals even as large as buffalo or gaur efficiently. Later we shall look at these qualities in more detail, but first, what are the tiger's characteristics as a species?

The tiger has a wider ecological tolerance than other big cats such as the lion or jaguar. Living in very diverse habitats, it has undergone modifications in size, coat and colour which justify its classification into several distinct subspecies. The type species is the Indian tiger, *Panthera tigris tigris*; it is still well-represented even though drastically reduced in numbers and limited in geographic distribution compared with its former range. Its present home is the Indian sub-continent, Nepal, Bhutan, Bangladesh, and Upper and Lower western Burma, and the total population numbers some 2500. The combined total population of the other six sub-species – Siberian, Chinese, Caspian, Sumatran, Indochinese and Javan – is dangerously low, probably numbering less than 1500 and scattered in isolated pockets far apart.

An average male Indian tiger measures ten feet from nose to tip of the tail and 36 inches at the shoulder. The skull is $14\frac{1}{4}$ inches long in the case of the male, 12 inches in females. The fur is short in summer but becomes longer in winter. The Siberian tiger, *P. tigris altaica*, is considerably larger, measuring some 13 feet in length, with a massive head, heavy hindquarters, and long, thick fur. The Chinese tiger, *P. tigris amoyensis*, is smaller than the Siberian or Manchurian tiger, somewhat darker and more closely striped, with a thick tail which ends abruptly without tapering. The tigers which crossed over to the Indonesian group of islands are smaller than the Indian tiger and have different markings. The Bali tiger was last seen in 1952 by a Dutch forest officer and was thought to

SUB-SPECIES OF THE TIGER

Caspian

Siberian

Javan

Sumatran

Indo-Malayan

Chinese

Indian

be extinct, but recently there have been reports that a few may survive; these tigers are said to be only the size of a leopard. In 1968 Mazak described as a new sub-species the tigers living in Indochina, Malaysia and eastern Burma; in Thailand they have been known to visit populated areas, and possibly because of this habit Mazak named *P. tigris corbetti* after Jim Corbett. The hunting records of the Sultan of Johore show that the average length of 35 of these Malaysian tigers, all adults, was 8 ft. 3 ins. (Medway 1969); in India, where a full-grown tiger measures nearly 10 ft., we would consider an animal of this size to be a cub. In warmer climates animals tend to decrease in size because an increase in the evaporation surface per unit of mass helps to dissipate heat: hence the smaller size of Javan, Sumatran and Indochinese tigers. Conversely, in a cold climate the larger body size and longer fur help to conserve heat, thus explaining the larger size of the Siberian tiger. Unexplained, however, is its failure to adapt its colour to merge into the snows of the long Siberian winters, where the tawny colour and black stripes must be a disadvantage for hunting.

Hypotheses on the origin and migrations of tigers depend on a few fossil finds, such as those from the Lena River system and some islands in the Arctic Ocean, as well as remains of Quaternary age from near Harbin in China (Pocock 1929). Others are known from the site of "Peking Man" at Choukoutien and from Java. Pocock concluded that the tiger migrated from Siberia to Java and entered India via Burma, with another branch of the migration leading to the Perso-Turkestan regions and the Caspian. Mazak (1965) and subsequent writers supported this theory, but Warner Fend (1972) suggested that the tiger entered India from China although he gives no evidence.

Palaeontologists consider that no mammals came to India from the east – there are no similarities with Chinese fauna – but that from time to time they arrived from the north-west. It is very surprising that there is so little evidence of the presence of leopards and tigers in India during the Tertiary period although there were elephants, rhinos, gaur, deer and wild boars. Predators follow their prey, and when migrations were taking place how could the leopard and tiger remain behind? However, the Pleistocene Pinjor Formation of the Upper Siwaliks has yielded remains of a feline with a skull slightly smaller than that of the present tiger but otherwise comparable.

The tiger's colour and pattern hint at its evolution in tall grasslands interspersed with forests, subjected to desiccation and perhaps grass fires. Such conditions did not prevail in Siberia during Tertiary and early Quaternary times, and it seems far more likely that the tiger entered India from the north-west like so many of its prey animals. The presence of the leopard in Sri Lanka and the absence of the tiger gives a clue to the time of the latter's arrival in India. The leopard is not a swimmer but the tiger is; the leopard may have reached the island before the straits separated it from the mainland, but the tiger may have arrived after the gap widened beyond his swimming capacity.

The Indian Tiger is a creature of hypnotic power and fascination. A glimpse through green foliage of the sleek golden body gliding by like a phantom is an experience that no words can describe. What a marvellous skin the animal has! The more one sees of this beautiful beast the more one is charmed by its gorgeous colour, the vivid pattern of the stripes on the glossy skin, the strength of the muscles and the grace of the tiger's movements. But the colours and patterns, of course, were not devised merely for our admiration: they serve as camouflage, allowing the tiger to surprise his prey in many different environments. The broken series of transverse stripes of various lengths and widths arise from the dorsal line and end towards the ventral surface of the body. These and the horizontal stripes on the limbs, the rings on the tail, the orange colour fading to fawn and white below, and the combination of exquisite dots and dashes on the face make a complicated and hypnotic pattern. In grassland the yellow of the body merges with dry grass and the broken black stripes resemble the shadows of the leaves. In bamboo forests the tiger blends with the yellow of the bamboo stems; when he is hiding under a sal or lantana bush the stripes look like shadows of the branches; in dry deciduous forests the brownish-yellow foliage and patchy shadows make a background against which the animal is almost invisible. Even when he is sitting cooling himself in water the dazzling sun confuses the eye and a tiger can easily be taken for a river boulder.

The tiger's pattern and colouring, which seem so conspicuous at close quarters, are completely deceptive in the jungle. The changing light and shade in the forest makes every tiger a bush and every bush a tiger. Many a time I have seen a tiger only after my elephant had almost stepped on it. Even in burnt forest a tiger merges with the pattern of the burnt and unburnt. grass. Even if you do manage to make out the tiger's contours, the moment you shift your view you will have great difficulty in rediscovering this huge, heavily-built animal who may be sitting hardly 20 feet away from you. No description can ever convey the many different aspects of a tiger seen in different environments, just as it can never convey the excitement of a sighting.

The foot markings display individual characters, but there are difficulties in trying to identify a particular tiger by this means when more than one is operating in one area, especially when they are of the same age and sex. George Schaller, working in Kanha National Park, depended on markings round the eyes; but these differ on each side and can also look different depending on the mood of the tiger and the angle from which they are viewed. The sighting of tigers under good lighting conditions – as, for example, lions can be viewed on the Serengeti plains in East Africa – is seldom possible, and the difficulties of photographing eye markings and whisker patterns for purposes of identification are enormous. If the individuals are seen repeatedly, as in Kanha Park or a zoo, facial characters can be recognized fairly easily; but they are of very limited application in general.

What is the purpose of the tiger's camouflage? Most of his hunting is done after dark, so it would seem that it is more a means of defence when he is resting during the day. But who is his enemy, other than man? The answer is if he were conspicuous creatures that are active during the day would announce his presence and he would get no peace. The tiger's pattern of double stripes enables him to merge with the landscape of reeds and elephant grass, and he can thus get to within striking distance of his prey without being seen. His black stripes also break the solid appearance of the tiger's outline during twilight – his principal hunting hours when in a man-free habitat.

The tiger lives alone. Curiously, he is one of the least studied animals, and even such a vital question as whether tigers live alone or in pairs or family units has been much disputed and was one of the major queries I set out to answer. The evidence for my conclusions that hunting in pairs is an exception I give later.

There are good reasons for the tiger's solitary way of life. Thick forest or woodland with limited visibility would be no help in the manoeuvres of

Tigress and grown-up cub in perfect camouflage

communal stalking or chasing. Woodlands are far less productive of prey than open country, and the presence of more than one predator in a given area would be uneconomic; sharing food would cause competition within the species, and there would be more chance of disturbing the prey. (Those who are familiar with bush warfare and sniper activity will know that it is the individual soldier who conceals himself for an effective kill.)

The individualistic behaviour of the tiger is thus an extremely efficient adaptive mechanism. His output of energy is fully compensated for by the input gained by exclusive feeding. By jealously guarding his kill and returning to eat the last scrap of meat he leaves very little for his camp-followers, although human hunters of course exploit this habit of "returning to the kill". Lions and wild dogs do not return as nothing is left after a pride or pack has finished its meal.

The tiger depends far more on hearing than on scent or sight, especially in closed forests where visibility is poor. Hunters know that the slightest metallic sound from their rifle will cause a tiger to bolt, and it is said that he can even hear the breathing of a hunter inside a hide or from a *machan*. Although he takes no notice of rustling branches or sweeping grass, the breaking of a dry twig under a human foot is another matter. A tiger's sense of hearing enables him to judge the species of his prey. Once I watched a sleeping tiger; he paid no attention when a mongoose walked through dry leaf litter, but lifted his head when a jackal passed the same way. With the first sound of rolling stones produced by a herd of sambar, however, he immediately got up and fixed his eyes in their direction.

A tiger has bulging eyes which give him a wide-angle view, but he finds it difficult to see an animal when it is standing still; the slightest flicker of a tail or ear, however, does not escape his notice. This applies especially at night, when a tiger will not be able to see prey animals standing in shadow, particularly if he himself is walking in moonlight. I found that tigers were unable to detect buffalo calves sitting in the shade even at a distance of five metres and in full view so long as the calves made no movement. But unfortunately for the prey as soon as they sight a predator they become nervous and fidgety and give themselves away.

All cats, of course, are well-known for their ability to see in darkness. A tiger's eyes are equipped with the tapetum, a special layer of cells; light entering the eye is reflected by the tapetum and falls on sensitive perceptive cells, enabling the tiger to see well at night. His eye has a circular pupil, unlike the vertical slit of the lesser cats, and for this reason he is allotted to the genus *Panthera* rather than *Felis*. But the function of opening the retina wide is the same, allowing all cats to hunt at night. This principle is copied in the electronic eye of the automatic camera.

At night a spotlight picks up reflections from animals' eyes and, with experience, it is not difficult to identify them by the size and spacing of the eyes. The commonest eye picked up by headlights along our roads is the amber spot of a nightjar. A constellation of twinkling blue stars indicates a herd of chital. Large round spots more than five feet above the ground represent sambar, though these are sometimes confused with those of nilgai. Comparative size, spacing and height help to differentiate between a tiger and a leopard. If it is on a tree it is always a leopard.

Nearly everyone who sees a tiger at night describes the eyes as burning red, and this became a means of identification. I too believed this until I had the opportunity of throwing my headlights on five tigers who were on a kill at Sariska. The various angles of their positions presented different reflections. It seems that when the light falls straight on to the eyes the colour of the reflected light appears bright yellow-red; but when the light falls on the sides of the eyes it is bluish-green. This is probably due to the colour of the cornea and the colourless aqueous humour; the cornea produces a bright colour and the latter the icy blue of water. I tested this theory on white tigers who have icy blue eyes with a blue cornea, and found that they do not give an amber-coloured reflection from any angle; the reflection is always bright blue.

According to a Burmese saying, "If a tiger had to depend on its nose it would starve to death." On the other hand, a Sanskrit couplet describes the tiger as ". . . an animal which has a highly developed sense of smell". Burmese trackers, aboriginals, tribes like the Gonds and Bhils of India, Manchurian trappers and the path-finders of Indonesia, as well as such authors as Hamilton, Smythies, Locke and Baze, believe that the tiger hunts by smell. But Baker, Glassford, Champion, Burton, Corbett, Singh and Anderson all reject the view that tigers hunt with the help of their nose. Schaller, too, could obtain no evidence to show that tigers use smell to locate their prey.

I have already mentioned how I sat in a tree hardly four metres from the ground and a tiger never sensed my presence until I made an accidental sound. Human smell, which is so instantly perceived by elephants and other animals, does not seem to attract the tiger's attention. I conducted some experiments at Delhi Zoo to test the power of smell of eight tigers of different origins. A freshly-killed pig was kept concealed on the wire of the tigers' open-air enclosure, a metre higher than the tigers' bodies. Two fully-grown hungry tigers and two tigresses passed one by one through the passage and none of them discovered the pig. After the carcass became so high that even the human nose could scent it from a distance of five metres the experiment was repeated. This time both the tigers and one of the tigresses first sniffed the ground and then the air and discovered the source. The other tigress failed. Then the experiment was done again with two other pairs of tigers; this time it was the tigers who failed to discover the pig whereas both tigresses tracked it down in four seconds after sniffing the air. This to me was a fairly good indication that tigers do not have an acute sense of smell, and that this power varies from animal to animal.

Since tigers have highly developed powers of hearing and keen sight – at least for moving objects – the scenting faculty is hardly used in hunting. But they do use their noses to perceive the visits of other tigers or tigresses by sniffing objects on the ground visited by them. In doing so a tiger touches the ground with his nose and sometimes even with the tip of the tongue. After smelling the places where visiting tigers have urinated, both sexes grimace by stretching out their tongue. Experiments showed that such an expression has nothing to do with courtship or mating behaviour or territorialism. I could produce this expression simply by spraying them with their own urine.

Tracing the presence of tigers by their body odour has been reported by hunters. To test which part of the body produces the odour I smelled all parts of a zoo tiger's body in four different seasons of the year, and I also made this investigation on courting and mating tigers. I could locate no focal point of smell. Since the tiger is a clean animal there is no question of excreta coming in contact with the body, or of any rotting meat sticking to it.

I made several attempts to smell tigers when they were at close quarters in Kanha, Ranthambhor and Sariska, but did not notice any odour. On the other hand, I did detect a tiger's smell, a mild mixture of an aromatic scent and rotting vegetation, while passing through a forest at night. I stopped my jeep and searched the bush, where I found a big tiger sitting. I went there again next morning but there was no smell. I searched for faeces or a spot where the tiger had urinated but there was nothing. The odour came from the tiger.

On another occasion while I was inspecting a kill I scented a tiger; I retraced my steps and discovered him, but he jumped away. I smelled the kill and the spot where the tiger was sitting, but neither emitted that characteristic odour. Another day while tracking a tiger I smelled him from a distance of ten to fifteen feet. And in 1973 I saw a tigress sitting 30 feet from the road in the Kachida valley of Ranthambhor at night; disturbed by my efforts to photograph her she got up and walked away. I did not follow her immediately, not wishing to disturb her further, but after ten minutes I started following her and at two places there was a distinct tiger smell. Each time I discovered her presence entirely by smell. On the first occasion the smell still persisted behind the bush where she had been, and on the second occasion I found the tigress sitting in a bush when I went closer to investigate the smell. Again she got up and walked away. Following her closely, sometimes just ahead of her and sometimes just behind, I got no smell whatever. This suggests that tigers and tigresses emit a scent, whether voluntarily or involuntarily, either when they are uneasy or as a defence mechanism.

So much for some of the tiger's endowments; but before examining his plan of campaign and method of attack I would like to look briefly at his limitations.

Powerful predators could produce imbalances in the ecology if nature had not provided a system of built-in limitations to act as safety valves. One of the brakes on the efficiency of the tiger is that he cannot easily walk over broken or thorny ground, so that a cross-country chase is beyond his powers. Once his prey are in country covered in prickly undergrowth and dry branches or rocky outcrops they are safe. The pads of the tiger's feet are soft, and I noticed in the zoo that whenever I transferred tigers from wooden-floored cells to ones with bricks their pads would bleed. I have often taken advantage of this limitation by putting thorn fences round my hides.

In tropical forests, especially the dry deciduous kind, the temperature sometimes touches 48°C, with hot winds. Animals concentrate at waterholes and hunting should be easy for the tiger, but the ground is baking hot and the rocks become frying pans: a tiger dare not walk there or his feet would be blistered in no time. The ungulates, whose hooves are insulated, take advantage of this and come to drink at the hottest time of the day, even in full view of a tiger cooling himself in a near-by pool.

A second limitation is that the tiger's formidable power and strength is good for only one or two springs, after which the prey is safe. Yet another limiting factor is caused by the alarm calls of birds and animals betraying the tiger's presence. Even the tiger's solitary way of hunting has its disadvantages; he cannot profit from group hunting when recuperating from injuries, nor can a tigress rely on others to bring her food immediately before and after giving birth. All these limitations ensure that predation is kept under control and a natural balance maintained.

Now for the plan of campaign. The tiger is a wanderer, and apparently wanders with no definite plan in mind. But within his "home range" he has a mental note of such features as day shelters, waterholes and places where food may be expected. (His periodical reappearances at these places is sometimes interpreted as visits to guard his territory). He seldom leaves his home range except to pursue receptive tigresses or when driven by desperate hunger. The walk is leisurely, with mouth open and the tail loop carelessly swinging from side to side. Once he locates his prey, however, there is nothing indefinite about his strategy. He does not make a straight approach but circles the animal to select a suitable route through cover. If the prey is on the move the tiger walks faster or sometimes runs to overtake it and take up his position in advance. In exposed situations he keeps his body close to the ground with his eyes on the target (cf colour photo no. 21.)

The last phase of the approach is extremely cautious. The tiger crouches, placing the hind feet in the spot vacated by the front feet and pausing from time to time to assess the situation by raising and lowering his head. Having made sure of the distance and the position of his prey, he makes doubly sure by drawing his head back and forth as if focusing, then slowly he raises his body, charges and springs. The attack itself is a sudden rush at full speed with front legs in the air and tail erect. On landing, the tiger holds the animal's neck as close to its own head as possible, with one paw on the shoulder and the other on the face, securing a firm hold with the canines and then exerting all his strength to bring the prey down.

Sometimes when he has underestimated the distance he becomes airborne with the first leap, touches the ground, and then pressing hard on the ground with his hind feet and arching his back he leaps into the air for a second time, and lands on the prey with all his weight. If he fails to make contact he abandons the attack and either tries another manoeuvre or gives up the chase. Such failures happen more often than successes. Stalking is a difficult exercise and the tiger prefers to post himself in a depression or grass cover on the way to a waterhole and wait for the prey to come within striking distance. An ambush attack involves little waste of energy and has a greater chance of success.

A buffalo herd is a formidable adversary, as is a solitary bull, and the tiger tries to pick out calves. He waits for his chance near a waterhole and stalks them through the long grass, practising hit-and-run guerrilla warfare. When he manages to pounce on a calf he merely disables it and then runs off to avoid a charge by the herd. The herd will abandon the disabled calf and the tiger then returns to kill it. In 1969 in the Manas Sanctuary of Assam a tiger got into a fight with a bull buffalo and after fighting the whole night both were found dead next morning. On another occasion a tiger killed a buffalo calf in the

STALKING ITS PREY

Prey located

stealthy approach

On closer sighting
the body is lowered

The head is moved backwards
and forwards as if
focusing on its target

The final rush

presence of its parents, dragged it away and started eating it. The parents watched helplessly, but probably they were more scared of the elephant with its load of visitors than of the tiger.

The tiger does not care to tackle a full-grown elephant and usually withdraws if a solitary tusker or a *mukna* (tuskless male) is grazing in the vicinity. At times, however, tigers lie in wait for calves who stray from the herd. They generally snap the trunk and profuse bleeding results in the calf's death. J. P. Sinha describes such an incident in Palamau. The tiger employs the same method of "attack and run" as in the case of buffalo, returning to feed after the herd has abandoned the disabled calf. But sometimes a miscalculation results in the tiger getting trampled and killed by elephants.

The technique of guerrilla warfare is practised also in the killing of rhinoceros calves, and a mother rhino is always worried about the safety of her young when a tiger is around. Nineteen rhino calves were killed by tigers in Kaziranga Sanctuary between 1966–9, and the loss of 11 calves was reported in the year 1968 alone.

The actual method adopted by the tiger in killing its prey has been the subject of much dispute. Does it seize its victim by the throat or hamstring it first? Baldwin, Forsyth, and Brander state that the neck is held, twisted and broken. Fletcher, Sanderson and Corbett speak of tigers seizing the throat. Inglish describes a tiger killing a boar by biting it above the shoulders, and also by giving a numbing blow with the forepaw followed by holding the throat and tearing open the jugular vein.

During my studies I found that for choice the tiger will first bite the back of the neck as close as possible to the skull. This dislocates and fractures the weakest joint, that of the axis and atlas vertebrae, and causes death by compression of the spinal cord. Where the animal is larger than the tiger the method was by holding the throat and killing by suffocation. Adolescent cubs can hardly reach the neck of a grown animal and they usually go for the throat. In the case of a charging gaur or buffalo, which has its head down and does not expose its throat, the tiger's only choice is the neck. If the neck hold is foiled, the next move is to hamstring the animal.

Some hunters have said that the tiger holds its prey and sucks its blood, but I have never found this to be the case. I never saw any major blood vessel cut or even damaged; blood flows only when the grip is released from some local blood vessel. Moreover, the tiger's mouth is not provided with a sucking mechanism: he can only lick with the help of his tongue. The theory that the jugular vein is punctured and that this causes death is also not supported by my observations.

I examined about 160 natural kills and more than 100 baits of buffalo calves. All female sambar were killed by holding the neck; in each case there were four clear holes, two on either side of the vertebral column as close to the

opposite: *I disturbed this tigress while she was feeding on her kill with her cubs.*
She followed me through the foliage and I had to scamper up a tree for safety.

previous page: *Also in Kanha: an intoxicated and sleepy adolescent tiger rests after a hard day's stalking.*

left: *Tiger courtship is noisy and violent, and culminates in temporary conflict. Yet when mating tigers keep each other constant company, and ignore almost everything around them — even human presence.*

above: *A tigress is a devoted mother. At the slightest danger to her cubs she will move them to a safe place, holding each cub's head between her canines. The cubs co-operate by remaining completely immobile.*

below: *These helpless 40 to 50-day-old cubs were discovered in a bamboo clump on a river bank in Kanha when their mother was on a hunting expedition. Cubs after 80 to 90 days easily follow their mother.*

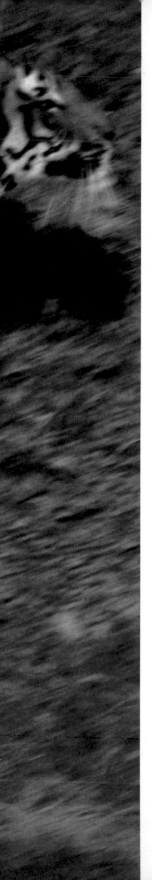

left: *This tiger was driven out in a shikar beat in Dholpur. With a spring from his arched body and hind legs he was airborne. Tigers make a hop, step and jump movement to reach their prey, knocking them down with their momentum.*

below: *Dalip, one of the famous white tigers of Rewa. His sharp canines and fine whiskers show that he is entering his prime.*

bottom: *The yellow grass and its shadows add to the black design on a tiger's body to confuse its prey.*

overleaf: *The extra yellow and red tone in this picture is due to the combined effect of dry grass, the afternoon light and, above all, the colour of the tigress, but I include it as it is one of the best portrait shots I have taken of a tiger in the wild. This tigress, surprised in a clearing of Kachida Valley, could not discover me in my covered jeep, and so gave me only a casual glance.*

(a)

(b)

(c)

(d)

(e)

THE KILL

The tiger grips its prey by the neck, so crushing the main joints and killing by compression. The top drawing (a) shows the head-on approach, (b) an attack from the side, in which the victim is forced to the ground. Tigers will also attack from behind (e) or go straight to the prey's throat, hoping to strangle it (c). Finally, it may seek simply to disable its prey (d) by attacking its hamstring.

head as possible. The spacing of the holes caused by the fangs gives an indication of the size of the tiger. In the case of stags, the tiger cannot reach the neck without his fangs coming into contact with the antlers, so he goes for the throat and the animal dies by suffocation. In one case I found the windpipe had been cut and forced out. In the case of live baits all kills were made by holding the neck, the fixed position of the buffalo calf making it easy for the tiger to adopt the hold he prefers. I also experimented by tying large buffaloes, and even then the tiger's choice was to hold the neck and bite close to the head. When a chain was tied round the neck, however, the tiger always avoided biting the neck or throat and the animal was eaten alive.

I found that natural kills gave no answer to the actual cause of death as during the subsequent dragging multiple injuries occur and the real cause is difficult to locate. The fixed position of a tied bait is unnatural so I decided to conduct an experiment. A captured tiger was put into a large enclosure with a deer weighing about 150 kg which was allowed to run about. After the tiger had killed he was driven away. I found that the joint of the atlas and axis vertebrae had been broken and bones close to the skull had been pulped into small pieces, injuring the spinal cord. I repeated the experiment and the result was the same. Death was definitely caused by compression of the spinal cord, much in the same way that a man meets his death by hanging. The experiments also enabled me to time the moment of death: if a proper grip has been secured, the time from first grip to the dropping of the dead body varies from 35 to 90 seconds.

Burton (1933) has given a graphic description of operation kill. The sequence of action is:

Rush – short scuffle – a choked bellow then absolute silence. Tiger stands with back of the prey's neck in jaws – opens jaws – the lifeless body of the victim falls on the ground with a helpless flop. Stands a few minutes fully alerted to the surroundings, gazing here and there – seizes the hind quarters and drags it away – after several tugs gives up the attempt and squatting at the tail of the carcass begins to tear it open.

This description holds good for the majority of cases when the kill is a staked live bait, with minor differences and short cuts due to the nature of the terrain, the relative size of prey and predator, and the individual habits of different tigers. The operation is so quick and neat that it has rarely been recorded; moreover, the situation is so exciting that the mind fails to register the details. For these reasons the precise technique of killing employed by the tiger has been as controversial as its power of smell.

How does the tiger start its meal? For hours on end I have watched and photographed tigers on a kill to get information on the technique. Invariably he starts by pulling out the hair from the skin of the haunches with his incisors. The cleaned space he then rubs with his file-like tongue to scrape away the skin.

He then bites into the meat to make it pulpy, lowers his face to one side and cuts open a patch with his molars. It is now that one hears chuckling sounds in the dark, but still he has not begun his dinner. The next operation is confirmed by the sound of the tearing of skin from the opened patch with the help of his canines by giving upward jerks while holding the carcass firmly between the forepaws. He does not use his claws for tearing, but they help him to grip. Sometimes this laborious process of dressing his dinner takes 20 to 30 minutes.

And then the meal begins. His first choice is the fatty tissues of the abdomen, intestines and muscular organs like the kidneys, heart, liver and lungs. In the case of large animals the tiger gets right inside the carcass in search of these organs, but sometimes he starts with the muscular parts of the haunches and works his way up. The rumen is carefully freed from attachments and pulled away; the tiger never allows the contents to mix with the flesh, and if this should happen accidentally I have seen tigers leaving in disgust. However, he relishes the intestines and pushes out their contents by pressing them with his incisors. The whole carcass is eaten except the flesh sticking to the head, the limb bones, vertebral columns and rib case, which he leaves for his camp followers. In the case of small animals no trace remains except for scattered antlers or horns and hooves; everything else is eaten, including bones and skin. The feeding process is very similar in the case of the lion but greatly differs in the leopard who starts with the soft belly, mainly because his jaws are not strong enough to break the bones. A punctured belly results in the mixing of the rumen contents with the flesh, but this does not worry the leopard, and the same applies to wild dogs and jackals. Evidence of a kill by a tiger is therefore well-defined.

The whole meal is not finished at one sitting. The first interval starts immediately after the kill has been made when the carcass is dragged to a safer place. The tiger may then go to a waterhole, drink, relax, and return to begin the cleaning process. The second recess is in about an hour's time after about 5 to 10 kg of the kill has been eaten. If a tiger is not hungry he will stroll away and return in the early hours of the morning. This provides an opportunity for other predators and scavengers, but the tiger always makes his presence known to scare the poachers. Sometimes, however, he stays away for longer and poaching does take place.

Once I was photographing a tigress on her kill in Sariska. The calls of sambar and chital in the distance confirmed that she had left the area and hardly 15 minutes after her departure a hyena arrived and started eating. It gobbled hurriedly and with the first warning call of a chital it bolted, but not before I had managed to get its photograph. The tigress returned, ate a little, withdrew to a bush and kept watch the whole day, occasionally scaring away crows, vultures, jackals and mongooses. By the following evening the carcass was high and the tigress had developed a keen appetite.

In the case of lions it is impossible to wait in this way as the carcass has to feed the whole pride. The leopard behaves like the tiger, guarding his unfinished kill and with the added advantage of being able to take it into a tree for safety. But a hungry tiger may finish a kill at one sitting with only short intervals of rest. Normally a prey weighing 150 kg – its dressed meat weighs about 60 kg – is finished in two nights, 20–30 kg being eaten on the first night.

I must admit that I found the apparently simple information as to how much a tiger eats in one night was most difficult to obtain since he eats at intervals, and, in between, other animals such as civets, jungle cats and even hyenas take a bite. As the tiger had not finished, I could not scare them away. The problem was still more difficult by moonlight when vultures roosting near by would land during the tiger's feeding intervals. The information I collected resulted only from lucky chances when everything went smoothly from the first weighing of the bait until the final weighing after the tiger had finished. Handling of the rumen sac was the most nauseating business, causing horror among my forest guards to whom even touching a dead animal is beneath their dignity. One is supposed to bathe and change all clothes before entering a rest house and when I simply washed my hands and ate my lunch on the spot they considered me a complete outcast.

A solitary tiger eats quietly, the only noise being the crunching of bones. When there are more than one, generally a tigress and her grown cubs, all try to feed simultaneously and such a feast is as noisy as that of a pride of lions

where each fights for the best place. With lions, however, the male has pre-
ference and the mothers follow with no thought for their cubs, whereas with
tigers the cubs feed first and the mother last.

The tiger is not a wanton killer. He usually kills only when he is hungry and
makes a full meal unless he is disturbed. Several times I have seen tigers pass by
baits and make no attempt to kill them; I then found in 45 cases out of 50 that
the tiger had had a full meal the previous night. Even when a tiger came to
drink at a waterhole where a bait was tied in full view he did not kill it. I also
provided baits on the tiger's usual route after he had made a kill and in 24 cases
he passed by without even stopping to look at the bait. In three cases he made
playful attacks without injuring the bait; and in another three cases he did kill
but did not eat. In two cases tigers returned to a partly-eaten kill and finding
another live bait tied in the same place, they ignored it and went for the half-
eaten one. Tigers prefer high meat as it is softer. Also, they do not want to have
to repeat the process of dressing their dinner, and if they kill the bait at all it
may be only in order to avoid the nuisance of its snorting during the dinner
hour.

A tiger does not often get the chance of scavenging because by the time he
arrives hyenas, jackals and vultures have usually done their work. Also he tends
to avoid animals killed by others to avoid confrontation with the unknown
owner. But a hungry tiger does not despise diseased meat: I found tigers feeding
on sambar that had died of hepatic septicaemia in Sariska in 1970. A predator
has immense immunity against disease and is himself a "zoo" of ecto- and endo-
parasites.

How far can a tiger carry its kill? James Butt mentions that a tiger has the
traction power of 30 men, and Singh speaks of a tiger dragging a full-grown
bullock over a 100 feet high hill through bushes to a ravine. Loukashkin (1938)
says that the Manchurian tiger can lift in its mouth a pig weighing 120 to 170
kg. I recall that once five of us could not get a buffalo calf on its feet, but the
same night a tigress killed it and pulled it about 300 metres through clumps of
grass and over the banks of a steep ravine. A tiger can also drag a full-grown
gaur or a young elephant. E. Smythies (1942) records that a tiger dragged
carcasses more than a mile, and I have seen tigers taking their kills for about
400 metres through rough country.

The method of transportation depends on the terrain and the weight of the
kill. A small animal is held by the neck and lifted to reduce friction. Sometimes
a tiger drags the animal between his forelegs, but if the prey is heavy he grips
its neck and pulls it backwards. The prey is never loaded on to his back as some
shikar stories would have it. A tigress with cubs will try to carry the carcass
to their hiding place, and this she does in two stages. First, she rejects the rumen
to make the carcass lighter, then eats a little, and afterwards carries it to her
cubs. If it is impossible for a tiger to drag his kill to a bush he tries to cover it

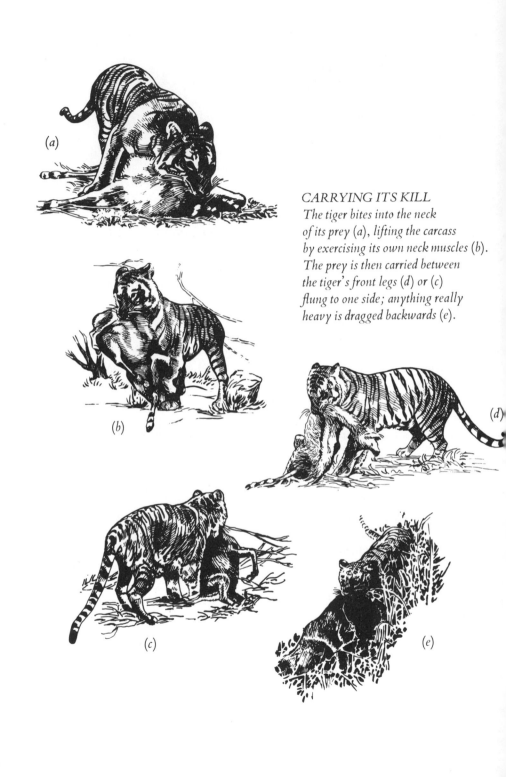

(a)

(b)

(d)

(c)

(e)

CARRYING ITS KILL
*The tiger bites into the neck
of its prey (a), lifting the carcass
by exercising its own neck muscles (b).
The prey is then carried between
the tiger's front legs (d) or (c)
flung to one side; anything really
heavy is dragged backwards (e).*

with grass or branches with leaves: in one instance a tiger kill was found covered with stones each as large as a coconut.

After devouring his kill on two successive nights a tiger usually spends the third night merely strolling and kills again on the fourth night. His average daily requirement is 10 to 12 kg of meat, which is the amount given to adult tigers in zoos; as they thrive on it I have assumed that this is the correct amount. An adult chital weighs 70 kg, of which 70% is available meat; one tiger, therefore, would need about 70 such animals per year. Since the annual rate of chital kills is 20% of the total population, a minimum of 350 animals is necessary to sustain one tiger for a year. The minimum number of tigers a reserve should have depends on the whole biotope complex, but if we take a figure of 30 tigers of all ages their annual food requirements can be maintained only if there is a population of at least 10,000 head of chital or 3600 sambar (which weighs on average 150 kg). These two species, which are found all over tigerland, form the bulk (67% according to Schaller, 1967) of the tiger's food. Wild boars, with an average weight of over 170 kg, are also an important item in the tiger's diet and these too occur in all parts of India.

There is little information available on the range requirements of chital or sambar, since the forage potential varies enormously in different habitats. But if one takes a good habitat in dry deciduous forest, a population of 10,000 chital would need an area of 30–35 sq miles. The optimum figure of 30 tigers in such an area is confirmed by several estimates. In 1830 there were 26 tigers in 20 sq miles in Booronpur; in 1941 there were 75 tigers in 250 sq miles of forest in Bundi. The present forests of India are not good forage areas as they are over-grazed by domestic cattle which are constantly guarded by their owners. Only if cattle grazing is eliminated along with other disturbing factors and an optimum number of prey built up can we expect to achieve a population of one tiger per square mile rather than the present state of one per ten square miles. Probably this will not happen except in the core areas of the tiger reserves.

The idea that the tiger is a territorial animal was challenged perhaps for the first time when a controversy started in the press following the death of a tiger named Sundar. An American zoologist, Dr John Seidensticker, came to the Sundarbans of West Bengal to try to tranquillize a tiger which had strayed into a village. The tiger died as a result, and the cause of death was attributed to a territorial dispute between Sundar and the resident tiger in whose domain he had been released. A post-mortem was done and the cause of death given as "deep wounds". When Dr Seidensticker met me in my office he admitted that his conclusions had been arrived at by a process of elimination. Leopards and hyenas are not found in the Sundarbans and the only other possible candidate who could have inflicted such wounds was another tiger. He did not realize that the wounds could have been caused by wild boars feeding on the carcass *after* the tiger's death; and he refused to believe that death could have been the result of weakness following an overdose of the tranquillizer. This practice yields limited data often at great expense, particularly in the Indian conditions of thick cover and undulating terrain. It was, in fact, folly to introduce a weakened tiger into an unknown area without gradual rehabilitation and an assured food supply for at least a few days. However, this would have reduced the drama of "operation release" which the foreign press was waiting for. The release was international news, but the death of poor Sundar made no stir except in the local press. I agree with the views of Dr Eton, the American ecologist, who said in his book on the cheetah that rare animals should never be darted as every single individual is precious.

The impression that tigers hold territory may be based on comparisons with the lion, or perhaps to some extent it is due to the anthropomorphic assumption that the king of the jungle must hold a kingdom. The spraying of urine on "boundaries" has been taken to indicate territorialism; but what good would it be if the territory is neither permanently held nor defended? I found that places which had been urinated on by tigers had no smell the next day. Even if a tiger could patrol a long perimeter of forest to re-establish his "boundaries" every few days, what would happen to the urine spray during the three months of tropical rains, or the winter nights of heavy dew? And what about the summers, when the hot sun and desiccating winds would remove the most pungent smell in a few hours?

However, ritualized urination is undoubtedly a fact – but for different reasons. Any conspicuous object like a tree or rock may receive a jet of urine but normally any other tiger visiting the area takes little notice of the smell. In the zoo, the same object is sprayed every day as soon as the tiger is released, but when a new tiger is introduced into the enclosure he cautiously approaches the spot, sniffs, jumps away and snarls. I conducted some experiments to test reactions further. Two heaps of hay, one sprayed with tiger urine and one fresh, were placed side by side. A one-year-old tiger, Jim, was dragged over the heaps; he walked over the fresh hay without protest, but in the case of the other heap he snarled and resisted. Presumably this reaction has something to do with information indicating "danger, there is another tiger about". Perhaps in the wild tigers take this hint and change course to avoid confrontation, as well as giving themselves time and space in which to move.

This also happens with other potential dangers, including the presence of human smell, a conclusion supported by my experiment of spraying human urine on the path leading to a tiger's kill. The spot was given a wide berth. We may assume, therefore, that spraying urine serves as a device to avoid unnecessary intraspecies confrontations, encouraging the distribution of members over a large area to allow for individual hunting. It is a spacing mechanism and not a territorial pillar-marking system.

To test the theory of territorialism I provided two baits at a distance of 400 metres from each other in the Kachida valley of Ranthambhor. On two different occasions both the baits were killed the same night at an interval of about two hours; they were eaten by two tigers which were within hearing range of each other, yet there was no fight – not even growls. Each carried on his own business. Old shikar notes even mention more than one tiger coming to the same kill and being shot one after the other, and I have observed tigers and tigresses killing baits one after another at Jharokha in Ranthambhor. Others have had similar experiences at Kanha. At times I have seen two tigers arriving at the same time; the weaker one was scared away from the bait, but the stronger one made no attempt to chase it from the area, as is normally done by all territorialists including lions, jackals, domestic dogs, nesting birds, and even human beings.

Since there are few large areas which can be reserved for the exclusive wanderings of a single tiger, the alternative is to share the range. Contrary to the Chinese proverb, one hill often holds two tigers. Several tigers may visit the same area but on different days or at different times of the day or night. They space themselves in such a way that confrontations are avoided.

I have photographed two tigers sharing a small shaded pool during the

THE EXPRESSIONS OF A TIGER

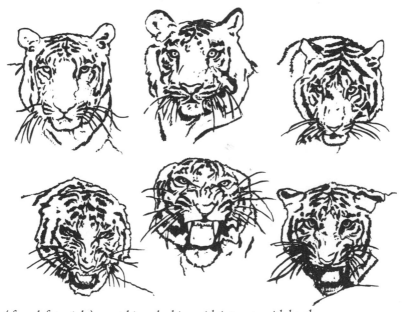

(from left to right): watching; looking with interest; with head lowered, interest intensified; (bottom three): angry dislike; warning growl, preparatory to action; low growl, made before withdrawal

Confrontations pass through a series of ceremonies, both animals having ample chance to withdraw at any stage. Fights last from between a few minutes to several hours.

hottest part of the day in June. Forsyth (1889) mentions driving five to seven tigers (all males) in a small beat; and Powell (1957) describes five tigers and a tigress sharing a small area. Schaller (1967) reports driving two tigers, three tigresses and two cubs in Corbett Park; I have examined the area and it is a reed patch of only a few hectares.

Conflicts do sometimes take place, as between two tigers courting one tigress in heat, or in the case of a mother protecting her cubs. Possession is nine-tenths of the law and a tiger who has been the first to locate a female in heat, or has made a kill purely by his own efforts, will fight for his rights. The instinct is inborn, and is further developed by training by the mother. I observed this behaviour in a cub about eight months old who had made a kill at Pandupole in April 1975. He was of course no match for his mother, but when she approached the kill while the cub was feeding she did so as a submissive individual respecting his right of ownership, almost as if she were begging for a favour. With the slightest protest from the cub she withdrew, probably in order to train him to be confident in asserting his rights. The protection of her cubs is every mother's responsibility and the slightest hint of aggression triggers off her defensive reaction either by escape or by distracting the aggressor by visual threats. Attack and elimination is adopted only as a last resort.

If confrontation between two tigers becomes unavoidable, the first step is to look the other straight in the eyes. If this does not work the next move is the fanning of the whiskers and baring of the canines. These visual threats build up tension, and in a few seconds vocalization comes into play. Each produces a hissing sound, which develops into a harsh coughing growl. The sound becomes louder and louder and the tigers come closer together until they are within arm's reach, when they sit on their haunches and start swinging their forepaws. At first the claws are sheathed, but a slight hit or scratch acts as an activator and they soon stand on their hind legs, with mouth open and eyes closed, swinging their arms. There is a terrifying deep-throated coughing sound, the fight gathers momentum and lasts for one or two minutes, and then the loser withdraws and runs away.

Such short confrontations are the most typical, but sometimes the fight goes on for hours. If one tiger manages to get hold of the other's neck it is broken and death is instantaneous. If a limb is broken the tiger suffers a lingering death. Sometimes while the two males are fighting the tigress slips away, or a third party appropriates the kill, but still the fight does not stop.

From the moment of the first visual contact until the battle actually begins each one has the opportunity to withdraw. The method is to appear to lose interest by looking away. This means submission: honour is satisfied, and the winner does not chase the loser. In most cases, therefore, the conflict consists of nothing more than a series of formalities, and it is very rare for a tiger to use his fangs or claws to kill a member of his species.

CHAPTER 2

Waiting for the tiger

The tiger is an elusive beast who does not follow rules. Frankly, in studying his behaviour I used no specific method but welcomed all sources of information. I found evidence in old shikar notes kept by the maharajas, case histories of poaching offences, taxidermists' records, zoo records, and personal interviews with a cross-section of people living close to tigers. Sometimes I used baits by tying up a buffalo calf or a wild piglet, but only to study specific behaviour patterns such as feeding habits. To keep a particular courting pair or a mother and cubs in the area, or to study the interaction of predator and prey, I provided baits near waterholes in Sariska and in the Kachida valley in Rajasthan. Hides near waterholes in Sariska during the summer proved particularly rewarding.

While sitting at waterholes to watch the relationship between the tiger and his prey, especially when he was not hunting, I learnt a lot about water. Nature allows no one to hoard this vital commodity to the disadvantage of others, every animal gets an equal opportunity to drink and no one goes thirsty. Confrontation is met by tolerance, illustrating the marvellous discipline of nature. A hot summer day followed by a night of full moon at a waterhole is the most rewarding experience possible for a naturalist, who is able to see nature's encyclopedia open page by page in front of his eyes.

Animals possess the power of discovering invisible waterholes. The technique is simple. Every patch of water attracts insects, especially mosquitoes and water-flies. Their presence is conspicuous because their flight is noticed by insectivorous birds, and when these dive their calls attract the attention of small mammals which in turn lead the larger mammals to discover the waterhole. In the deciduous forests which form nearly 80% of tigerland water becomes a problem – especially from April to June. The streams dry up and all that remains are a few scattered pools. The situation becomes acute in the dry deciduous forests of western Madhya Pradesh, Rajasthan and southern Bihar, and it deteriorates still further with the failure of the monsoon, which happens almost every third year. In the long summer days the water requirement of animals, especially the larger ones like elephants, gaur (*Bos gaurus*) and sambar deer (*Cervus unicolor*), as well as big birds like peacocks, is greater. They have to travel long distances to waterholes, which become the nerve centres of activity in the jungle.

I have spent countless days and nights at such waterholes, waiting and watching. A typical example will illustrate the routine – and the rewards.

Travelling by bus to my field station in Sariska I shout "Kalighati" and the driver stops with a jerk; he hardly expected any passenger, least of all me, to alight at this lonely spot in the middle of the forest late in the evening. The bus goes on and I am left all by myself. "Kalighati" means a black valley, and a long time ago the name was appropriate as the forest was thick and impenetrable and its floor was always dark. The fact that there are still tigers in the valley shows that its environmental quality has not deteriorated all that much. The landscape is one of well-clothed rolling hills, sheer quartzite walls of the Aravali range, hog-back crests and narrow valleys. I have returned to this fascinating country for the last twenty-three years, at different seasons and at different times of the day, even arranging to be there on the same day year after year to confirm my observations. In August the whole valley is lusciously green, then as winter approaches the foliage turns copper-brown and the grasses become yellow. In spring the leaves dry on the trees and with a gentle breeze they start falling. By March the forest is leafless and bone dry, its floor covered with a cushion of fallen leaves inches thick.

On this particular occasion I looked around for help but there was none. On the lonely hut hung a padlock. Evidently the forest guard was out on his rounds, and I sat on my box to wait. A few peacocks arrived, and some tree-pies and red-vented bulbuls began to drink at the bird bath. Within minutes there were more than fifty peacocks around but they took no notice of me. The last rays of the sun were striking the hilltops and I was losing all hope of the forest guard's return: he might have gone on leave, or to collect his pay and rations. Then at last he appeared from behind a bush, a short man dressed in bleached khaki with an axe over his shoulder.

Bhanwar Singh, as later he introduced himself, has been there for 15 years, mostly entirely alone. His life is routine. In the morning he goes out to patrol his beat and look for poachers, including wood poachers, and drives the cattle away. In the afternoon he returns, cleans the watch-tower and prepares it for visitors. He pumps water from the well for the wild animals, provides carrots for chital, corn for pigs, salt for sambar; and he ties a bait for tigers. This duty he performs unwillingly as he dislikes the cruel killing of a tethered buffalo calf. Unfortunately the tourists expect it and it is part of his official work.

On the way to the hide he had made for me he told me all about what had happened since my last visit, about the tigers' kills, the tourists' luck in seeing tigers, petty quarrels with his officers, his home leave, the marriage proposal he had received from a neighbouring village, and finally his marriage. Bhanwar Singh – or "Bhanwaria", as I call him – feels free with me because he comes from Jodhpur and we speak the same dialect.

Soon we were at the waterhole and I inspected the grass hide, which was cosy but flimsy. A few thorn bushes had been placed round it to discourage the predator from approaching too closely, but I insist on branches without leaves

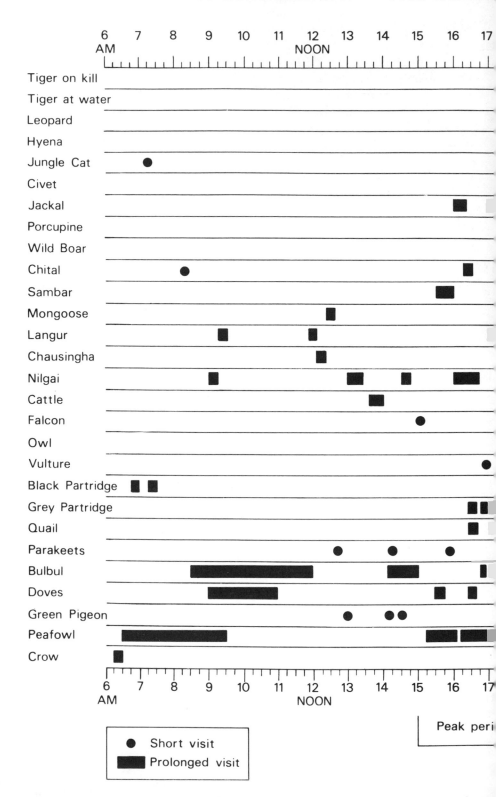

A SUMMER'S DAY − Wild animals

Short visit
Prolonged visit

Peak peri

ghati waterhole in time and space

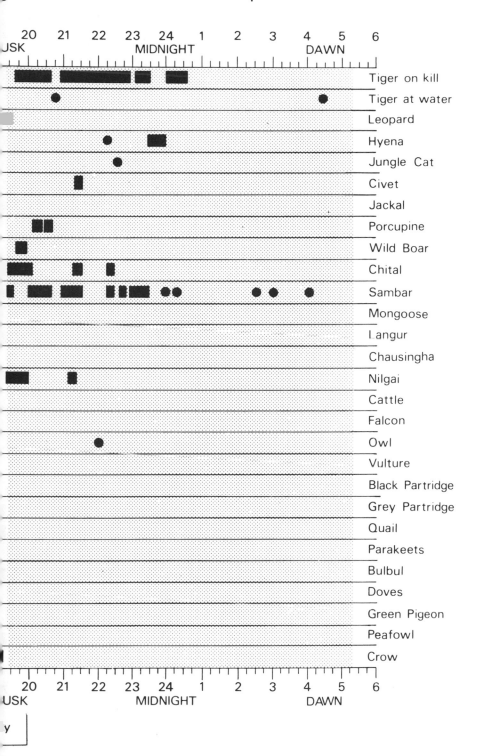

	20	21	22	23	24	1	2	3	4	5	6	
USK					MIDNIGHT				DAWN			

Tiger on kill
Tiger at water
Leopard
Hyena
Jungle Cat
Civet
Jackal
Porcupine
Wild Boar
Chital
Sambar
Mongoose
Langur
Chausingha
Nilgai
Cattle
Falcon
Owl
Vulture
Black Partridge
Grey Partridge
Quail
Parakeets
Bulbul
Doves
Green Pigeon
Peafowl
Crow

	20	21	22	23	24	1	2	3	4	5	6
USK					MIDNIGHT				DAWN		

y

Red wattled lapwing

as otherwise they attract browsers and one cannot scare them away for fear of being discovered by the tiger. The game warden never approved of my sitting close to a bait in such a flimsy hide and was always anxious to know first thing in the morning if I was still alive.

It was impossible to stand up in the hide so I dived inside and made a soft landing on the cushions. The first job was to adjust camera angles, flash-unit positions and lenses so as to be ready in total darkness without making the slightest noise. For night work the lenses have to be focused in advance and fixed with Sellotape; the only adjustment that has to be made at the time is the diaphragm and I have familiarized myself with this by long practice. Winter nights in hides can be terribly cold, and frost often persists in these forest depressions even after sunrise, so I make myself as comfortable as possible with foam-rubber cushions, sleeping bag and extra quilt. Old clothing is best as it does not make a noise when rubbed, and gloves are necessary on frosty nights as it is too cold to remove the covering from lenses with bare fingers.

In the summer I have an ice box with soft drinks and oranges, but I avoid food and anything containing sugar as it attracts ants and makes the hide uncomfortable. Hides near water always attract mosquitoes and flies so I use an insect repellent. Other equipment includes a luminous watch to record the times of arrival of animals and their duration of stay, a counter, a stopwatch and a thermometer to record the temperature. For relieving oneself I keep a few bottles.

I always go alone and do not even take books to divert the attention in case a valuable opportunity is lost. Animals like chausingha, the four-horned antelope (*Tetracerus quadricornis*), visit water only once in 24 hours and stay for less than two minutes. They come during the day, but one never knows which two minutes they will choose, so it may involve a tense and tiring wait of many hours. I never carry a gun as it gives a false sense of security and one could be provoked to use it out of nervousness rather than need. Also, arms attract the attention of dacoits and other outlaws. Once in the Chambal ravines I had to explain the use of a telephoto lens to a group of dacoits; they did not believe me until one of them had triggered off my camera three times without hearing a bang.

On the occasion of which I was speaking, "Bhanwaria" closed the hide with a thorn bush, passed me his axe (not for defence, but for making adjustments inside the hide) and left me. There was still some light, and although the animals had been disturbed by our presence they soon regained confidence. First came the peafowl with a "honk, honk" to inspect the hide and, finding no disturbance inside, proceeded to the waterhole; I counted 32 peahens including a few chicks. A few months earlier when I visited the place the peahens had their August brood. The birds bring their chicks to the water with great caution and the slightest disturbance causes them to stop drinking, extend their necks and raise the neck feathers in excitement. Soon a few gorgeously feathered peacocks arrived and they were even more cautious. While the male went to the water-hole one hen came close to my hide and looked straight in; I did not even flicker my eyelids and, reassured, she proceeded to drink. When the peacocks lowered their heads to reach the water the beautiful metallic tail-feathers with their moons and crescents went up in the air, then as the equally lovely blue necks rose from the water the tails went down. This see-saw continued for ten to twelve times in each case, the fan-like crests adding grace to the movement of their bodies. Then more peahens arrived and the entire shore of the waterhole was filled with birds. Sariska has probably the highest concentration of peafowl in the world and Kalighati is the centre. Every day more than 100 birds arrive for their morning and evening drink. A few smaller birds such as partidges and quails waited their turn at a short distance and the whole scene was transformed with movement.

The sudden appearance of langurs disturbed the birds but soon they were sharing the waterhole. The monkeys came in small groups, mothers with babies clinging to their breasts, yearlings and adults; but the leader, a robust male, sat at some distance watching the troop. Langurs at a waterhole present an amusing caricature of human behaviour. The leader sat facing me, looked hard and bared his teeth, then he cautiously lowered his head, clasped the ground firmly and sipped. Except for drinking langurs have no use for water, but although they never take a bath they groom each other constantly and are the cleanest of all primates. The dominant male drank for over two minutes, raised his head and looked in all directions and then had another long drink. Hearing the click of my camera he gazed in my direction but was unable to locate the source of the sound, so all he could do was to bare his teeth again in protest. Confidently he walked off and disappeared. Langurs select a certain mud-free spot for drinking and all crowd together; they are tolerant of the presence of chital, nilgai and peafowl, but not of pigs.

The light was fading and only one peahen remained, then she too returned to the trees to roost. When it was almost dark a huge blue bull or nilgai (*Boselaphus tragocamelus*) arrived and stopped about ten feet from the water; although the waterhole was free he wanted to be sure that no predator was around. A massive, muscular beast, he stood on the shore and lowered his head but he could not reach the water. The blue bull has a backward slanting body and when the water is lower than ground level it is difficult for him to reach. He dropped on his knees and started drinking, but soon raised his head, the drops trickling from his mouth. This was the closest look I had ever had at the sharp, spiky horns, tufted beard and huge eyes of the majestic blue bull. After another short drink he was off, bouncing away like Humpty Dumpty. The whole visit lasted two-and-a-half minutes.

Next a jackal trotted to the waterhole, walked nervously around, then lowered his head and tucked his tail between his legs. After lapping up some water he remained half-submerged, presumably to quench the heat of the day. His mate joined him, and a large herd of chital watched and waited for the jackals to clear off. They stayed too long for a pair of red-legged lapwing, who launched aerial attacks until the jackals left. Then the delicate-footed chital (Axis deer, *Axis axis*) approached the shore, a doe followed by another doe with a fawn. The three drank close together, almost touching faces, although the

lapwing and Vavanus lizard

whole shoreline was vacant; probably in this way they gained confidence. Soon they were followed by does, fawns, yearlings and stags in such numbers that there was no room at the waterhole. For 45 minutes they drank in turns undisturbed in the darkness; chital are diurnal but here as in many other places they have become nocturnal owing to human disturbance.

All this time, of course, I had been taking notes. The recording of observations in total darkness is a problem. I tried talking quietly on to a tape, but even that is too loud. I tried using a small pencil torch under a blanket, but in the blackness of a moonless night in the jungle the slightest light is visible outside the hide. Eventually I had to resort to writing in a notebook in the dark. Once my pen is on the page I do not lift it until the sheet is finished and these scribbled notes can be deciphered next day to record a fair copy on specially designed punch cards. Although my friends laugh at my doing so, I prefer to use a roll of toilet paper when writing notes. It provides continuity, and while writing I get a philosophical feeling, as if I were preparing someone's horoscope on long rolls!

After the chital had left the waterhole a sambar doe arrived and, since the chital were still in the vicinity, she did not stop to verify that the coast was clear. (Wild animals are very much guided by signs, signals and alarms from their co-sharers of the habitat. Even the slightest signal is noted, and acted upon.) She was joined by her fawn, and within ten minutes there were no chital on the scene. More sambar does arrived and then, very cautiously, a stag. More stags appeared and they formed into a stag party in a separate group from the does. There were five of them, yet there was no quarrel. Occasionally one of them raised his snout towards me and sniffed the air, stamping his forefeet on the ground and nervously raising and lowering his tail. Soon the waterhole was full of sambar. At first one entered the water, then two more who sat down to wallow. The first stag urinated into the water, unconcerned that he would be drinking it soon after. The full moon came out and I could count more than 20 sambar. Then a wild boar arrived and stood there snorting; he was joined by others and one started butting the sambar, who promptly left the waterhole.

Priority at a waterhole is obviously determined by the capacity of a species or individual to inflict harm on the others. Smaller birds yield to bigger birds, which in turn yield to mammals. Does and cows yield to stags and bulls. Among males the size and effectiveness of the weapon is the ruling factor, and even stags surrender to the wild boar's tusks. But he himself gives way to the bad-tempered porcupine, whose backward thrust impales his adversary with a battery of spears. Predators, including birds such as falcons and owls, take priority over all as they are equipped with claws, pointed canines, or sharp beaks.

As I waited in my hide and the jingling of crickets filled the air I suddenly heard a metallic "dhank", the alarm call of a sambar. At that time of the

evening the danger is 99% certain to be a leopard or a tiger – most probably a
tiger, I thought, as I knew that one lived on that hill. The cramped four hours I
had spent in the hide were forgotten in my excitement. I rearranged and checked
my photographic equipment, opened up the peephole, and reassured myself
of the position of the flimsy gate. I had already fixed tapes on the lenses after
focusing on the shoreline. A few sambar and chital were drinking normally and
even when the tiger's roar from the near-by hill could be clearly heard there
was no panic. Animals calculate the distance from the predator by the pitch
of the sound, and react accordingly.

The moon rose higher and faintly I saw the forms of chital and a family
group of wild boars. For more than an hour there was no further alarm call,
but this did not damp my hopes as I knew the tiger was there. If he had left the
valley the animals would have given fading alarm calls and their silence indicated that he was waiting somewhere in the vicinity. When a predator is
resting, even in full view, his prey do not make a sound as a sitting predator is no
danger to them.

My hopes further revived when a chital gave a low alarm call; since chital
live on the plains the call confirmed that the predator had moved down from
the hill slope. A few more chital took up the call, clearly demarcating their
enemy's movements. Eventually all the animals stopped drinking and turned
their heads towards the direction of the alarm. Then there was complete silence
as if nothing had happened, and a whole hour passed. But the tiger could appear
at any moment, and I slowly opened my water bottle and sipped to clear my
throat, as a single cough could ruin everything.

At that moment the silence and darkness were shattered by a distant flashing
of lights and with it my hopes disappeared. A mini-bus rolled in with a load of
talkative tourists. Jai Singh, the game warden, had promised them a glimpse of a
tiger and, failing to find one, he flashed his spotlight on my hide. He started

Chausinga antelope

talking about my research and told his audience about how I would spend a cold night in the company of tigers without any weapons. Some wondered, some pitied, while others wished me luck. Mercifully the warden did not know about the alarm calls so they left me to it, and I cursed them for ruining my chances.

I am not against people occupying the watch-tower while I am in my hide, but unfortunately many of the tourists are exhausted after a day of climbing steps to temples, or are suffering from jet-lag, and within minutes of their arrival they start snoring. Generally they are elderly and cannot control their cough, and it is always difficult for them to refrain from talking, especially after an exciting day seeing "Kama Sutra" carvings or buying jewels in Jaipur! A whisper is enough to make a tiger go elsewhere, and the glow of a cigarette bright enough to scare him away. We welcome disciplined tourists and those who are really interested in the wildlife, but many merely want to add the tiger to their list with the temples and the Taj. An influx of non-serious tourists is not what our reserves need.

After the noise of the mini-bus faded away, complete silence prevailed again. Sambar came back to the waterhole and the normal activity of the jungle was resumed. Suddenly – within ten minutes of the mini-bus leaving – peacocks called and the langurs with their "Kho ka kookho" confirmed the movement of the tiger. In fact, the tiger had been waiting for the bus's visit, so he could finally come and drink in peace. Once I had realized this I was able to use this information to ensure that tigers came to the hole at an earlier hour. A blue bull which was at the waterhole stopped drinking and fixed his head in the direction of the calls, then he became very nervous, gave a muffled bellow and joined in the general stampede. The waterhole was deserted.

A muffled sound of rolling rocks and the flapping of a heavy bird came from behind the hide. It was a horned owl, and the resident lapwing cried "Did you do it, did you do it?" and took to his wings. A moment later I saw a huge figure, of an animal larger than I had ever seen. The dim moonlight did not allow me to make out its contours precisely, but from my low angle it appeared bigger than a buffalo. It proceeded to the waterhole and, sitting on its haunches, lowered its forelegs and head into the water. The lapping sound continued for over ten minutes, then the animal rose and walked off. It was the tiger, and in the faint light and atmosphere of tension and excitement he had appeared enormous.

While I was watching tigers at the Sulkhan river pool in Kanha in April 1971 one arrived at 10 a.m. when the sun was beginning to get warm. He crouched, started lapping, then stood up, turned and lowered his hind legs and sat down half submerged in the shaded pool. After about an hour he sat down under a tree, and he repeated his visits to the water six times that day. This alternate

drenching and drying keeps the tiger cool during the hottest hours. I also saw a
film with Maharaja Bhim Singh of Kotah which showed that tigers frequently
visit water to soak themselves for an hour or so and then come out; the hot
winds provide a cooling effect when they blow on the tiger's wet body. As
soon as the water evaporates and the body gets dry, the tiger goes into the
water for another long bath. Alternately wetting and drying himself, the tiger
passes the hot day.

On another occasion in May 1971 I had spent the day in the same hide at
Sariska. Evening fell and I was watching a bait when a tiger arrived. He lowered
his body and rushed at the victim, there was a choked bellow and the tiger stood
motionless with the head of the calf in his mouth. I could hear his heavy
breathing, and after 20 seconds he opened his jaws and the lifeless body fell
down with a thud. For a minute the tiger stood still, then walked away completely unconcerned for a drink. After ten minutes I heard repeated calls of a lapwing. The tiger came back to the kill, gave a few tugs and dragged the carcass a
short distance. Next I heard the sound of tearing skin and the crushing of bones.

These sounds were clearly heard by some sambar hinds and a stag, who stood
on the shore barely 45 feet from the tiger. They were nervous, but this did not
prevent the stag from drinking for two minutes, pausing for a few seconds and
drinking again, after which he trotted off. Similarly some chital drank and went
away, and finally a porcupine arrived and was quite unconcerned. The tiger,
busy munching, paid no attention to the juicy prey within his reach. Recently,
in May 1977, at Sariska, I saw a sambar doe and two fawns sitting in an ash-
patch absolutely unconcerned while a tigress and her grown-up cub fed in full
view hardly a hundred yards or so away. Even when my jeep disturbed the
tigers and they moved away this did not bother the sambar. Animals know that
the tiger, unlike man, is satisfied with what he has killed for the day and is not
concerned with tomorrow. He takes only what he needs and does not kill for
the sake of killing. There is a perfect understanding between predator and prey.
For the first time I felt ashamed of being a man, who is not trusted even by the
jackals, much less the deer and antelopes.

After the tiger had eaten for an hour he had had enough. Leaving half his
kill he went away, to return the next day. He could not stay to guard it owing
to human disturbance by day in that valley. Within a quarter of an hour a
hyena arrived and hurriedly tore at the open hindquarters, broke off the leg
and carried it off. Then came a jungle cat who circled the carcass and climbed
up on to it. She was nervous, but at last started nibbling. Meanwhile animals
continued to come to the waterhole in ones and twos, unconcerned at the
threat of death so close by. Another jungle cat tried to approach and there were
growls at the kill. A resident ratel which lived in a near-by bush then punctured
the rumen which released an awful smell, and I had to open the thorn cover of
the hide for ventilation.

The moon shifted behind the western hills and shadow filled the valley. In the early hours just before dawn one small creature arrived, but I knew of its presence only from the sounds of something being torn. When the eastern sky began to lighten it was possible to confirm my suspicion that it was a jackal. He was busy pulling at the intestines, and was far more interested in offal than in solid meat. Every time he managed to pull a piece off he trotted away, returning after five or ten minutes, and soon after his mate also came out to feed.

Sunlight illuminated the kill and I saw that the buffalo was half-eaten. A big bird landed with a thud, then a few more landed and walked confidently up to the carcass and drove off the jackals. Any further attempts on the animals' part were repelled by a show of strong claws, and it was only after persistent begging by the jackals that after a while they were given a little room to continue feeding. Normally vultures arrive late as they have to soar high to discover a kill. If they are roosting within viewing distance they generally wait for the light, but sometimes they arrive for a moonlit dinner. Since vultures are so slow to get off the ground they avoid confrontations with a tiger on his kill, preferring to wait till the day is well advanced and the tiger has left.

More birds landed and I counted 42, but not all of them were visible at any one time as some were right inside the carcass. Soon there was no room at all for the jackals. The big birds shrieked as they gulped the meat, while the jackals looked on helplessly. The common vulture is not fitted with a cutting mechanism, so the whole process consists of tearing, stretching and pulling in reverse gear. After about half an hour the birds began to lose interest and sat basking in the morning sun. By 9 a.m. they had all left, and all that remained of the tiger's kill was the skeleton, head and hooves. All this time the tree-pies were anxiously awaiting their turn, and now that the vultures had moved off they started picking the fragments of meat still sticking to the bone, all fighting for the best place. The peafowl took no notice; all they were interested in was their morning drink at the pool, and I took the opportunity to photograph them with back-lighting to add depth to the scene.

As the day became warm activity slowed down except for visits by red-vented bulbuls, doves, rock pigeons and occasional orioles, green pigeons and parakeets. Sometimes a swallow would dive down swiftly to drink, or a king-fisher to fish. When the heat was dazzling a chausingha came along with his doe and fawn, but they were in view for less than three minutes. By 1 p.m. the heat in the closed hide became unbearable and I knew that nothing would happen until the stream of birds started arriving in the evening, so I called it a day. The first thing I did was to go to the nearest well and pour over myself buckets and buckets of water. I too needed a waterhole.

On some occasions in Ranthambhor and Sariska I was able to follow tigers in a jeep at night, and in Kanha on elephant back or on foot during the day. The

tigers were not disturbed either by the jeep or the elephant and amply re-
warded my curiosity. I found elephant rides an uncomfortable and tiring
exercise because, unlike horses, an elephant keeps three feet on the ground and
lifts only one at a time. This results in the shifting of the centre of gravity with
every step with consequent rocking movements. The ride is still more uncomfortable when the elephant crosses a watercourse: one feels as though one is
on a giant whirligig every time it lifts its leg. Any attempt to resist the movement tires the rider in no time, but by leaving the body relaxed to harmonize
with the elephant's movements the strain can be reduced considerably. When
climbing or descending a slope the rider is thrown backwards and forwards
respectively, and if he does not hold the rails of the howdah firmly he is likely
to fall off. Although it is the elephant that does the walking, shoes are still
needed to protect one's feet from the branches.

Even when standing the elephant is seldom steady, but shifts its weight from
one side to the other, lifts its trunk to grip the nearest branch or clump of grass,
then thrashes it on the ground or on one of its front legs before putting it into
its mouth. Often when I thought the elephant was steady and was about to
click my camera shutter it started inhaling or exhaling, resulting in camera
shake. Successful photographs from elephant-top were a combination of instrument efficiency and a quick draw, but mostly good luck. After many failures I
learned that if the elephant is made to sit one can take a shake-free picture.

However, in spite of these handicaps the ease with which the elephant
wades through the water-hyacinth-infested swamps of Kaziranga, or the tall
grasses of the Manas or Corbett Parks, crosses the ditches and ravines of Kanha
and approaches grazing herds and sleeping tigers silently, all make it an ideal
mobile *machan* for study and photography. In the majority of tigerlands there
is no substitute for an elephant. To have a sitting elephant, incidentally, means
there is a far more level position from which to photograph, and a greater
opportunity to compose a photo with a feel of the natural background to it, but
at the same time it is cruel to the elephant, who finds any sitting position
particularly awkward.

In open forests and scrublands the jeep is a most versatile vehicle and is a great
relief from tiring elephant rides. Wild animals get used to inanimate transport
quite quickly and after a cursory investigation they ignore it and resume
grazing. When it is necessary to drive across country through thick foliage or
bushes one is dependent on the skill of the driver and I found Fateh Singh,
assistant director at Ranthambhor, excellent at the steering wheel.

On one occasion he accompanied me when I was camping at the ruins of
Jogimahal. At that time I was convalescing from heart trouble and was strictly
forbidden to exert myself or get excited, but with a camera in the field this was
impossible. I was following a herd of chital and a troop of langurs, and the light
was giving excellent colour contrasts. The master stag left the herd to challenge

an intruder and soon they were entangled. They were in a small, well-lit open patch, but my jeep was in the forest with no way out. I was in despair at losing this opportunity to photograph fighting chital as I watched helplessly.

Suddenly Fateh Singh virtually bulldozed through the trees and put me in the open patch in front of the stags. Amazingly, they completely ignored our approach and continued fighting for the next ten minutes, occasionally resting with antlers entangled, separating and fighting again. Eventually the intruder managed to push his tine into the shoulder of the dominant stag, causing the latter to flee. The victor triumphantly took command of the harem of does and the other stags accepted him as their new leader.

Driving efficiency is particularly important when you are sitting on the bonnet of the jeep to get a quick picture. Any sudden jerk is likely to throw you in front of the vehicle and may prove fatal. This happened in the case of the famous wildlife photographer Ylla who lost her life at Bharatpur in just such an accident. She was photographing a bullock cart race from the bonnet of a Land-Rover when the wheels hit a clump of grass and she fell flat on her head. After two days in a coma she died. I was at Bharatpur at the time. Photography while the vehicle is in motion is never satisfactory, and it is essential not only to stop but to switch off the engine at the right moment. Animals ignore a uniform noise but allowing the vehicle to roll with switched-off engine scares them: probably they take the silent monster to be some curious animal moving towards them. An open jeep is not ideal, as the animals note one's hand movements, so I prefer a closed jeep which provides suitable cover.

My classmate from the Forest College, Jagdeesh Mishra, had an amazing mastery of the art of approaching wild herds with a jeep. When he took anyone round Palamau Park he always tried to give them the closest possible view of the elephants. He knows most of them by name and never forgets those which have given him trouble. I once tried to frame a cow elephant which was busy pushing trees down and Mishra put the jeep in reverse and backed a few metres. The animal stopped her activity and looked at us, raising her trunk to try to catch our scent. Then she advanced a few steps and stared, at the same time making a drumming sound. All of a sudden the entire herd stopped grazing and the cow elephant charged. Our jeep was already in reverse and Mishra continued to drive backwards rapidly. Meanwhile another elephant appeared from a depression and tried to block our way, and the slightest hesitation on the driver's part would have been fatal. One of the elephants of this herd had made pulp of a Fiat not long before. The charging cow followed for some distance and then stopped, staring at the retreating jeep and thumping her front feet in anger.

Early next morning I returned to find the area littered with broken trees, looking as though it was the site of some inefficient forestry operation. Apparently one of the cow elephants was about to give birth and was looking for

a safe maternity ward, so her companions were helping her by clearing the ground to fortify her hiding place. The trees had been pushed all to one side, giving us a clue to the direction of the elephants' movements. The morning was completely silent except for a faint sound coming from a thickly covered ravine, where evidently the herd had retired to rest. This road-blocking behaviour by pulling down trees is a peculiarity of the elephants of Palamau, which number only about 30 and are a recent invasion of the late 1930s. They are believed to have escaped from the elephant camp of the Raja of Sirguja, a famous tiger hunter.

As there was no chance of elephant photography we were discussing the next move when I heard the distant roar of a tiger. It was repeated twice at an interval of 30 seconds. The night before we had left a buffalo calf as bait, and the sound we heard might have been the last call of a tiger which had eaten a good meal and was about to retire for a day's rest. On investigating the place where the bait had been tied we found that the calf had indeed been carried off. Christian Zuber, the wildlife photographer, was busy filming the drag mark and remains of the calf. It seemed that the tiger had come to the bait after Zuber and his charming wife had abandoned the hide the night before, and the animal must have been watching them the whole time. Zuber was not the only one to be duped like this; the then Chief Conservator of Forests, Shri S. P. Shahi, and many others had been the repeated victims of the tiger's cunning. The villain had taken more than 60 baits without obliging even the Park Director.

On examination I found several causes of their failure to film or photograph the tiger. One was that the hide was not properly located and designed. The first principle of hide-making is that the hide should merge with the landscape, and for that purpose only local material should be used. Thus on river banks or on rocky areas local stone is vital; similarly grass should be used in meadow hides and brushwood in scrublands. In open country one needs a 3 ft deep pit with local thatching to merge with the environment. On one occasion the hide was a massive structure, with three big windows for projecting the cameras, and these openings gave the tiger a clear view of the inside of the hide and any movement within. He could also hear all sounds. I advised them to close all three windows and to leave open only a few very small peepholes, just sufficient to project a lens at eye level in a sitting position. Another defect I noticed was the manner in which the bait was tied; the tree could have created an obstruction between the cameraman in the hide and the animal attacking the bait. We solved this problem by anchoring a wire loop round a log buried two-and-a-half feet in the ground. This done, I elected to try my luck and sat there the next evening, but unfortunately the herd of elephants decided to graze in the same area. The tiger was scared and did not turn up. With burning torches, my rescue party escorted me back to camp.

Certainly I had more failures than successes. There were occasions when I travelled hundreds of miles along dusty forest tracks without meeting any wild animals except a hare or a jackal. Even in the famous tiger forests of North Kheri in Uttar Pradesh driving through the night I saw only a few chital. Cruising for over 1000 km in creeks around the islands in the Sundarbans, spending sleepless nights, I failed to see a tiger even though I found fresh pug marks on almost every island. For days on end sometimes I waited at hides in the hope of getting a glimpse of a tiger without success. On such occasions I had to be content with collecting corroboratory evidence such as disturbed grass, footprints, droppings, drag-lines of kills and the carcasses of prey which showed individual methods of killing, even claw marks on tree trunks. There were also noises: the alarm calls of chital and sambar, the nervous dog-like bark of a barking deer, the muffled bellow of a nilgai, the snort of a gaur, the sneeze of a chinkara, the hooting of an owl, the cough of a peacock or a langur, and occasionally the great roar itself coming from a distant hill. Even when I did see a tiger it passed so quickly that few details registered in my mind, much less in my notebook or camera film. Attempt after attempt proved frustrating, but success when it came dispelled all the previous depression. All the same, I came to realize that failure could be as important as success from the ecological point of view, negative information being just as much a record very often as something positive.

There were times when luck was on my side and I would find myself spending days in the company of a tigress with cubs, or of tigers relaxing in streams or pools or guarding their kill. On one glorious night after another tigers would come to dine on their kill and keep me company till dawn. I made many thrilling discoveries, such as the times when I photographed courting tigers, a tigress carrying a cub in her mouth or one bringing up a record litter of five cubs.

Successful photographs are distressingly rare, sometimes owing to the presence of tourists, sometimes (which is worse) due to my own fault. Once after a hectic day I rushed to Kalighati waterhole and entered my hide to see the usual stream of chital and sambar coming to drink but no sign of a tiger. The cool breeze lulled me to sleep and the next I heard was a lapping sound. It was dawn. I looked around and there was the tiger. His pug marks showed that twice he had come close to my hide and I knew nothing about it. My wife tells me that when tired I snore heavily and no doubt the tiger was puzzled at such curious noises in his land.

There are worse things to look into than the eyes of a tiger. In my Kachida hide in May 1971 while I was observing sambar at the waterhole I found that a stone was obstructing my view. After the sambar had gone I pushed the stone out of the way and was getting ready for a fresh shot when I saw a cobra face to face through the lens opening and hardly 20 inches from me. Movement in the cramped hide was impossible so I gave a hiss and the reptile raised its hood. It turned away, but I hardly had time to breathe before it had dropped into the hide from the other peephole and there it was behind my camera box. I do not recall what I did, but the snake must have slunk away. I have never been so frightened in my life even when facing tigers at close quarters, such as the time when a tigress with three cubs surrounded my hide and tried to take the roof off to discover the source of the flashing light.

Studying a tiger is always thrilling, but if not carried out with sufficient care and knowledge it can be dangerous. I had some very anxious moments in Kanha Park when for a whole day I hung precariously from a tree while a tigress with two small cubs prowled below making angry attempts to get at the outsize "vulture" up in the branches. My choice had been a bad one as the tree forked not very high above the ground and the branch on which I perched was almost horizontal. The tigress discovered my presence while her cubs were feeding and she stood under the tree with murder on her mind. I froze and made no attempt to climb higher for fear of catching hold of a dead branch and falling. The tigress raised her forelimbs on the trunk, scratched the bark in frustration and then sat down. I wondered how long I could remain in this position, and whenever I made a move the tigress rushed to the tree. I had an eight-hour ordeal until the camp elephant came and lifted me off.

On other occasions I had to hold my breath when a tiger, to confirm his suspicions, came close to my flimsy grass hide. Some of my close-up pictures are the products of sheer foolhardiness; but then, it is just these risks that give tiger-watching its special thrill.

I enjoyed every minute of my stay in stuffy hides, sometimes sweating in a temperature of 46°C, at other times shivering beside a frozen pool. Perhaps my most uncomfortable experience was while watching birds rather than tigers, sitting on floating hides in the fresh-water swamps at Bharatpur to observe the behaviour of Saras cranes on their nests. The atmosphere was almost un-bearably hot, humid and oppressive, and any movement shook the raft and made it conspicuous. I watched from sunrise to sunset, seated precariously almost on the surface of the mosquito-infested marsh; but I forgot the glare of the August sun and my discomfort in the fascination of watching the cranes' nest-building activities, their share in the duties of incubating the eggs, and the dance and trumpeting calls in unison at the time of the changing of the guard. The cranes put me to shame for my own shortcomings as a father.

The technique of photographing from a hide was unknown to me until I met Dr Salim Ali, the greatest living authority on the birds of India. At our first meeting I invited him to lunch and noticed that he was only nibbling salad. To my horror I saw that the main dish was green pigeon: it was August, the close season. My wife tried to pretend it was a small chicken, but Salim only smiled. After that I saw him almost every year, and in 1969 when he got the Phillips Medal from IUCN I went to congratulate him and presented him with a one rupee coin. In Rajasthan tradition such a gift conveys the highest respect, and Salim valued it. When I saw him later after he had been presented with the Paul Getty award of $50,000 I reminded him that this was not the first gift of cash he had received.

By photographing and taking notes over long periods of time in some places I came to know the animals and birds almost by name, or at least by their morphological peculiarities such as deformities, injuries and battle scars. I saw them when they first came with their mothers, then as youngsters, then with their mates, and finally with their own young. Sometimes when I missed a certain individual I would be afraid it had been killed or trapped, only to be reassured by seeing it the next day or on the next trip. Such encounters always make me happy and I experience a sense of family reunion.

Although I identified with these creatures they never trusted me: the under-standing was all one-sided. Even my scent sends them bolting. I have wondered whether it was my fault, but then I tell myself that it is nothing personal but an inbuilt fear of man which the animals have developed because human action has exceeded the natural limits of predation. Man is the embodiment of un-predictable danger, so I could never be accepted as part of the ecology of tigerland and can only remain a secret witness to the animals' lives.

CHAPTER 3

Family bonds

During my wanderings in tiger country I have never met anyone who has watched the courtship and mating of tigers from beginning to end. Tulsinath, a shikar officer of Udaipur, told me that he only once saw a mating pair, and for a few minutes at the most. Much of the evidence cited is no more than the odd noises which hearers associated with mating tigers.

On 10 December 1970 luck favoured me when I was in the Kachida valley at my field station of Ranthambhor. In the late evening my headlights caught a tiger. I followed him for about a mile, overtook him, and after about 20 minutes went to see if he was coming to my bait. By then there was a pair. The bigger tiger turned aside to the left and the smaller one, presumably a tigress, slipped into a bush to the right. Not wanting to disturb them I switched off the headlights and proceeded in reverse till I was round a turning, then accelerated to be ready in my hide. An hour passed but there was no sound except the occasional tinkling of the buffalo bell. Then I heard two roars at an interval of one minute, followed by three more after fifteen minutes. The valley echoed with the roars, but the only response was a distant call from a sambar. Suddenly the buffalo got up and the continued tinkling of the bell made it clear that he was very nervous. Soon I made out a sleek animal that rushed in and gripped the calf, and this was followed by the usual noises of a scuffle and a long-drawn moan.

I did not switch on the light for fear of scaring the tigers and had to make my observations by moonlight. The tigress tugged at the carcass five times, then the tiger came and pulled at the haunches of the dead calf, and with the first jerk it was free. The tiger dragged it through the bush but, being unable to free the animal's head, he settled down to eat on the spot. He was behind a bush and I could only hear crunching noises. The tigress remained sitting in the grass about fifteen feet away. After about half an hour there were some growls and the tiger left the carcass and went and sat on a rock near by. The tigress then had her turn at tearing and munching. Feeding alternately and occasionally resting they continued their dinner until 2 a.m., when they both disappeared.

I heard nothing until shortly after 4 a.m., when there was a cry followed by a strange metallic sound. With my zoo experience it was clear to me that the tigers were engaged in their love-play. Similar noises were heard at intervals of about half an hour, but I resisted the temptation to switch on the spotlight and awaited the dawn. When at last the light improved I could see both of them asleep on the bank of the stream. The tigress got up, smelled a patch of grass by almost touching the ground, and put her tongue out. She then went up to the tiger and rubbed her body against his, turned her back and walked away. He followed and there was a short chase, then she sat down in a crouching position. The tiger made the most of his opportunity and mated with her. After five seconds the tigress began to make low growling sounds – "Oaar Oaaa" – and the tiger, lowering his head and grasping the nape of the tigress's neck, gave a metallic high-pitched squeal – "Aee Ooaa" – trailing off into "Aee Aee". Soon the lady lost patience, turned round angrily and growled, whereupon they separated.

However, not long after the tigress got up and the entire process, including the mock quarrel, was repeated. By now I could not see them but the durations and intervals of the sounds were fairly regular and distinct and were within recording distance of my tape recorder. Occasionally the tiger roared with pleasure but the tigress did not respond. I came out of my hide at 10 a.m. thinking that the bright light would stop their courting but it did not. They mated again on the forest road and then retired to a thick bamboo grove. To my astonishment as I was returning to Jharokha tower I saw yet another tiger within 50 metres of the courting couple. I stayed there the whole day and recorded the times of the courting noises: 11 a.m., 12.30 p.m., 2.32 p.m., 6 p.m. and 9.15 p.m. The final mating sounds I heard at 11 p.m., after which there was silence for the rest of the night.

The carcass remained half-eaten, but the pair did not return to their meal. I posted my assistants to keep a watch, but no tigers came that day. The following night the couple was heard mating in another valley four miles away. I traced the footprints and compared them with the others; they were the same.

Tigers do not respond to the roars of others except when they are courting, but vocalization by a tigress in oestrus is a means of attracting the attention of the male. The call made by a tigress is something like "Aung oo oo aongh", or "Aooch aooch aoonch aounch aoo". The tiger's call is similar but more deep-throated, louder and shorter. Apart from the mating calls already described, when two tigers meet, whether they be male and female or a mother and cubs, they make little sound; but a "Brru brru" is a greeting which shows that they accept each other as friends, and I depend on this when deciding whether strange tigers are suitable to share an enclosure in a zoo and whether they are likely to accept one another as mates.

Unlike tigers, when lions start roaring they continue for a minute or two and this induces others to join the chorus. But tigers are silent animals, and this makes for greater efficiency as predators. They may roar to express satisfaction after a good meal, but this does not happen invariably. In March 1974 I watched a tiger eating a sambar and the whole night long there was no sound. Then soon after 5 a.m. he began roaring and continued for a whole hour, after which there was no call throughout the day, and the following night he returned to the kill and ate in complete silence. Many hunters say that tigers mimic the "ponking" call of sambars; but why should they do so, when it would alert other sambars? Perhaps it is a way of flushing out other kinds of prey.

Opinions differ as to whether there is a definite mating season for tigers. According to Baikov (1925), in Manchuria the December nights are famous for the nerve-shattering roars of mating tigers, and legends tell of the tying of men to trees at these times as a form of capital punishment. In India, Morris (1937) and Singh (1959) record a long mating period from November to April, while Schaller (1967) shortens it to November–February. My personal communications with other authorities confirm that tigers mate during the cold season (December to early March). Colonel Rice (1857), who hunted tigers mostly during his summer leave, mentions tigers breeding in June and says that the courting period is March. Wordrop (1925) gives autumn as the courting period.

My 49 records from the zoos of Rajasthan and Delhi show that courtship was observed 23 times during the cold season – 5 times in December, 9 times in January and 9 times in February – and 13 times in the hot season – 6 times in May, 7 times in June. During the remaining months mating did occur, but only 3 times in March, twice each in April, September and October. We may conclude, therefore, that although tigers mate at all times of the year, there are two peak seasons, a major one in winter and a minor one in summer.

In Delhi Zoo I kept notes of the reproductive behaviour of five pairs of tigers, following them through three successive breeding periods, and found that on an average a tigress is receptive for a period of 6·3 days. I also took the time interval between the last day of oestrus and the first day of the next, but this was only possible with the tigresses who did not mate. The times varied considerably, ranging from 13 to 59 days in the case of Ratna and from 13 to 37 days with Rosy. Sadleir (1966) calculates the inter-oestrus period as 51 days, the range being 46–52, but he took the mid-oestrus to the following mid-oestrus interval. According to this method, the average for two tigresses in Delhi Zoo, Rosy and Ratna, comes to 49·4, with a range of 34–61. In Basle Zoo 41 records of one tigress show the inter-oestrus period to be 51·9 days (range 20–84), and with another tigress the average from 18 observations was 52·2 days (range 27–83).

Other useful information about the reproductive biology of the tigress concerns the interval between the last litter and the next oestrus. I collected records on this from tigresses of both the Rajasthan and Delhi Zoos; excluding abortions and stillbirths, the range was from 75 to 592 days. The average was 384 days, enough time to rear the previous litter. An interesting fact emerges from these records: if a tigress loses her litter she comes into oestrus within only a few days (Sukeshi 10 days, Asharfi 12 days, Rani 29 days), an evolutionary

opposite: *A herd of nilgai arrived for an exclusive afternoon drink on a hot day at Kalighati, Sariska.*

above top: *Langurs avoid water, except for drinking. Here one of them sensed my presence, and is trying to confirm his doubts.*

above: *Tigers are the only big cats who love water. I found this pregnant tigress cooling herself in the Sulkhan river pool. Elephants pour water into their mouths by means of their trunks, gibbons soak their hands and either drain or lick the water from them but most animals suck in water like a suction pump. Dogs and the cat are exceptions; they use their tongues.*

right: *A small herd of wild buffaloes in Borbhil in Kaziranga, immediately after a heavy downpour of rain.*

left: *A golden oriole came during the hottest part of a dazzling May morning.*

right: *The kingfisher came at 1.00 pm; then, every 15 to 20 minutes, it dived headlong into the water to cool itself.*

far right: *Sunset in the fresh water swamps of Bharatpur.*

below: *Everyone observes silence at a waterhole except the talkative blossom-headed parakeets who arrive in ones and twos and can mount to a dozen or more.*

overleaf: *This chital herd waited till nightfall before visiting a Kalighati waterhole. They were there for an hour, then a female sambar arrived. She was followed by a few more does, who took possession of the whole waterhole. The mixed herd was the transition phase, each creature keeping to a strict time-table so that a confrontation or conflict was avoided.*

COURTSHIP PATTERNS

A proposal may be made by (a) a tiger kissing a tigress or (b) a tigress rubbing her body against his. (c) the tigress presents herself (d) at the moment of climax the tiger holds the skin round the tigress's neck and gives a metallic, high-pitched cry (e) the tigress feels insecure and protests to be free (f) a brief confrontation, often leading to injury (g) they stand on their haunches and swing their arms: the male's role is always defensive (h) the tigress lies on her back and relaxes

opposite above: *Tall grassland in Kaziranga, the home of the one-horn rhino, a 500 sq. kms. area supporting 800 rhinos, 600 buffaloes, 500 elephants, 250 swamp deer, 800 wild boar, 5000 hog deer and 30 tigers.* below: *Swamp deer of the Terai lands of the North.*

process for the survival of the species. Sometimes zoo authorities try to induce breeding for commercial production by removing the cubs from their mother as soon as they have been weaned, or sometimes even less than a month from birth. This induces a tigress to breed faster. Normally in the wild she returns to oestrus within 18 to 20 months, a period needed for her to train her cubs to be efficient predators.

On the first day of oestrus the frequency of copulation is low, increasing on the third day to as many as 52 times. From the fifth day on it declines. My observations show that mating continues day and night at varying intervals of 5 to 20 minutes, and the duration of copulation varies from 15 to 30 seconds.

Captive pairs mate more during the day-time and sleep during the night. What happens in the wild? The pairs seem to retire to secluded areas of the forest to engage in love-play during the day. They do not eat much, but do search for food during the night. The myth that the tiger makes the kill to show his masculine dominance is simply not true. Four records show that it is the tigress who kills the prey: two were made by me at Jharokha, Ranthambhor, and similar observations were made on two other occasions by the game warden of Ban Vihar.

Since tigers do not live in fixed pairs, any available tiger mates with any tigress in heat. Courtship is exclusive, company is constant, and there is no chance of a tiger courting another tigress at the same time; if a weaker male does turn up he is driven away by the stronger one. Tigers live alone almost before they are adolescent, so inevitably their courtship starts with trial and error. If both partners are inexperienced it obviously will take them longer to learn the art of love.

When the zoo tiger Jim was introduced to Rosy after both had achieved maturity neither knew what to do; they approached each other cautiously and then separated with blows. Personal safety is more important than the sexual urge, at least on the first few occasions, and in the wild a couple may come together and separate time after time until mutual confidence has been gained. The copulatory process is such that the tigress has to present herself in a most vulnerable position, exposing her neck to a bite and instant death if the tiger is so inclined. In the case of animals living in groups or prides like lions there are plenty of opportunities to see what is happening; two novices rarely come together as there is always an experienced partner available. With tigers, although errors in courtship have been known to prove fatal, when one of the partners is experienced mating is usually easy, safe and successful.

In one case I saw a tigress mounting a tiger; she displayed the full range of a male's copulatory role. This was to arouse the tiger to play an active part and the trick worked. I have never seen two males attempting to indulge in homosexuality, which is quite common in the case of deer and antelopes. The reason is probably that they go their own ways before reaching maturity and perhaps never witness any sexual act while they are young.

When strangers meet at first the tigress growls and snarls, with all the body muscles taut. Gradually they come closer, whisker to whisker, but continue to snarl. Mutual confidence is soon established and the love-play begins.

The tigress "kisses" the tiger – bites him gently – turns, rubs her body against his, raises her tail, and finally presents herself by sitting with forelimbs fully extended and hind-legs more than half-bent. The tiger mounts her in a half-knees-bent position without putting any pressure on her body and she emits low, deep "Oaar oaaa" sounds. As the act comes to a climax, the tiger lowers his head and grips the skin folds of her neck firmly but carefully; this position helps both to achieve proper orientation at the time of the climax. The tiger then gives the peculiar high-pitched squeal described earlier in this chapter, the tigress growls, and finally gives a sudden jerk to dislodge the male. She turns round to face the tiger and starts boxing. At times this is accompanied by high-pitched noises and the planting of superficial scratches on each other.

The tigress now feels exhausted and lies motionless on her side; then she rolls on her back, fluttering her limbs in the air. The tiger stands or sits by her side and watches her movements; even the slightest flicker of her tail receives his attention. After about five minutes she lifts her head. Now the male comes nearer and smells her, and sometimes he kisses her. She gets up and moves, he follows closely. She again presents herself and allows him to mount.

Occasionally one comes across a misogynist: a tiger lived for sixteen years in Jaipur Zoo but never mated. He refused to share an enclosure with any tigresses even when they were in heat, and he actually killed two of them.

No wild tigers have been marked or collared and followed up from mating to parturition, and there are many speculations about the gestation period. Estimates vary as follows: Eckstein and Zuckerman 98–109 days; Bourlière 105–6; Crandall 100–8; Perry 14 to 16 weeks; M. D. Chaturvedi three-and-a-half months. My study of four tigresses in repeated pregnancies (16 times in all) works out at 96–110 days, the majority falling between 100 to 104 and the average being 102 days. In one case at Delhi Zoo I allowed a tigress to mate for one-and-a-half days (18–19 January 1968) and three cubs were born on 3 May. Nothing can be more specific than this record of a gestation period of 103 days.

Pregnancy cannot be detected for the first two-and-a-half months, becoming obvious by the bulging belly only in the last ten days. At this stage a tigress is most vulnerable to enemies and to starvation. No one helps her to find food, not even the tiger who mated with her a couple of months ago. Therefore she has to complete her maternity duties in the shortest possible time, and this also explains the short gestation period as an evolutionary adaptation.

No one, as far as I know, has witnessed the birth of tiger cubs in the wild. But my finds of newly-born cubs indicate that a tigress looks for a secluded corner in tall grass, bushes or other thick cover, even an overhanging rock or a big hollow log, in which to give birth. Trampled grass provides a mattress, but otherwise there are no preparations. All the cubs are delivered in an area of about a square metre, preferably in a corner, thus ensuring that the cubs are closely grouped for care and feeding. When Radha delivered her five cubs at Delhi Zoo in 1967 she had the space of a whole enclosure 20 ft by 15 ft, but her entire litter was born within a radius of one metre.

At the zoo I always tried to be present when tigresses were giving birth, both out of interest and in order to help if possible if there was a chance of loss by trampling or starvation by neglect. My studies of six cases showed that soon after the tigress becomes restless she exerts pressure and the emergence of the cubs is generally quick. The cubs appear at an interval of 10–20 minutes and the whole process is over in an hour, although Vindhya took as long as 18 hours to deliver five cubs. Such a long-drawn parturition is painful and exhausting, but after each delivery the tigress gets good nourishment by eating the embryonic sac, cord and placenta.

I remember a superstition of my childhood that if a mare delivered a colt during the day-time it was considered a bad omen which might cause the death of a king, maharaja or other local ruler. It was then necessary to spread some fantastic rumour of an unnatural occurrence to counteract the inauspicious event. Parturition by day was considered unnatural, and it is certainly less common than night births: out of eleven litters at Delhi Zoo only two were delivered during the day. Presumably at night the tigress feels more secure and is able to deliver her cubs in peace, and no doubt this applies to any other animal too.

The first ever recorded observation on litter size was by the Mughal emperor Jahangir, a noted naturalist of the early seventeenth century who would have made an excellent zoo director: he mentions the birth of three cubs. Two to three cubs in a litter is normal. My records of 49 litters in Indian zoos show an average of 2.9, and the average from 55 litters in the white tiger family is 2.75. However, the average survival rate in zoos is only 1.9, and in the wild it may be assumed that only one cub per litter survives. Vindhya and Radha each produced five cubs in a litter, and in May 1963 I witnessed Rani delivering six cubs. Six cubs were also born in the white tiger family in the National Zoological Park, Washington. Six seems to be the maximum number, and J. W. Best's (Berriff, 1932) evidence of seven foetuses is baffling. In December 1976 I saw a "pride" of tigers in Ranthambhor consisting of the mother and five cubs aged about 8–10 months, possibly a record for successful rearing in the wild.

Just as there seem to be two peak periods of mating, so there are two peak periods of birth, with the major one in the summer (March-June) and a second during the rains (August-October). Nature favours the best opportunities for survival, and cubbing is directly related to the climatic factor. Cubs born in the

BIRTH OF A TIGER
(a) A pregnant tigress about to
litter (b) she licks her vulva and
(c) exerts pressure on her hind
quarters (d) she either stands and
continues to exert pressure until
a protuberance appears or (e) sits,
one leg raised for easy delivery
(f) she waits until the litter
is complete before (g) freeing each
cub from its sac and drying them

spring are big enough to follow their mother when the rains break, and those
born at the beginning of the monsoon period are inactive for the three months
that the rains last (in this case of course the cubs must have their nursery under
shelter and above flood level). There are local variations depending on climatic
conditions. Records of the births of cubs in Jaipur and Delhi Zoos again show
two distinct peaks.

My records at Delhi Zoo show that the first cry of the cubs is heard within 3
to 30 minutes of birth, and the tigress then starts licking them and freeing them
from the umbilical cord. As soon as they have been cleaned the cubs try to
approach the mother's teats. While watching the birth of the four cubs of the
white tigress Homa on 20 May 1976 I noticed that the infants took no notice of
the teats until they had been fully dried. Homa's third cub cried and cried
within three minutes of birth when he was only half-cleaned, but the mother,
who was still in labour, was already so exhausted that she did not even lift her
head. The cub then rolled away from her hindquarters and landed near her
mouth; this gave her an opportunity to continue licking him, which she did
with her head resting on a piece of meat. The cub did not approach the teats
for another six hours, although generally the infants are successful in obtaining
their first meal from one to four hours after birth.

Pioneer exploration by blind cubs is a fumbling process, and I found they
hit the mother at any point from her head to her tail. The cubs' approach to the
teats is said to be based on thermoradian attraction – i.e. the mother's body
heat acts as a guide. But sometimes the mother seems to cause an obstruction:
Homa raised a barrier by crossing her legs. Aggressive cubs are able to cross
over the legs and reach the teats, and once there they grip and cling, holding
fast to the hair of the mother's belly. The first contact lasts only for about 5–10

minutes, but if the approach is delayed it is cause for concern, for a cub may die of starvation, as the mother takes no initiative to help except for putting herself in a position to allow an easy approach. Right from birth cubs have to struggle, and deaths are governed by natural selection.

It is the movement of the cubs that arouses the tigress's maternal instincts; if they are stillborn she makes a few attempts to clean them and then ignores them completely. Two of our tigresses on becoming mothers for the first time were scared of the moving bundles of flesh they had produced; they snarled at them and finally abandoned them, and the cubs died of starvation. As with courtship, parenthood is at first by trial and error. As tigresses live alone there is no opportunity to learn by others' experiences; however, by the time of their second litter they have gained experience, and by the third litter they are devoted mothers ready to risk their lives to save their cubs. Some tigresses, like our Ratna and Radha, are good mothers even with their first litter; but they are exceptions.

Some tigresses are temperamental mothers who abandon their cubs at the slightest provocation. Rani, a tigress of the Delhi Zoo, left her cubs because one of them was treated for an ear injury; she smelled the ointment and immediately started snarling, and she would not even tolerate her other two cubs whom she had been suckling a few minutes earlier. The tigress Asharfi abandoned her cubs because she became confused. She and Vindhya had litters of 30 and 41 days old respectively, and Asharfi happened to see the other tigress with her cubs; she then seemed to be puzzled about the identity of her own and began to resent them. Her three cubs were removed for hand rearing, and Asharfi was kept alone for three days in the zoo hospital. I then reintroduced her cubs one by one. At first she was suspicious, but soon started licking them. It was a great family reunion.

The popular belief that cubs handled by humans are abandoned by their mother is not supported by my observations; I handled the cubs of four different tigresses within an hour of their birth and none showed any concern or resentment.

There is no substantiated record of tigresses eating their young, although both cats and lionesses sometimes do this. When I read a report that a white tigress at Bristol Zoo had eaten her cub I was puzzled. The only evidence given was the presence of small bones and hairs in the faeces of the tigress, and I find it difficult to agree with the conclusion that was drawn. Our tigers at Delhi Zoo swallowed splinters of bone with their meat but none were found in their stools. How then could cartilaginous infant bones be discovered in the mother's faeces? Nor is the presence of infant's hair convincing, as the mother constantly licks her cubs and naturally some of the hair is passed in her faeces. In one case a dead cub left beside the mother was ignored although she was hungry. However, there have been cases where tigers shot in the early hours of the night were eaten by a tiger arriving at the bait later (personal communications Pillai 1954, Roongta 1962, Debroy, 1976).

All predator babies are born blind, for a very good reason. The helpless infants are forced to stay at home and the mother is able to find them on return from her hunting expedition. If they were able to wander about they would soon be the victim of some predator or scavenger. For the first few days the cubs have a membrane over their eyes; this period is usually from three to five days, but sometimes it takes up to twelve days before the membrane splits. (I even knew a cub which was born with one eye open, and its other eye opened next day.) Once the eyes are opened the cubs can still see very little due to opacity, and it is about two months before they can see clearly. Not before then, and more usually after three months, are they able to follow their mother.

Tigresses are unusual in having no home help. Lions have baby-sitters and foster-mothers who will take on the cubs if the mother dies. Wolves and jackals have guards to protect the nursery. An otter husband runs a home delivery service of fish for his nursing wife. I once saw a most touching case of fatherly devotion in a langur family. The mother died when her baby was hardly ten days old and no other female langurs were available in the zoo at the time. The father took on the duties; since he had no milk he used to pulp banana, mix it with his saliva and force it into the baby's mouth. This worked well, and when the baby was hungry it would suck at its father's lips. But there is no father, uncle or aunt for the tiger cub and the sole responsibility for raising and training a litter is the mother's.

Tigers are extremely clean animals. Tigresses never take a single feather or fibre of meat inside their nurseries, and they keep their cubs spotless by constant licking. Every speck of blood from their prey is removed from their own body with the help of a rough tongue. Water is for cooling rather than bathing, but they never urinate or defecate into it as do deer and cattle. I have watched them closely in zoos and saw that for this purpose they always left their lair and walked a short distance away. Travelling on forest tracks I always found tiger faeces to one side or away from the road altogether.

I made detailed observations of the duration of mother-cub contacts in the case of four tigresses in Delhi Zoo. During the first 24 hours suckling continues for about 70% of the daylight hours. This is reduced to 60% after ten days, and to 30% after 40 days; after 90 days less than 10% of daylight hours is spent in suckling. Zoo cubs are not allowed even to lick meat until they are about 40 days old; after that they get a little meat supplement to the mother's milk, and they are completely weaned by the time they are 90 to 100 days old. At this stage I weighed the cubs before and after meals and found that they ate up to 1 kg of meat per day.

According to Glassford and Somerville, a tigress provides regurgitated meat for her cubs. This practice is common in the case of dogs and jackals –

and also among cormorants, spoonbills and storks – and I have noticed it among lionesses. It sounds very logical, but I did not find a single piece of evidence to support regurgitation among tigers either in the wild or in zoos.

In order to keep an eye on her unweaned cubs for as long as possible, the tigress brings back her own dinner and eats it at home. After the cubs have been weaned the mother always feeds last – a very different style to lions and lionesses, whose cubs are kept away from the kill until all the adults have finished and may even die of starvation. To test the forbearance of tigresses I made some experiments at Delhi Zoo. Vindhya was kept hungry for four days and her six-months-old cubs were fed regularly in a separate enclosure in full view of the tigress. On the fifth day mother and cubs were given meat together. Every time a piece was thrown the cubs were allowed to get it; even when all three cubs had a piece each the mother allowed the greediest one to snatch an extra piece. She showed no resentment; on the contrary, she went away from the cubs and sat down by herself. This experiment was repeated with three other tigresses and the results were all similar.

Observations in the field also confirm these experiments. In April 1975 a tigress with two grown cubs aged about nine months in the Pandupole valley of Sariska were given regular baits. Every time the tigress would stay about 20 metres away while the bigger cub killed or disabled the calf. Then the other cub would join in and both would eat, growling and quarrelling. Mother always came last, or if she did start feeding before they had finished she would choose some difficult place, leaving the easier portions for the cubs. If either cub protested while she was eating she would withdraw until the young ones were satisfied.

While the cubs are still in the nursery the mother will not tolerate any intrusion; either she eliminates the enemy or she moves the cubs to a safer place. Transportation is difficult as she has to carry them one by one, holding the neck and part of the head between her canines and molars. A tigress never grips the cubs by the nape of the neck as is done by domestic cats. The distance she carries them is regulated so that she is able to keep a watch over both those already shifted and those that remain. The cubs co-operate and are totally submissive, making no noise or awkward movements and coiling their bodies into the shape of a comma. If a tigress meets a human being while shifting her cubs she is liable to attack, and most accidents take place when a tigress with cubs is approached too close by woodcutters or other people in the forest. She attacks to ensure the safety of her cubs, purely out of maternal love.

At this stage a tigress avoids any other tiger, including the one who has fathered her cubs. He is not counted as a member of the family, and if the mother dies the cubs starve. Infant mortality in tiger cubs is high.

A tigress discharges her maternal responsibilities admirably through an elaborate course of training. Even when the cubs are three months old and

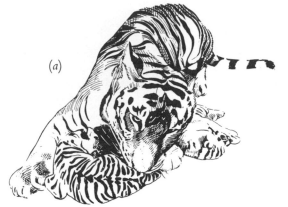

(*a*) *the tigress will often massage her young, either to improve circulation or bowel movement* (*b*) *cubs co-operate in this transport system, remaining coiled up and silent* (*c*) *displeasure is expressed by either a cough or a growl* (*d*) *tigresses are devoted mothers – and* (*e*) *the affection is returned*

eating nothing but meat they are not yet allowed to go hunting with their mother but share whatever she brings home. They remain hidden in a bush until she calls them with a soft "aunh".

In 1971 at Kanha I was able to watch the progress of a tigress with two cubs. Quite often I saw her tracks and the tiny footprints of the cubs in the soft earth on roads, or in wet sand in a stream bed, but I did not actually sight the family until the first week in December when the mother brought her cubs to feed on a live bait. Even then I only caught a glimpse of something yellow streaking through the grass. Sometimes she would kill the buffalo calf, drag it into the near-by undergrowth and then lead the cubs to their dinner. First she had removed the heavy rumen to make the carcass light enough for transport, then she peeled the skin off the thoracic region and exposed the fatty tissue for her cubs.

The cubs grew fast and by late December they were about six months old, but even then they were not permitted to accompany their mother after sunrise. With the first bird call at dawn they would leave the kill and obediently go to their hiding place for the whole day, while the mother stayed to guard the kill. Once in a while she would go and check the cubs, then return to the kill again. One day I tried to discover the cubs' hiding place. The mother was with them and, giving a mild warning growl, she came towards me. For ten minutes she sat in the open watching me, then she got up and went to a clump of grass some distance away. Doubtless she was trying to divert my attention from the cubs, just as a plover will give a "broken wing" display.

A chance to photograph the cubs came to me as a New Year's gift. At 8 a.m. the tigress and cubs were feeding on the kill, but as soon as they were aware of my presence the cubs went off to a near-by hill. I intercepted them and did manage to get a few pictures, but the bamboo clumps and grass blades obstructed the view and in any case a shaded subject was not what I wanted. I waited the whole day hoping that the tigress would bring the cubs for another feed, but they did not reappear. Next morning I approached the kill from the side of the hill so as to block the passage of the cubs, and this plan worked. Finding me coming from the side of their escape route the cubs were puzzled and hid themselves in the grass near the kill, where the tigress was busy feeding. When I approached the cubs she came close and gave a mild cough-like noise; the cubs obeyed the command, came out of hiding, crossed the stream and went into grass cover on the opposite bank. The tigress started to follow them but some crows landing on the kill attracted her attention and she came back. She sat about 20 feet away from the kill guarding it and for about an hour she seemed to doze, but was alert enough to open her eyes if a bird flew past the kill.

Then she returned to the kill and started to peel off the skin. After exposing an entire side of the front of the carcass she gave a long drawn-out "aunh" and repeated it three times. She went to the stream bed and stretched her neck to see if the cubs were coming. Getting no response, she set out to fetch them, following the route taken earlier by the cubs. She walked a little way, stood, called, and again walked on, searching the thickets one after the other. She was not sure of their hiding place and kept on calling them. Soon a distant metallic cry was heard; she stopped and watched, again gave three calls and advanced a little further. The two cubs came out to meet her and there was a happy reunion. She purred and licked them, then led them down the hill into the stream bed and on to the kill, making a long detour.

I next saw the whole family on the kill but did not approach closely as the cubs seemed hungry. They ate for 45 minutes while the tigress sat watching them about 20 feet away. Replete at last, the cubs joined their mother across the stream and all three left the area.

However, the tigress had not gone far before she became aware of poachers and she rushed back to the kill. The cubs meanwhile entered a small pool, first the male cub who ventured far from the shore. The female cub did not risk a swim and was content with paddling. In December Kanha is frosty at night and the water of the stream was cold, but this did not prevent them enjoying their bath. The tigress, having eaten, walked back to the cubs and all joined in a Japanese-style bath for about twenty minutes. After that they did not return to the kill, and the remains were finished off by crows and vultures.

On another occasion I was able to watch a tigress training her cubs to make the actual kill. Before dark the tigress began to watch the bait from the bank of a stream, but she did not approach until it was completely dark. I have seen tigers killing the calf instantly by gripping its neck, and the longest kill I have observed took 1 min 28 secs, even though the job is usually done in half a minute. The tigress disabled the calf by biting its haunches and when it was unable to stand she summoned her cubs with a low "aunch". They started playing with the bait, holding it by the neck and biting its back. Eventually the tigress bit strongly into the haunches and opened the body, and the cubs

The mother tigress makes a kill – with an unwanted helping hand from one of her male cubs

Sleeping after love-play; actual mating lasts for fifteen
to thirty seconds only, and takes place as often as 50 times a day

started feeding on the exposed flesh. The whole affair seemed very cruel as they were eating the calf alive, but it was all part of their training. At last the poor calf died in a sitting position, but the tiger family did not feed properly all through the night, merely taking a few bites and then going off for a stroll.

I waited for the dawn, when I could see the whole family sitting near the carcass. By 8.30 a.m. a bright patch of sunlight lit up the tigress, and the cubs came up to her, licking, hugging and purring. Even that cold morning light was not to the taste of the tigress, and she retired to the shade. As the light grew stronger the cubs stopped feeding and left the scene. All day long the tigress guarded the kill, and by the evening the cubs were ready for more food. They descended the bank, checked to see that everything was all right, then advanced a few more feet. The male cub arrived first, licked his mother and went to the carcass to feed. His sister followed and went through the routine of good manners, purring and kissing her mother before going to the table. The tigress did not eat, but stayed to guard her cubs.

Tigers, unlike lions, love water; but this seems to be adaptive rather than instinctive and the mother has to train her cubs to like it. I once had the opportunity to watch three cubs having their first swimming lesson. The tigress entered the water and sat facing the shore, but the cubs stopped on the edge. After about ten minutes of noisy protests one of them tried to approach its mother, who purred encouragingly. Finally it jumped in, and when she thought it had had enough she grasped it in her mouth and deposited it on the shore. Then she seized the other two, one by one, doused them in water and brought them back to join their bolder brother.

To verify this behaviour, in 1967 I experimented on the tigress Vindhya and her three cubs in Delhi Zoo. The tigress sat in the water and called the cubs. Two of them followed her, and then there was tragedy. One slipped past her into deeper water, paddled its limbs frantically, but drifted further and further out. It made no sound and she did not notice its plight, and the cub was drowned. She went to fetch the third cub, submerged it in water, and carefully put it back on the grass; but the drowned cub was completely forgotten. By the following day the other two cubs had lost all fear of the water and from then on enjoyed their daily swim; but they avoided the deep water.

By the age of six months tiger cubs start exploring and stalking, but they do not stray more than about 50 metres from their mother. Their quarry consists of small birds and chital fawns, but sometimes they even manage to put down a chital doe, and they are not afraid of big animals. The cubs whose swimming exploits I have just described enjoyed stalking me from different directions, but I never knew when the playful stalk might turn into the real thing.

By the time cubs are about eight months old they participate in hunting and claim priority for everything killed. The tigress is indulgent, but only if she is sure of their safety. If the prey is a large animal she allows them to approach only after it has been killed or so disabled that it can inflict no harm on the cubs.

In June 1970 I watched a tigress with her three cubs of about eleven months old stalking a gaur herd in Kanha. It is not easy to pull down a full-grown gaur, and the cubs kept having to retreat from the bull who was guarding the herd. However, the mother did not interfere but just sat watching the cubs while they learned their lesson.

The possessive instinct and increased appetite brings competition into the family circle, which begins to break up when the cubs are aged 18 to 22 months. The more aggressive cubs leave earlier and male cubs separate earlier than females. From hunting records giving the lengths of solitary cubs shot it is possible to work out their approximate age, about 13 months in the case of males and 20 months for females. It can happen that a tiger comes to court the mother and drives away the adolescent cubs, forcing them to disperse. If there is plenty of food and the courting tiger is tolerant, or unable to drive the grown cubs away, all members of the family may be seen together. For some time they stay together and hunt in a group, but eventually they separate as a result of competition. If a male and female cub reach maturity before they separate they may mate.

Sometimes after a tiger has courted the tigress and leaves, the cubs and the mother may reunite. To test this behaviour I experimented with the tigress Asharfi. While she was mating with the tiger Arjun in November 1966 her cub stayed away, although they were in the same enclosure; but at night the tiger was removed and the mother stayed with her cub – Gita – and after the mating period was over they were together again all the time. When Asharfi delivered her next litter, however, she did not allow Gita to come near. The experiment was repeated with the tigress Vindhya, with the same results.

Invariably when the tigress is about to give birth to a new litter she leaves the older cubs and looks for a secret, undisturbed place, and this prolonged absence often causes permanent separation. No hunting records report cubs of different litters living together when the infants are less than three months old; the tigress will not tolerate any intruders until the newborn cubs are able to run and hide themselves in the case of an emergency. I have seen a tigress at Kanha leaving her kill and running away with her young cubs when an adult tiger happened to enter the area. Once the new cubs can fend for themselves their mother will sometimes let a tiger, or even cubs from a previous litter, join the family group; but such associations are rare.

A tiger and tigress are seldom seen together unless they are courting. At Delhi Zoo I carefully watched contacts between the two sexes; when the tigress was not in oestrus physical contact was almost nil and the male and the female took different routes and occupied different corners. According to records from Gauripore, out of 496 tigers shot on 455 occasions, pairs were shot on only 23 occasions (hardly 5%). I also examined 188 hunting records from Jaipur and discovered that on only three occasions were tigers in pairs when flushed from the forest. In all my 25 years' wanderings in tigerland I saw pairs on only twelve occasions, and in every case the tigers were courting. The tiger is a solitary individual, who lives by himself.

CHAPTER 4

Tigerland and its inhabitants

India is unique in having three out of the world's six bio-geographic zones: Ethiopian, Palaearctic and Oriental. No other country, or even continent, has more than two. The Gir forest in the north-west with its *Acacia* and *Commiphora* trees, habitat of the Asiatic lion, is an example of the Ethiopian region. The Palaearctic region in the temperate zone consists of coniferous forests and Himalayan pastures, which merge into snow-clad hills supporting only moss and lichens; it is inhabited by the Kashmiri stag or hangul, ibex, markhor, snow leopard and bears both black and brown. The Oriental region covers the rest of India, with tropical forests on hills and plains, great river basins and deltaic areas. Here live the animals which we associate so essentially with India: tigers; sambar, chital and other deer; the gaur and the Indian buffalo; langur and other monkeys; and of course pythons and cobras.

In its richness and variety of wildlife India can best be compared with Africa, paradise of big game and in particular the "big five": elephant, rhinoceros,

buffalo, giraffe and hippopotamus. India has representatives of the first three: the Indian elephant (*Elephas maximus*), the Indian one-horned rhino (*Rhinoceros unicornis*), and the Indian buffalo (*Bubalus bubalis*). The gaur (*Bos gaurus*) compares with the hippopotamus in weight; and the long-necked, long-faced nilgai or blue bull (*Boselaphus tragocamelus*) makes up for the giraffe. Palaeontologists have even found fossil giraffes and hippos in the Tertiary beds of the Siwalik Hills in north-western India and Pakistan.

Africa is renowed for its antelopes and gazelles, but India too has these, as well as nine species of deer which Africa lacks altogether. This is the highest number of deer species found in any one country. Sambar and chital and the barking deer (or muntjac) are found over a wide range, but others such as swamp deer and musk deer are becoming rare. Hog deer (*Axis porcinus*) have a limited distribution in the Gangetic and Brahmaputra plains but are in no danger of extinction. Mouse deer, though not a true deer, live in forests in the Indian peninsula. As their name suggests, they look more like rodents.

Mouse deer or chevrotain

Of the 500 species of mammals in India, representing almost all the Orders, 21 are found nowhere else. These include the blackbuck (*Antilope cervicapra*), sole representative of the genus *Antilope*; and the only antelope with two pairs of horns, the chausingha (*Tetracerus quadricornis*) which has no close relatives anywhere in the world. The nilgai and chital are also unique to India, as well as the curious sloth bear (*Melursus ursinus*).

In its exceptional richness in cats of various kinds, and in the presence of bears and wolves, India can rightly claim the title of "the kingdom of predators". Nowhere else are the lion and tiger found together in one country. India also has leopards, and the cheetah became extinct there only during the early 1950s. In the temperate zone of the north lives the snow leopard (*Panthera uncia*) and in the Shillong plateau of the east is a member of a different genus, the clouded leopard (*Neofelis nebulosa*), an arboreal predator magnificent in its colour and markings.

Among the lesser killers are eight species of cats including the caracal, golden cat, fishing cat, leopard cat and marbled cat. There are wild dogs (*Cuon alpinus*), mongooses, foxes, three kinds of otters, eight civets, five badgers, and various

Indian fox

scavengers like the striped hyena, jackal and ratel.

Just as the waters of the Nile are famous for crocodiles, so India too has its aquatic predators. The *Crocodilus porosus* of the Sundarbans and the coasts of Orissa are just as large as the crocodiles of Africa; another species, the marsh crocodile (*C. palustris*), inhabits the rivers and lakes; and the narrow-snouted gavial (*Gavialis gangeticus*) is unrepresented in Africa. Fish life varies from the sporting trout and mahseer of the mountain streams to the carps of tropical waters. The butterflies of Sikkim and the moths of the Assam valley are as colourful as those of Brazil or Madagascar. Above all, the spectrum of India's bird life is truly fabulous. It seems almost unbelievable that one can identify over a hundred species of birds within an hour in almost any garden, forest, bushland or patch of open savanna anywhere in India.

Magar crocodile

Altogether there are over 2040 species of birds in India, whereas the whole continent of Africa, which is ten times as large, has only 2500; and in North America, excluding Mexico, more than fifteen times the area of India, there are a mere 775 species. Barbets, rollers, shrikes, bee-eaters, sun birds and weaver birds are almost equally represented in India and Africa. The progenitor of the domestic fowl is the red jungle fowl (*Gallus gallus*), and pheasants of many kinds and hues penetrate far up into the Himalayas. The tallest flight bird, the Saras crane (*Grus antigone*), is part of the landscape of the north Indian plains.

But the title of India's national bird goes to the peacock (*Pavo cristatus*) which attracted the attention of Alexander the Great and whose splendour has earned it a prominent place in Indian literature.

Unique features of India's avifauna are the quarter of a million resident and migratory birds in Bharatpur Sanctuary, which has already been mentioned, and the half-million nesting flamingos in the Rann of Kutch.

India's flora is as outstanding as its fauna. Overwhelmed by the grandeur of the landscape, the freshness of the air of the Himalayas and the beauty of the flowers, the most splendid Mughal emperor Shahjahan exclaimed: "If there is paradise on earth it is this, it is this, it is this!"

The stately sal (*Shorea robusta*), known for its hardwood, and the teak (*Tectona grandis*), the standard timber of commerce, are distributed over most of the country: the sal prevails in the north and north-east, while the teak covers the entire peninsula including the Western Ghats. The most expensive wood is the rosewood (*Dalbergia latifolia*); it bears no resemblance to any quality of the rose, but nothing, not even the rose, excels the sweet aromatic fragrance of sandalwood (*Santalum album*), a partially parasitic plant whose weight and value equal that of gold. A paste of sandalwood produced by rubbing it on stone is said to be a cure for headache – but as one of our poets rightly observed, the effort of producing the paste is worse than the headache. Before man knew of paper the bark of the birch tree, *Betula*, which peels off in sheets, was used for writing, and birches occur up to the last limits of the tree line in the Himalayas. Indian sages wrote down their experiences on such pages and civilization has inherited much of its knowledge from the birch trees of India.

Among the wild flowers and shrubs I would mention the asters, irises and primulas of the Himalayan meadows; and the red, mauve and yellow rhododendrons mixed with horse chestnuts of the temperate region. In the plains the whole landscape is set ablaze during the short spring period with the flowering of the flame of the forest (*Butea monosperma*). In the dry forests the valleys are enriched by the crow flower (*Erythrina indica*), the purple and white bauhinias, the thick, flashy flowers of the silk cotton tree (*Bombax malabaricum*), and the lemon-yellow flower and bell-shaped buds of amaltas (*Cassia fistula*). During the summer in the hot humid jungles of the east the colourful arboreal and terrestrial orchids are set like jewels among the trees.

A paradox of nature are the bamboos, which flower only once, at the very end of their lives. Such climbers as the tigerlily (*Gloriosa superba*) and *Butea superba* of the deciduous forests fully justify their specific names by their gorgeous flowers and riotous colouring. Except in the valley of Kashmir the Indian autumn is not as colourful as in temperate Europe or North America: the sal, terminalias, fig and Kusim trees (*Schleichera trigura*) colour the landscape in early summer, when the leaves are red. In the dry deciduous tropics the scene in late winter is generally red, yellow and brown, particularly owing to the foliage

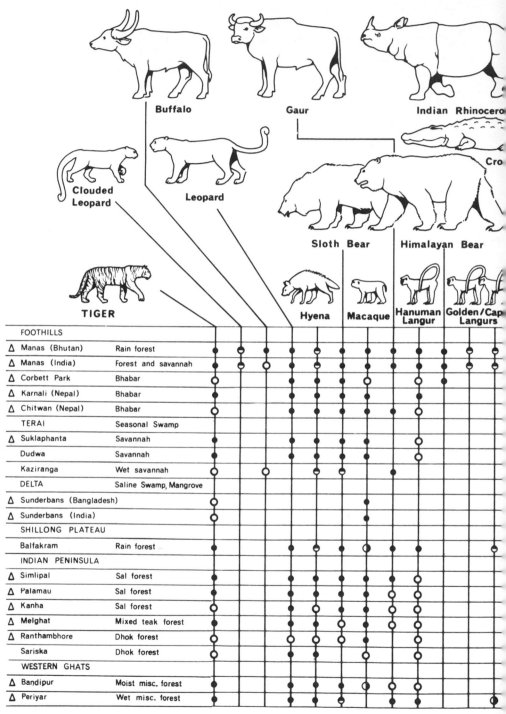

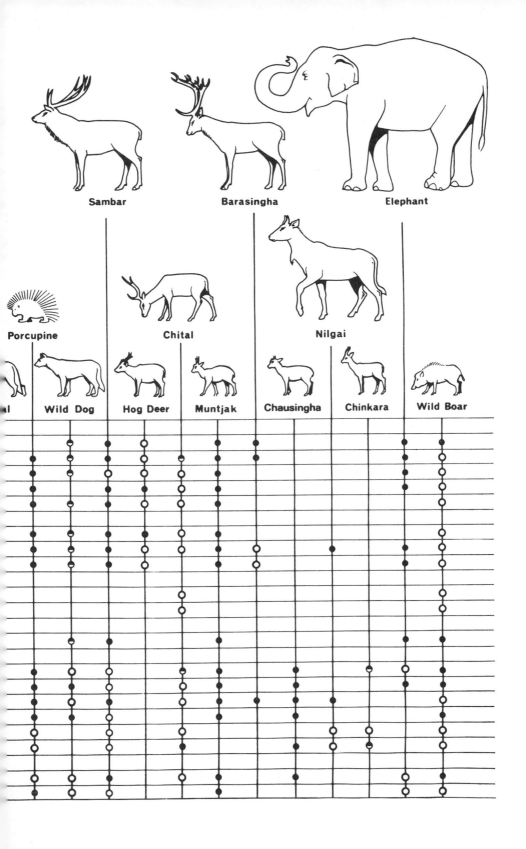

Sambar Barasingha Elephant

Porcupine Chital Nilgai

al Wild Dog Hog Deer Muntjak Chausingha Chinkara Wild Boar

of the dhok (*Anogeissus pendula*) mixed with *Grewia tilifolia* and karaya (*Sterculia urens*) which turn colour before falling. Then, after the early summer when the forests are leafless and drab, they become luscious green in the monsoon.

There are trees with open seeds (conifers) and those with the seed closed in a hard covering (coconut) which can remain dormant for years. But trees in the delta have viviparous seeds which germinate before falling to the ground. The mahuwa tree (*Madhuca indica*) is actually a standing brewery: its fleshy flowers have a high sugar content which ferments and intoxicates the consumer. Wild animals enjoy it immensely. The common weed cannabis (*C. sativa*) sometimes intoxicates beyond recovery when its leaves are chewed. Among the carnivorous plants is *Nepenthes*, the famous pitcher plant, which is found in extremely limited spots among the dripping rocks of Meghalaya. Perhaps these few examples will give some idea of the extraordinary trees and plants that give India its unique character.

Until recently the whole of tigerland was one unit with no physical barriers and there was free interbreeding throughout this huge range. Nowadays tigers are isolated into four separate regions: the north-east, including the Gangetic delta of the Sundarbans; the north-west, with the foothills of the Himalayas and the plains running parallel to them known as the Terai; the Indian peninsula, including the arid lands of Rajasthan, the central plateau and the Eastern Ghats; and the Western Ghats. Information about the tiger's habitat based on old shikar notes is only of historic interest because conditions have changed so rapidly during the last 50 years. In order to obtain first-hand knowledge of the present status of the tiger, therefore, I visited each of the main regions.

I started in the north-east in the State of Arunachal Pradesh, formerly known as the North-East Frontier Agency, and worked my way across the Assam valley to the southern banks of the Brahmaputra to Meghalaya. The northern part of this region is characterized by high humidity and thick mists which, together with the hot sun and the soft rock of the outer Himalayas, encourage luxuriant vegetation. The tropical forests of tall trees and woody climbers have a heavy undergrowth of shrubs, evergreens, bamboos (*Dendrocalamus hamiltonii*) and wild bananas. Although the cover is excellent and there is plenty of water, evergreen forests are no place for tigers because of the limited number of prey animals. Hardly 1% of the plants provide suitable forage for browsers, and ungulates do not like such dense cover. Predators such as the clouded leopard and golden cat live mostly on arboreal primates.

On the fringe of the forests where rivers descend to the plains are grasslands, the equivalent of the Bhabar and the Terai and known in Bengal as the *duars*, so called because they are the gateways to the East. There are also open patches nside the evergreen forests where shrubs and grasses grow, some of them the former site of villages. These grasslands, whether wet or dry, large or small, are burnt annually by the people to provide good grazing for their cattle. Savanna vegetation such as this is known as "preclimax", i.e. the stage before the "climax" type which the climate could support.

These savannas are ideal for sambar, wild boar, buffalo and gaur, hog deer and swamp deer. Rhinoceroses are found in the well-watered tall grasslands and elephants come to graze on the wet savannas. Such a combination of hunting grounds in open country and resting places in thick forest, all within an hour's stroll, is a perfect habitat for the tiger.

We can judge the truth of this statement by referring to the old hunting records (1880–1907) of the former princely State of Cooch Behar in West Bengal; during these 27 years no less than 295 tigers were shot. In the adjoining area of Gauripur in Assam over 500 tigers were shot by the Raja of Gauripur during the first half of this century. Similarly in Manipur 189 tigers were killed in the 14 years between 1910 and 1924. Colonel Pollock mentions that in 1877 tigers were more plentiful in Assam than in Burma; and in Burma, according to Prater, no less than 1382 tigers were shot in only four years (1928–32). Today there are hardly more than 200 tigers left in the entire region north of the Brahmaputra, including the foothills of Bhutan.

The Royal Bengal Tiger of the Sundarbans has become a legend. Living an almost amphibious life in the saline swamps, these tigers were once a nightmare to the local people owing to their man-eating habits.

It is impossible to get the feel of the Sundarbans without actually experiencing it. A network of estuaries, creeks and islands, this fringe of the Ganges delta extends for 270 km along the coast of the Bay of Bengal. Most of the area is inundated twice a day by the tide and occasionally all of it is flooded as the result of a cyclone. It is hot and humid and there is practically no fresh water for drinking. Mangroves are well adapted to live in saline marshes. The spiky pneumatophores stick up above the mud to breathe. Thick mats of stilt roots of *Rhizophora* and other plants firmly anchor them in loose soil. Dwarfpalm (*Phoenix paludosa*) adds its charm to the landscape. This dense wall of evergreens obstructs the view so that it is impossible to get an idea of the Sundarbans from a boat; the ideal way is to hover over the delta below 1000 feet in an aircraft, as I once did, or walk through the dense vegetation.

My first visit to the Sundarbans was in the first week of April 1972, an important week because it is then that permits for honey-collecting are issued by the forester. Early in the morning the leader of each party bathes, offers his *pooja* (prayer) to Ban Bibi, a forest goddess, to get her blessing and protection from tigers, and then goes to his *dingi* (a small boat from which the English word "dinghy" is derived). About 40 boats line up and as the sun rises the forester fires a gun, whereupon they all go off as fast as they can to search for beehives. I followed them through the mangrove forest in a boat and during my week's stay no accidents were reported, but I was told that 35 men were killed by tigers during the season.

After several visits I found that this challenging habitat came to fascinate me, and in particular the strategy used by tigers to overcome the difficulties. I found walking through the mud with the feet entangled in innumerable roots a tremendous strain, yet the tiger will carefully pick his way through the spikes. He subsists on an extremely narrow range of prey, mainly wild boars and chital which he chases over the coastal sand dunes and slushy creeks; but occasionally he resorts to rhesus monkeys, reptiles, fish and crabs. The only other predator is the crocodile, and occasionally the two come into conflict; yet tigers will swim across sizeable creeks, even in rough weather when there are high waves.

In every part of the forests I visited, including the islands, there were fresh pug marks of tigers and an estimate of about 180 in the Indian side of the Sundarbans Reserve may not be far wrong. This is the highest concentration of tigers in India, about one tiger per 7 sq km of land area. The main reason must be that human disturbance in this very specialized and hostile environment is minimal. In 1907 Daniel Johnson stated that "Cosum Bazaar Islands and the Potelle evergreen jungles are overrun with tigers and there is no chance of their annihilation", and as late as 1914–15 86 tigers were shot in one year in the Sundarbans. Yet until Project Tiger got under way they were never protected. Now a substantial area (2000 sq km) has been demarcated as a Reserve and the population is building up.

The tiger's home in the north-west, in the foothills of the Himalayas, is the region made famous by Jim Corbett and the site of the present Corbett National Park. I have known this country ever since my college days as most of my forest training was done in the Siwalik forests of Dehra Dun. The outer Siwalik Hills have an ancient geological history and large numbers of mammalian fossils have been found there – even fossil tigers.

The topography consists of *duns* (valleys) and *chaurs* (plains) trapped between the outer and inner Himalayas, intersected by streams which flow only during the rains. Summers are hot but frost is common in winter and the annual rainfall is over 80 inches. Both hills and valleys are clothed in sal forests which stay green and cool during the summer. On the unstable slopes of the hills dry deciduous shrubs and grasses provide enough food for prey animals and sufficient cover to allow predators to stalk.

On the open *chaurs* or grasslands hundreds of deer – sambar, chital, hog deer and barking deer – and wild boar feed at dawn and during the late afternoon, retiring to the cover of tall trees in the middle of the day. Sambar and barking deer live in the forest cover. Elephants, too, inhabit a small part of the western region of the forests of Uttar Pradesh, occasionally straying further east. The

A sambar in silhouette

deciduous forests are rich in bird life, and the hill rivers support the marsh crocodile and gavial. The most famous tiger habitats of this region are the Chitwan valley of Nepal, the Cheela and Dun valleys of Dehra Dun, the Corbett National Park, and their adjoining forests.

The southern limit of the foothills region is known as the "Terai", meaning "moist land"; formerly marshy, much of this area has been drained by agriculturalists from the plains to the south. This flat country once supported dense pockets of sal and laurels alternating with tall grass savannas, which still remain in some parts. The potential of such country for tigers is obvious and no doubt all these pockets had considerable populations of tigers at one time.

In the fresh-water swamps cane (*Calamus tenius*) is dominant, and these marshlands were once checkered with open patches called *chandars* overgrown with tall elephant grass. Even now the few *chandars* which have escaped the forest plantation programme or the encroachment of agriculture are ideal homes for tigers: Dudwa Sanctuary in Uttar Pradesh is one example. Good cover adjoining grasslands where deer and wild boar are plentiful is just the country the tiger likes.

To evaluate the condition of the habitat in the past I again resorted to hunting records which need not be quoted in detail here. It is enough to mention that between 1946 and 1970, the year when hunting was banned, 166 tigers were shot in the Kheri-Pilibhit area alone in the Terai; equal numbers must have been killed in the Siwaliks. In the whole of the Himalayan foothills only just over 300 tigers are left, including some 80 tigers in Nepal.

The triangular mass of peninsular India, land of the Rajas, is of tremendous geographical complexity. Bounded by ranges of hills, the plateaus and escarpments, plains and peneplains, are cut by numerous ridges and narrow valleys.

The hot, dry climate supports deciduous forests with occasional belts of evergreen along the streams. These forests support a large population of deer, antelopes and wild boars; they are also the home of the sloth bear and the stronghold of tigers. Leopards were once common and still survive, though in a precarious condition. Carnivores of all kinds – wild cats, wild dogs, civets, hyenas and jackals – are found throughout the region.

As already mentioned, the wildlife – especially tigers – of this land of the maharajas has been both hunted and preserved from time immemorial, and the meticulously-kept hunting records are of great value in giving an insight into the former distribution and population of tigers. To give just two examples: Colonel William Rice was allowed to shoot 93 tigers in the forests of Nimach adjoining Rajasthan (now in Madhya Pradesh) 1850–4; and in more recent times 334 tigers were bagged in the small princely State of Kotah from 1920 to 1965. Adjoining Kotah is the district of Bundi, my first posting. The Maharaja of Bundi, who lent me his hunting diaries, was very upset about the destruction of the tiger's habitat there.

I was also privileged to be allowed to see the records of the Maharaja of Rewa. In this small State, home of the famous white tigers, the number of tigers shot between 1923 and 1969 was 364. And in Jattygaon Khandesh (a district in Bombay Presidency, now part of Maharashtra) the slaughter of tigers in 1821–8 amounted to 1053; bounty was claimed on this number as "vermin" and many others must have been killed but were unrecorded.

This whole region of peninsular India holds about half the total population of Indian tigers remaining today. The total is estimated at about 2500, so the remainder in this entire region is about equal to the numbers killed in the one district of Jattygaon Khandesh in seven years. No wonder that desperate remedies had to be taken, and out of the nine Reserves now created for tiger preservation five are in peninsular India (Ranthambhor, Kanha, Melghat, Palamau, and Similipal).

Those who came to India by sea from the West first saw the sheer wall of the Western Ghats, also known as the Sahyadri Range. It starts from south of the Tapti River and ends in the southernmost part of Kerala, a distance of 1000 kilometres.

In investigating this part of tigerland I divided the area into three main units. The northern region includes the Dangs, the Rajpipla of Gujarat, and the hills of Nasik, separated by two gaps. The middle region is situated between the 10°N parallel and the Nilgiri mountains, running for about 640 km close to the coast of the Arabian Sea. When viewed from the eastern range it seems to be cut up into terraces, or mesas and buttes. Consisting of horizontal sheets of lava, it has given rise to the characteristic landscape of the Deccan trap. Finally, the third region stretches southwards from the Palghat gap.

The western aspect of the range prevents the moisture-laden winds coming from the Arabian Sea from penetrating inland, so the region receives heavy monsoon rains (maximum 250 inches). The mean annual temperature is close to 27°C, and the high temperature and good rainfall results in a luxuriant growth of vegetation. The whole region is forested, but there are minor differences in the three units. The northern region supports only deciduous forests, some moist, some dry. The wetter forests of the middle section are dominated by *Terminalia Bombax*, rose wood trees and the famous teak. In the Southern Ghats evergreen or semi-evergreen forests are found over large areas. A special feature is rolling grasslands interspersed with dense pockets of evergreen forest called *shola*.

This variation is reflected in the distribution of the wildlife. Whereas deer and wild boar are found throughout the region, the gaur is absent in the north, and elephants (except for small groups that stray into the North Kanara of Karnataka) are found only south of Bangalore. The dense evergreen forests are rich in monkeys – Nilgiri langur, common langur, lion-tailed monkey and bonnet monkey – and the clown-like slender loris is found in the semi-evergreen and deciduous forests. Wild dogs and leopards live throughout the region, and so do tigers. For the most part the fauna is dispersed, though there are a few concentrations, for example at Periyar where there is an artificial lake, *sholas*, and the rolling meadows of the higher Ghats. Elephants are the dominating feature among the fauna, along with leopards, wild dogs, gaur and sambar; there are no chital on the western aspect of the Ghats. Flying squirrels glide through the trees, and hornbills, both Malabar grey and pied, and the grey jungle fowl are conspicuous among the birds.

A cross-section through any point of the Western Ghats cuts across two or more habitats, making it easy for animals to shift from one to the other in the course of a day, or even during one feeding stroll. With such a wide range of food, waterholes and shelter, the Western Ghats are one of the richest strongholds of wildlife in India.

As to tigers, I was sad to read in the District Manual of Coimbatore that 93 were poisoned in the year 1874 as part of the British Government's tiger eradication programme. The notes of G. P. Sanderson mention plentiful tigers in Mysore in 1882, and in 1900 C. E. M. Russell considered that their extinction in this area would be far-off. In 1911 F. W. F. Fletcher described Wynnad, then in Madras Presidency and now in Kerala State, as a happy-hunting ground where tigers were extremely numerous and a dozen used to be killed every year. He also says that the annual sport of the local people was the netting and spearing of tigers.

The tiger shoots of the late Maharaja of Mysore were a regular feature, and he and his guests shot 69 tigers between 1945 and 1967. Tigers were even found on the island of Bombay as late as 1929, as evidenced by J. J. Sutari's shoot.

By the end of 1972 it was estimated that only 191 tigers were left in the whole of the region of the Western Ghats.

There are fifteen major and distinctive ecosystems of tigerland, with four principal types of habitat: evergreen and semi-evergreen in the Assam valley and the Western Ghats; moist deciduous in the Himalayan foothills and the Terai plains, in central peninsular India and including the Eastern Ghats, and a belt in the Western Ghats; dry deciduous forest in the rest of the tiger habitat (outer Siwaliks, the Aravali range, the entire Vindhyan system extending from Rajasthan and Madhya Pradesh to Bihar and the Deccan plateau of Maharashtra and Andhra Pradesh) and the swamps of the Sundarbans.

Based on my ecological studies I have attempted a diagrammatic represent-ation of the distribution of predators and prey in these habitats today (including the very specialized delta region of the Sundarbans). Circles have been divided according to the proportion of forest land in each habitat type; gaps and incomplete circles show discontinuous and partial distribution respectively. The tiger occurs in all parts of India except the deserts and the Himalayas, while the leopard inhabits all areas except the deltaic swamps of the Sundarbans.

Each one of the three main habitat types consists of thickets, open woodlands and savanna. The extent of each sub-type depends on the influence of climatic and other factors, but I found during my wanderings that in the evergreen habitat thicket predominates. Open woodlands are few, and savannas are limited to river banks, riverine islands and areas of abandoned cultivation. The moist deciduous habitat is more uniform, with thick cover along the streams, open woodlands on rock formations and poor soils with grassy patches. Again, savanna-type vegetation is found on newly formed islands and banks of rivers, areas of changed river courses and abandoned cultivation. In the dry deciduous habitat, in contrast to the evergreen type, thickets are very limited. They are found in strips along streams and in patches on the foothills of the Vindhyan escarpments. Most of the country is open woodland, with savanna on hilltops and on slopes where the soil is shallow due to the geological formation and erosion.

The evergreen thickets have plenty of water and shelter but are poor in food for browsing. The open woodlands and savannas, though limited in extent, are rich in forage. The moist deciduous habitat has enough thickets for shelter and sufficient open woodland and savanna to support ungulates. The distribution of the sub-types is uniform, waterholes are plentiful, and almost all areas are occupied by wild animals.

The dry deciduous forests are more productive and richer in forage than any of the other habitat types and can support larger concentrations and a wider range of ungulates – and hence tigers. This was amply demonstrated by the records of the princely preserves of Rajasthan, Gwalior and Rewa during the first quarter of this century. The present deterioration is due to over-grazing and competition for water by domestic cattle, and the disturbance caused by man, including poaching for skins. During the summer scarcity of water helps to reduce grazing pressure on poorer areas and so saves the habitat from deterioration. This fact is sometimes forgotten by enthusiastic wildlifers who regard the provision of water as an act of charity.

I remember a small spring in Kachida valley where I spent all my summer leave for many years. It was surrounded by trees and shrubs, and the animals could approach to drink under cover. When I visited it in 1963 I found a hundred people working there, putting the finishing touches to a large dam and the whole area, including my hide, was submerged. Within a year all the trees had died and the large sheet of water was largely ignored by the animals. On one side the pools became contaminated by seepage containing lime and iron rust. My opportunity came when the Inspector General of Forests visited the site: I was given the green light to breach the dam and the clear spring recovered.

Nature's checks and balances need a better understanding before we tamper with them with our sketchy knowledge of the ecology of tigerland. The co-existence of India's rich wildlife and the extraordinarily high concentration of human population – 80% of whom still live outside the urban areas and many in the forests – show a remarkable adjustment on the part of nature.

The wild predator controls the population of his prey and thus automatically safeguards himself. If a hunter develops new techniques its prey soon adopts new methods of defence. Hunters and hunted are adapted to one another in the long evolutionary process. Predators even exercise family planning, killing or neglecting their offspring if litters become too large. No prey species has ever become extinct as a result of predation, whereas instances are on record where the destruction of a natural predator has upset the balance of nature and created conditions difficult even for human life.

Let us take as an example a small area of the Bharatpur Sanctuary. There used to be a few leopards that kept the wood poachers away, at least at night, and owing to their presence the village dogs did not dare enter the Sanctuary. The cattle population was kept under control by the leopards thinning out their calves. Then in 1962 the last leopard was shot by the Maharaja, who enjoyed exclusive rights even though it was a Sanctuary. The result is that large areas of forest have been lost; the chital population has deteriorated as a result of hunting by dogs, and feral cattle have become a problem not only in the Sanctuary but in the neighbouring agricultural fields.

The tiger is at the apex of nature's pyramid and controls the whole eco-system. By thinning out his prey he prevents over-use of vegetation and saves the land from destruction. He acts as a sentinel to protect the forests, some of which have been saved solely because wood poachers lacked the courage to enter them at night when the forest guard is asleep.

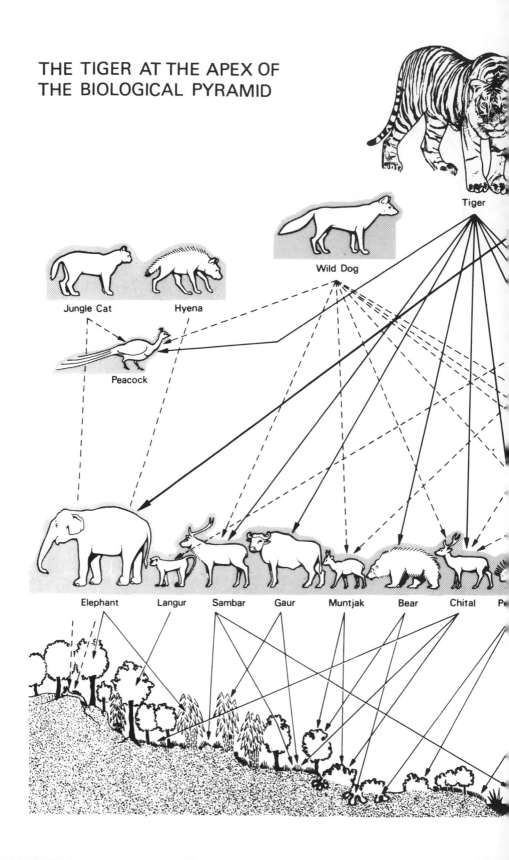

THE TIGER AT THE APEX OF
THE BIOLOGICAL PYRAMID

Tiger

Wild Dog

Jungle Cat

Hyena

Peacock

Elephant   Langur   Sambar   Gaur   Muntjak   Bear   Chital   P

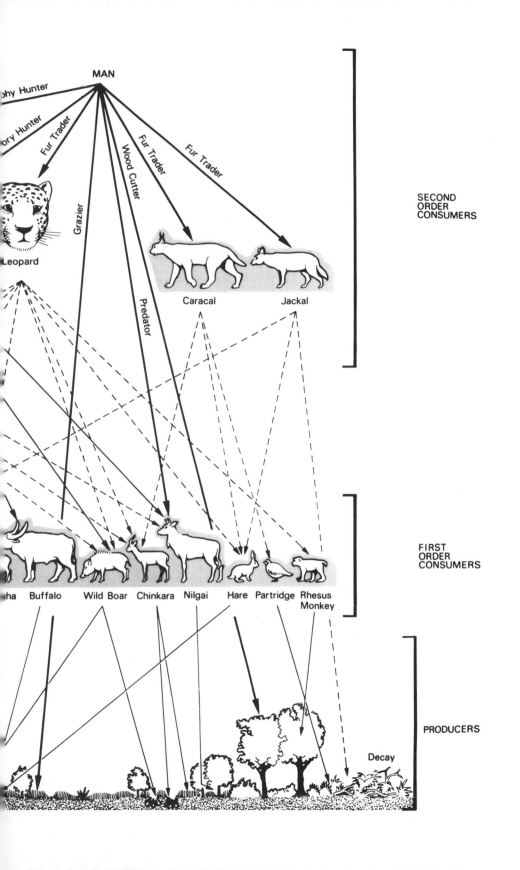

MAN

ohy Hunter

ory Hunter

Fur Trader

Grazier

Wood Cutter

Fur Trader

Fur Trader

Predator

Leopard

Caracal

Jackal

SECOND
ORDER
CONSUMERS

ha   Buffalo   Wild Boar   Chinkara   Nilgai   Hare   Partridge   Rhesus
                                                                  Monkey

FIRST
ORDER
CONSUMERS

Decay

PRODUCERS

CHAPTER 5

The tiger's prey

The species preyed on by the tiger have selective feeding habits, thus avoiding competition. This is achieved in two ways: by modifications in their physical structure, and by adopting different ways of life. Those living in the woodlands and rain forests, for example, lack the sharp sight of the herds of the open savannas but have acute powers of hearing and smell. In order not to be conspicuous they live in small groups of 6–8 (except when they converge in meadows, where they swell to enormous numbers) and, since relying on speed would be impractical among the trees, they adopt camouflage and "freeze" to escape detection. We have also seen how the tiger is adapted to the ecology of woodlands and forests by camouflage, acute hearing, and ambush rather than speed over long distances.

One of the most important ecological links in tigerland is the elephant. Because of its massive bulk and extravagant consumption of forage the elephant is generally thought to be a destroyer of the habitat, but this is far from true. It plays an important role by knocking down trees and so maintaining the habitat in the best condition for other wildlife. The tall trees are out of reach of other herbivores, but the keen eye of the elephant selects them – they form less than 1% in the evergreen forests. Since elephants live in herds their tree-felling activities make a real impact in opening up the forests, encouraging the growth of new trees and grasses. They also make paths through impenetrable undergrowth. As soon as a herd leaves an area others come to feed on the left-overs; and, attracted by such a host of ungulates, the tiger makes a bee-line for the place where the elephants have rampaged. Waterholes dug out in sandy river beds by elephants provide a life-line for all the animals of the area during summer when most of the watercourses dry up. And elephant and tiger are well aware of each other's company. Tigers will look out for stray elephant calves, whom they will disable. The victims are then left behind when the herd moves on. However, should a tiger make a wrong decision the result may prove fatal, for he can find himself in the middle of an elephant stampede.

Their present distribution shows that elephants used to be found all over India except in areas of very low rainfall. Now the herds have been broken up, segregated by extensive cultivation and other factors. They are now confined to: the foothills of the Himalayas; the entire eastern region; the eastern and central forests of Orissa, with a stray herd also in southern Bihar; and the Western Ghats of Karnataka, Tamil Nadu and Kerala. Despite trapping and

opposite: *A study of Jim.*

left: *This caracal*
...vered feeding a
...distance from a
...road in Sariska
... the rains. He is
...food off his nose.

left: *An old lioness*
...Gir Forests of Gujarat;
...ne of 182 Asiatic
...eft in the Indian wild.

right: *Leopards are*
...al creatures who
...eir food on to the
...ranches of a tree to be
...reach of tigers or
...s.

right: *Never before*
...eam of seven wild
...en photographed
...r. This pack had
...a herd of chital and
...lanning a pack hunt.

above left: T
armour-plated
Indian rhino.

below left: T
common vultu
I saw a carcass
of 150 kgs.
demolished by
vultures withi
half an hour.

above right:
leader challeng
a lone tusker:
resulting battle
was brisk, sho
and decisive, u
the intruder be
driven away.

below right:
jackal was per
aware of my
presence and
kept a wary e
on me through
his meal.

insets: A tigress cleans a patch of blood from her nose before starting to feed, tearing at her victim's haunch.

main picture: A family dinner is a noisy affair, as everyone jostles for a better place. Yet this mother took no part in the meal and watched till her cubs had finished. Then she helped herself to the few left-overs — which hardly made up a meal.

sales to zoos, the elephant population is stable. Few male Indian elephants have tusks, and they are little hunted for ivory.

The gaur (*Bos gaurus*) occupies the same ecological niche as the elephant but, since the gaur is incapable of knocking down trees, he profits from the elephant's left-overs. Elephants cannot negotiate steep slopes but the gaur can do so with ease. Found in the forested foothills of the Himalayas, the central highlands and the Western Ghats, gaur are purely woodland animals. They live in herds of about 20 individuals, passing the day in the forest and coming out in the late afternoon to feed on bamboo shoots, shrubs and coarse grasses. The bulls are glossy black and very muscular; fine specimens may weigh as much as 1000 kilos.

Gaur have an acute sense of smell. They apprehend danger from a distance and walk away from it, but when cornered they form a strong ring with bulls and cows facing the predator, snorting and challenging. However, if a single individual is cornered by more than one tiger it has no chance. In one instance in Kanha National Park I found a solitary bull that had been killed by three tigers, probably a tigress and her two adolescent cubs. On another occasion I witnessed two bulls snorting and pushing a pair of tiger cubs away from the herd, with no fear of the tigress who was sitting hardly 50 feet away.

These large animals are not easy victims for predators, so when their numbers increase beyond the carrying capacity of the area they are usually almost wiped out by a rinderpest epidemic, only to build up their numbers gradually once again. Mostly the disease is spread by domestic cattle which act as carriers, reducing the gaur population much earlier than it actually needs to be thinned. The epidemic of 1968 reduced the population of gaur in Bandipur and Mudumalai Sanctuaries to just a few individuals.

Wild buffalo (*Bubalus bubalis*) occupy the same habitat of tall grasslands and, in the eastern region, along the waterside, but they eat coarse, dry grasses which are not relished by elephants and gaur. Living in small herds of ten to fifteen, they are wary creatures and take to flight at the slightest scent of danger.

The Indian rhinoceros (*Rhinoceros unicornis*) is sometimes found in the same areas as wild buffalo, as in Kaziranga National Park, and their requirements are much the same. Segregation is effected by the migratory habits of buffaloes, who cover a large area in search of food, whereas the rhino has a very limited range. The Indian rhinoceros is found in the foothill forests of Jaldapara in West Bengal and Manas in Assam, as well as in the wet savannas of Kaziranga on the banks of the Brahmaputra. Every year during the monsoon the land is flooded, and after the rains swamps and pools known as *bheels* are formed. The fertile soil, hot sun and plentiful water support a luxuriant growth of tall reeds and elephant grass, a habitat ideally suited to the rhino. Nearly 800 live in Kaziranga National Park, which extends over 500 sq km, another 300 live in other sanctuaries in India, with 250–300 in Nepal (including Chitwan).

opposite: *A two-year-old and two adult langur grooming themselves in Ranthambhor. Their long tails help them to maintain balance while leaping from tree to tree.*

Rhinos have an acute sense of smell but their sight is poor – similar in fact to an elephant's. When confronted with anything unexpected they either snort and retreat or charge the intruder. The armour-plated rhino takes little notice of tigers, but young calves may be killed by them. In 1968 the Forest Department actually suggested that tigers should be killed because they were taking such a heavy toll of rhino calves. Rhinos live solitary lives except during the breeding season (April-May) when more than one male courts a cow in heat. Rivals may inflict deep wounds on each other, which they heal by wallowing in the mud; but sometimes the wounds become septic and the animal may die of septicaemia. Such natural deaths are much fewer than those caused by poaching; attracted by the very high price of rhino horn, poachers always lurk round the sanctuaries. The widely-held superstition about the aphrodisiac quality of the horn once reduced the rhino population to eleven. This was in 1910, since when strict protection and a dedicated staff has brought the numbers up to 1100. Even this has been considered to be too high by empirical observation, but the rich biome, which is renewed every year by burning and flooding, could certainly support more.

Sambar, chital, hog deer, swamp deer, barking deer, nilgai and wild boar form the main prey species of the tiger. They occur in the same geographical range but their ways of life differ. Sambar, barking deer and wild boar live in hilly thickets and woodlands. The sambar (*Cervus unicolor*) is a browser as well as a grazer and ranges over rough hill slopes, valleys and lake shores. It can browse up to a height of nine feet when standing on its hind legs, can clear up to eleven feet to reach some particularly choice fruit, and will wade through up to seven feet of water to feed on aquatic vegetation, especially lotus and water-lilies, and even trapha and algae. This range of feeding habits, both terrestrial and aquatic, explains the wide distribution of sambar throughout the country. In peninsular India they attain a larger size and have longer antlers than those living in the foothills of the Himalayas.

I have already mentioned that a single "ponk" or "dhank" repeated after a short interval is a sure indication of the presence of a tiger. This alarm call is normally given by the sambar when it sees the predator on the prowl or otherwise senses danger, including man. It has a curious way of verifying danger; first, the ruff of hair round the neck is raised, the tail becomes erect, and the animal starts stamping the ground; then it begins to sniff the air and sometimes walks forward to ascertain the source of its uneasiness. This habit comes in handy for a tiger waiting in ambush. Older males with big antlers are particularly cautious when approaching waterholes: probably they know their limitations, for the antlers are apt to become entangled when the stag is fleeing through the bush. Stags without antlers, or with antlers in velvet, fall easy prey to the tiger; and indeed sambar are the main item in the tiger's diet in wood-

Chital

lands. Although cautious, the sambar is no coward – he ignores jackals and jungle cats, for instance – and he does not take to flight unless the danger is unavoidable.

Stags live mostly in stag parties of from two to four for most of the year except for the rutting season in January-February. By then the antlers are well developed and hard, and each stag possesses a small harem of two to three does. To be a master stag is not easy, for he constantly has to chase away rivals and at the same time court the hinds in heat. Rutting battles sometimes lead to casualties. In January 1974 I came across two stags fighting in the open near a waterhole when the light was beginning to fade. For about fifteen minutes they fought, separated, and battled again, after which the stag with the smaller antlers had had enough. The victor did not chase his rival, and the hinds took no notice of the fight at all. The winning stag then had exclusive courtship rights to the hinds in heat. Occasionally he tossed grass, bushes and branches with his antlers, while foam trickled from his mouth. The fruits of the zizyphus tree which are rich in sugar ripen during the rutting period, producing wine in the stomach and the stags literally get intoxicated. But, unlike chital and swamp deer which give rutting calls, the sambar's courtship is a silent affair.

In peninsular India the fawns are dropped in October when the grass is high, so concealing the young from predators. In the flood plains of Assam the breeding period is different; there I saw courting pairs in May-June, and the fawns are born in January after the floods are over and the land is drained. This change of breeding period from winter to summer is an adaptive mechanism to ensure better reproductive success.

During my visits to the Kachida valley in March I always found stag parties of as many as six to eight members separate from the does. After the antlers are dropped the males become close friends again, proving that disarmament is an essential prerequisite for peace. Mothers and fawns also live in small herds. Standing close together they merge into the background, making it difficult for a predator to isolate a particular individual for attack. But the deers' main defence is the swiftness with which they are able to scatter in different directions through thick bush.

Tigers post themselves in depressions along the tracks leading to waterholes and spring out suddenly on their victims. According to my count, out of a hundred kills of sambar by tigers 62 were hinds and 28 fawns; 80% of these kills were within 50 metres of the waterhole. These figures may be biased because discovery of kills near waterholes is easy, but there is no doubt that these are the places where sambar are common and provide an easy prey.

Chital or axis deer (*Axis axis*) feed mainly on short, tender grasses and herbs. They live in forests interspersed with open land so that they can rest in the shady groves and feed in the meadows. Their habitat forms a transitional zone between that of the sambar and the nilgai, but they do not compete with the sambar as they stay mostly in the meadows. Chital will browse on shrubs and fallen leaves and can stand on their hind legs to pluck leaves and fruits from a height of up to six feet.

When danger threatens chital stand motionless with neck outstretched, their big eyes focused in the direction from which the strange sound has come. They group themselves so close together that it is difficult even for humans to distinguish individuals, a device to confuse the predator. Each herd has a sentinel, usually a doe, who gives the alert signal the moment she spots danger by sight, sound or scent. By their pitch and frequency, the calls become conspicuous when a predator is on the prowl; even small cats or jackals make the sentinel nervous. But a tiger can be in full view and she will give no call if he is resting. Once I saw two chital does within less than 50 feet of a tigress with two cubs who were on their way to rest in the shade. The chital looked at her and bolted, but gave no alarm call until they were about 200 feet away.

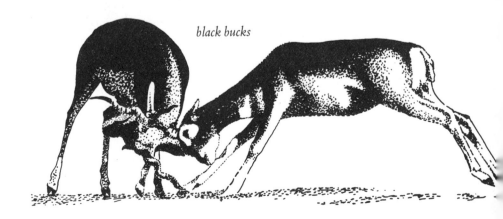

black bucks

I saw chital throughout tigerland except in areas of very high rainfall in Kerala and the entire eastern region, and also those with low precipitation where waterholes are limited, such as the Aravalis and Melghat. The availability of water is a limiting factor to their distribution. Surprisingly, the chital lives on sea water in the Sundarbans and thrives in brackish creeks.

Their courting season is the spring, and they live in herds of 30–40 members, both stags and does. Several herds unite during the course of a day at waterholes or grazing grounds. In Kanha during the rains, when luscious grass had attracted their attention, I was amazed to see their numbers swelling to over a thousand. They move daily from cover to open pasture and back to cover, selecting high ground which can give them a clear view of approaching predators when they are resting. While the herd is sitting they all look in different directions to keep watch, but even so one or other of the herd falls victim to the big cat almost every day. The chital is one of the staple foods of the tiger in the Terai and the forests of the Sundarbans.

Herds of swamp deer (*Cervus duvauceli*) numbering several hundred were a common sight in the open grasslands of the Terai region of U.P., north Bihar, the Nepal Terai and in the Brahmaputra valleys. But with the loss of much of these lands and over-hunting swamp deer are now confined to a few pockets in Dudwa in Uttar Pradesh, the Terai of Nepal, and the wet savannas of the Brahmaputra valley, where a few thousand still survive. There are about 500–520 head in Kaziranga and about 2000 in Dudwa. They feed on coarse grasses and were once a staple food of tigers in the swampy country of the northern and eastern regions of India.

Another race of swamp deer, *Cervus duvauceli branderi*, was once found over large tracts of the central highlands. A deer of the hard ground, it differs from the common sub-species in having a narrower split in the hoof (the wide split is an adaptation to swampy ground). It was named after Brander, the first naturalist of the Central Provinces.

Swamp deer are stupid animals; confronted with danger, instead of escaping they group themselves in confusion and call in distress, almost as if they were hypnotized. A predator can practically walk up and pluck one out without any difficulty. They live in small herds which can increase and decrease significantly during the course of even a single day. Unlike sambar, they like to graze in meadows and rest in woodlands close by. In the cold season the stags are magnificent, dark tan in colour, their antlers hung with bunches of grass indicating that they are in prime condition for mating. The master stag, with hay covering his face, looks much like an Indian bridegroom, and his mating call sounds like a country musical instrument played inexpertly and for too long. He constantly chases his bride and is completely engrossed in this romantic pursuit, but after a week he courts another hind, and then another. Romance does not always run smoothly, and rival stags are always looking for an opportunity to muscle in; the master stag has to guard his bride constantly. As for the hinds, it does not matter to them who courts them. The drama lasts for a short period of four weeks from mid-December to mid-January, but, as in the case of the sambar, in the Assam region of floodplains the courting season is May-June.

The hard ground species is now in danger of extinction, and there are just over 215 of them left in Kanha National Park. George Schaller discovered that brucellosis, a disease which causes abortions in hinds as in domestic cows, was probably responsible for the dwindling numbers. Others who based their theories on casual impressions blamed the tigers of Kanha, and at one stage it was suggested that the tiger should be eliminated from the Park. When Kanha was included under Project Tiger there were protests: these people did not realize that the heavy predation by tigers was the result of over-baiting in the meadows by researchers and photographic enthusiasts, causing the tiger population to increase to an artificially high level. When Dr Schaller left and the baiting site was shifted the kills of swamp deer were reduced from sixteen in 1963-5 to four in 1971-2. The following year when Cloud Martin studied the ecology of the deer he attributed the reduction in their numbers to the deterioration of the grassland due to over-burning. The tiger was absolved and Kanha is now one of the best tiger reserves in the country.

The hog deer (Axis porcinus) is found only in the foothills of the Himalayas and the open savannas of the Gangetic and Brahmaputra plains. They share the habitat with elephants, gaur and buffalo – that is, mainly tall grasslands. The stag is a well-built animal, capable of defending itself against enemies bigger than itself. But a tigress likes to train her cubs on a doe that she has killed. I once saw two cubs trying unsuccessfully to bite into a hog deer; they had to go and fetch their mother, who opened up the haunches before dinner could begin.

A bark coming from a hillside in Meghalaya far from any dogs can be puzzling, as I found when I was camping there. The alarm call of the barking deer or muntjac (Muntiacus muntjak) sounds just like a dog. These animals are found over a wide range of habitats from the sub-montane, sub-tropical Himalayas to the semi-evergreen and deciduous forests of India, but they do not live in the arid zones, the delta, or the Terai plains. Although they stand only 20 inches high at the shoulder, the bucks are strong fighters and are armed with short but sharp antlers and well-developed canine teeth. They are able to command their own grazing ground and may take advantage of their small size by slipping underneath a bigger animal to rip open its belly. But confrontations are rare.

The barking deer is associated with sambar in peninsular India and in the sub-montane forests, utilizing the uneaten foliage inside bushes which the sambar cannot reach. These small deer cannot approach water plants, nor do they graze in grasslands, preferring hilly country. They live mostly in pairs or in small family groups not exceeding six, and their restricted population appears to be due to their specific food requirements. They are not much hunted by tigers unless they are very hungry, though a tigress likes such small game for training her cubs.

The nilgai antelope (*Boselaphus tragocamelus*) dominates the scene in the dry deciduous forests, especially in the tiger habitats of Rajasthan, parts of Madhya Pradesh, southern Uttar Pradesh, Bihar and Andhra Pradesh. It feeds on dry, coarse grasses and its long neck allows it to reach high branches, but the backward slant of its body does not enable it to climb hills with ease or to stand on its hind legs and it is therefore confined to open forests.

The nilgai (*nil*, "blue"; *gai*, "cow") enjoys religious protection as its name is akin to that of the sacred cow. With such a name, the body of an awkward horse, and the beard of a goat, it has had its genealogy disputed on a number of occasions in the law courts. The nilgai is in fact India's largest antelope, comparable to the African eland. Although it is not often prey to the tiger, it is still a major ungulate of tigerland – and one of the least studied. Since it is the animal of my homeland, Rajasthan, my fascination for its size, shape, colour and social system is only natural.

In this area nilgai herds are a common sight. They consist of schools of bulls, mature as well as recently admitted immature bulls, and feminine herds, which consist of light-coloured cows with calves of varying ages from newborn to the young of previous years. Solitary males, segregated either by choice or forced to do so by rivals, may also be seen.

Resting nilgai herd

The nilgai is known as the blue bull since it has a bluish tinge to its dark coat. It looks docile, but this appearance is deceptive. I once saw two bulls disputing their property, which was not territory but a cow in heat. They challenged each other with short calls, then started circling round with their bodies strained and arched. Slowly they closed the circle and finally attacked; they did not use their horns to tangle but fell down on their knees and pushed each other with their necks. It literally became a neck-to-neck fight, with the necks twisted and twined like giraffes in combat. They did not bite but tried to prod the soft flank of the opponent with their strong pointed horns. The stronger bull then charged furiously with neck held high and his broom-like tail raised up like a victory flag. He was looking for a chance to gore the hindquarters of his opponent who, for fear of exposing these soft quarters to danger, went round and round a bush with his tail between his legs. In this way he avoided the charge, but the fight was decisive and the lighter-coloured bull was chased away from the cows in oestrus. During such fights the bulls are blind to events around them, including human onlookers. But disputes are sometimes settled without a fight, simply by the ritualistic display of the arched body, after which the dominant males join the female herds for mating.

Each well-grown bull will appropriate at least two females. There is no courtship ceremony and no love call except that occasionally a cow bleats like a buffalo. A bull simply chases the female relentlessly, guarding the cow herd at all costs and driving away rivals. But while he is so occupied a second-in-command will take the opportunity to mate. The mating period lasts almost the whole year round, but the peak is in the cold season (November-January) when the bulls are at their best with their blue-black bodies gleaming. I used to visit Ranthambhor and Sariska every winter to record the courtship of the nilgai, but I still feel there is much to be learned. Only recently the first blue bull ever to be collared, at Ranthambhor, has yielded interesting information about its range of movement and herd formation.

Soon after the mating is over in mid-February the bulls leave the cows and form herds of their own. These include immature bulls whose coats are just turning black, who now leave their mothers' herds to join adult bull schools. The feminine parties consist of 10-12 members, but bull parties, with members of all ages, may consist of as many as 20. As the cows have now left them there is no cause for fighting, but young bulls who have not yet mated sometimes indulge in trials of strength. These playful mock battles are probably a preparation for next year's real ones. A bull party is therefore always active, some intimidating others with heads raised and bodies bent, closing in on each other and circling, or chasing one another. Some play with bushes, even pushing their horns into the ground when in a fighting mood.

Nilgai are very careful when grazing, even more so when they are resting. For this they select an open patch and members of the herd sit with their backs together, each guarding an allotted side. When danger threatens the animals stand up and give strange muffled bellows. The noise is so curious that unless one actually sees a nilgai bellowing one would never believe this to be its call.

The young are born in September-October when the grass is high enough to hide them until they are up on their legs, which happens about eight hours after birth. Twins are quite common, and life is a communal affair, any fawn suckling any lactating cow as if it were a milk bar. I have seen as many as five calves, including one almost a year old, suckling one cow.

The males have a habit of dropping their pellets at the same place day after day, and many observers have confused this habit with territorial markings and the renewal of boundary "pillars". However, cows do not follow this rule. I have never come across a tiger waiting near these places of defecation, probably because an adult bull with its sharp horns is too much even for a tiger to tackle. The females are of course more vulnerable, especially from February to April and again in September-October when they are about to drop their calves, and the bulls give them no protection.

Chinkara

The little chinkara gazelles (*Gazella gazella*) are associates of the nilgai in open land and share the same habitat as sambar in the dry areas of tigerland, but their small size and efficiency in climbing precipitous hills eliminates any competition between them and either of the others. Living in dry deciduous woodlands, the chinkara is able to penetrate deep into thorny bushes and feed on forage left untouched by sambar.

The buck is a very elegant creature with its lyre-shaped horns and graceful, well-shaped body on lanky legs. The females too carry horns, but they are small, straight and unimpressive. Chinkara are found in pairs or small family groups of three to six, and during the courting season in March unsuccessful bucks stay together. A courting buck will hit the doe with his front legs: this means a proposal. The buck is a fearless fighter and does not hesitate to challenge a rival much larger in size.

When a chinkara stands motionless it is difficult to make out, as its light-brown coat and white belly merge so well into the background of dry, broken country, especially during the hottest part of the day when shadows are minimal. Only its restless tail exposing the white rump makes it conspicuous. In size and appearance chinkara resemble the Thomson's gazelle of East Africa; both inhabit semi-desert country and both can stand dehydration.

The chinkara is seldom hunted by tigers but falls an easy victim to a hungry tigress with growing cubs. She will either spring out from ambush at a water-hole or manoeuvre to stalk them in open grassland much like a lioness.

Blackbuck (*Antilope cervicapra*), the only member of the genus *Antilope*, once roamed in thousands all over the plains of India, but their numbers have been reduced to a few hundreds in isolated pockets. They occur in Gujarat, parts of Bihar, Orissa, Uttar Pradesh, Madhy Pradesh and Tamil Nadu, but above all in Rajasthan. The former richness of the blackbuck population, which still lingers in Dholi Sanctuary near Jodhpur, was largely due to religious protection given by the Vishnoi community. Members of this sect follow 20 principles in life, of which one was the protection of the blackbuck. About 22 blackbuck are trapped in the Kanha meadows, a wholly unsuitable habitat. How they came to be there is an unsolved mystery; it may have been a fancy idea of some wildlife enthusiast. Because of the open habitat in which they normally live and their telescopic sight blackbuck are not on the tiger's hunting list, although they have always been inhabitants of tigerland.

Sariska is the only place where the four-horned chausingha antelopes (*Tetracerus quadricornis*) can be seen easily during day-time, and I have spent hours observing them. They share the same habitat as sambar, living in hilly, moist, deciduous dry forests, open deciduous woodlands, feeding on the lower bushes and even entering thickets to utilize an unused feeding niche. Chausingha live in pairs or small family groups and do not exert any conspicuous pressure on the habitat. Their walk is elegant, gentle yet gracefully jerky. Although mostly preyed upon by leopards, they sometimes cross the path of a tigress with cubs, and their alarm call resembles the low "ponk" of a sambar. Their other enemy is the jackal, who attempts to kill the fawns.

The wild boar (*Sus scrofa*) is found all over the country, including even the swamps of the Sundarbans. It is a fearless beast and goes to waterholes without much anxiety about the possible presence of a tiger. The tiger is well aware of the boar's strength and ferocity, and normally does not accept a challenge.

female black bucks

But awkward confrontations can occur at a waterhole and then the battle is generally fought to the death. In 1961 in Kotah forests a wild boar and a tiger fought for almost a whole night; the tiger ripped the boar open, and the boar charged back and disabled the tiger. Eventually the boar was killed, but the wounded tiger was in no mood for a meal and left the victim in disgust, never to return.

The thick muscles and extra layers of fat round a boar's neck are too much for a tiger to bite through and his canines can hardly reach the vertebral column to make a quick kill. Naturally the tiger prefers killing by holding the victim's throat. Small fatty piglets are his particular favourite. In my samples of tigers' faeces collected at Kanha, Sariska and Ranthambhor I found that almost every third one contained pig hair. The rate of production of piglets is large – 10–12 per litter every year. If it went on at this rate very soon the habitat would be destroyed by the pig's habit of digging up roots, preventing the regeneration of trees. Therefore their number is kept under control by all predators, including the tiger. Even jackals and wild dogs like them. Nature's concern for their survival as a species takes account of heavy predation by this over-production of young, and equally counteracts over-production by heavy predation. Thus the mystery called the "balance of nature" is again maintained.

The wild boar is known for its acute powers of hearing and smell. It lives in small family groups, and both mother and father take care of the young. Solitary males are also commonly seen: these will have defected, or be rejected individuals who have been turned out of the family. When boars fight for possession of a sow in heat they stand on their hind legs to butt. The battles are noisy and alert the whole forest.

Wild boars are omnivorous, feeding on any organic matter such as succulent roots and tubers. They also scavenge the predators' left-overs, eating even soft bones. At a kill the boar is extra-cautious, gobbling the meat in haste for fear of the owner's return. Sometimes when a boar arrives to appropriate a tiger's kill he himself becomes a kill. Otherwise, because his food is mainly subterraneous, he does not come into conflict with any other animal except occasionally with porcupines.

Porcupine

While studying tigers in Sariska I witnessed the extraordinary courage of porcupines (*Hystrix indica*). I had provided corn for them and for wild boars in a small patch where a bait was tied for tigers. By sunset a tigress and four almost full-grown cubs arrived; one of them killed the buffalo calf and all joined in to eat the dinner. As darkness fell three porcupines appeared and, without any fear, started picking up the corn. When they had finished they scared the tigers with rattling quills in order to get a few grains left near the bait. The tigers gave way.

On the same day I saw a porcupine walking between two sitting tigers. One of them stood up and followed, but the spiny creature showed no anxiety and after walking a few steps the tiger returned.

That something covered in a mass of hard, sharp quills can be the prey of tigers is difficult to believe, but it does happen. Porcupines attract a tiger's attention either out of curiosity or hunger. He is able to kill the rodent outright, but often the quills get planted in his throat, jaws or foot-pads. Such wounds turn septic, rendering the tiger unfit to hunt effectively. Tulsinath Singh, a shikar officer of the ex-Maharaja of Udaipur, once recovered quills from a tiger's stomach and found that they had caused gastric ulcers. Colonel Kerari Singh recovered two quills from the jaw muscles of a tigress, and according to Corbett such animals generally become man-eaters. In my own studies I found that four tigers' faeces indicated the presence of porcupine quills, and in a case at Bastar I noticed clumps of quills half-digested.

No animal other than the tiger takes up a challenge with a porcupine. An infuriated porcupine is a big ball of sharply-pointed black and white spikes (actually modified hair). The longest quill is over a foot long. The animal attacks in reverse gear at top speed, releasing its quills into its victim's body by a special mechanism. It does not shoot so much as release its quills, but it does so at such speed that "shooting" is often the word used to describe it.

The porcupine is purely nocturnal, coming out of burrows or rocky crevices in thick bush well after dark to feed on roots, fallen fruits, even carrion. It will gnaw bark in such a way that the tree is girdled and dies. This operation has selective value, for the dead tree makes way for new growth and thus helps to ensure food supplies for the future.

There are other animals which help in maintaining a good supply of food for the prey populations: troops of monkeys and flocks of parakeets.

Once I went early in the morning to take some pictures of nilgai and to my surprise found that there was not a single animal in the valley although the zizyphus trees were in full fruit. Then, as the day became warmer, a troop of langurs arrived and started feeding. Soon the place became a hive of activity, with sambar, nilgai, chital, jackals and wild boars. Due to the primates' energetic activity in the tree-tops and their wasteful feeding habits, leaves, flowers and fruits – rich in proteins and vitamins – drop to the ground and are picked up by the monkeys' followers. But for the langurs this food range would be beyond the reach of the ungulates.

Thus an interesting ungulate-primate association has developed. The chital, for example, is usually under a tree where a troop of langurs is feeding, and the nilgai also follows the langurs wherever they go. Not only do the ungulates have the advantage of an extra food supply, but the monkeys act as tree-top sentinels while the former are feeding. However, it works the other way too. Conspicuous activity by the monkeys attracts the attention of predators, who know that it indicates the presence of other prey animals. The whole system is interlinked, and who takes most advantage of whom is anyone's guess.

On spotting a moving tiger, the common langur (*Presbytis entellus*) gives an alarm call – "khok, khok kakookho" – and repeats it until the tiger is out of sight. They then give an all clear signal by a repeated "hoop, hoop, hoop". Langurs are nervous animals, and sometimes when a tiger stands below their roosting tree and roars one or two fall like over-ripe fruits into his mouth. One reason for this is that langur are the favourite food of leopards, who will climb to their roosting places with ease. Instead of climbing further up the tree the langur will fall to the ground in order to climb up another tree, and so falls an easy victim. A tigress will also try to kill a langur as a training manoeuvre for her cubs.

The langur feeds on leaves, shoots and fruits in the jungle and lives in troops ranging between 10 and 30 members. Troops hold territories, with dominant and co-dominant leaders who guard their members tenaciously. Life is peaceful and co-operative; babies are considered as members of the commune and looked after by all adults. The young are brownish-red at birth, become blackish-red, and finally change to white with jet-black faces. Female langurs are devoted to their babies, who cling to the mother's breasts until they are six weeks old. They cling so tightly that the mother is able to leap from tree-top to tree-top without fear of losing them.

The death of a langur is a pathetic sight. Once my speeding car killed one and I stopped to place the body to one side of the road. I then witnessed the mourning of the whole troop as one by one the senior members came close and seemed to whisper something into the ears of the dead monkey – perhaps never to trust man. Sometimes when an infant dies the mother carries the body around for days.

The langur is the most widespread species of primate in India, extending from the Himalayas over the entire peninsula, from the scrub forests to the evergreen habitat of Assam. Geographical variations have been noticed in different localities – those in the south are darker than those in the north – but no sub-species have been identified. The common langur has several cousins, however: the golden langur (*Presbytis geei*); the capped langur (*P. pileatus*) found in the dense forests of Assam; and the Nilgiri langur (*P. johni*) of the tropical forests of the Western Ghats in Kerala. All three species are rare, and all extremely photogenic.

Stoutly built with short limbs, the rhesus monkey (*Macaca mulatta*) is an unfriendly animal which acts as an informer by his chattering alarm call. Like the langur, he drops sufficient fruit to attract a following of herbivores. Once when I was sitting in the Kachida valley the nilgai and sambar suddenly started giving alarm calls. A troop of langurs bolted and slowly a solitary rhesus came in sight. Life resumed its normal course only after he departed, for the rhesus is vicious and temperamental. Rhesus monkeys are the only primates which habitually drink saline water and hence they are able to live in the Sundarbans. Their counterpart in the south is the bonnet monkey (*Macaca radiata*), with its characteristic hair style and long dragging tail. There are also a few local sub-species in Assam.

Primates are not normally part of the tiger's food, but they add activity to tigerland – quite apart from their ecological value in providing fruits and other extra foods for the ungulates, and in running an informer service. Ecologically monkeys have never been taken seriously. They have always been considered as destroyers of crops, including forest growth, and this has been partly responsible for their large-scale capture. The demand for forest-dwelling primates free from communicable disease for medical research has resulted in great losses to the monkey population. With the disappearance of the associates which provided extra food, the ungulates and their predators have also abandoned the forests, which are now sterile wildlife deserts. The important monkey link needs protection.

We have studied the wide spectrum of the prey range of the tiger, and the way each animal fits into its proper niche. But this is only part of the life of the animal kingdom of tigerland, only one food chain among thousands. Although the tiger is the principal predator of his land, he in no way holds it exclusively. He shares the habitat with his co-predators and camp followers.

Common langur

CHAPTER 6

Co-predators and camp followers

Tolerance and peaceful coexistence is the law of nature. We have seen that prey animals avoid competition by selective use of the habitat, and this is demonstrated equally by the ways of life of the seemingly more competitive predators. They too have different levels of operation even within the same niche, and they have various ways of interaction with the tiger.

Predators living in open country must adopt different tactics to those who hunt in the forest, but various alternatives are available. In the savanna, if a predator were to depend on stalking a herd over long distances he would soon tire; a better method is to go in for sudden speed, and the cheetah is a magnificent example of this style of hunting. The strategy of lions is to drive the prey towards one member of the pride who is lying in wait for a short-distance attack. Or the teamwork may depend on a sustained chase in relays, as in the case of wolves, wild dogs and hyenas.

The leopard (*Panthera pardus*) lives either alone or in pairs in many types of country, preferring glades with trees and rocks to allow him to survey the terrain unnoticed; from this vantage point he can plan his attack as close to his prey as possible. The tiger's hunting methods, described in chapter 1, are similar in many ways. They are co-predators in so far as small mammals and fawns are concerned, but the overlap is limited to a very few species (mainly chital and wild boar). Leopards are far more versatile than tigers and their diet includes monkeys, peafowl, dogs and domestic poultry, all of which are usually ignored by the tiger. For this reason these two large predators can exist in the same region without undue competition.

No detailed study has been made to try to find out the index of overlap, as has been done in the case of the lion and leopard in South Africa (20% overlap according to Horn, 1966), or leopard and cheetah (75% according to Eaton).

Whenever I go to Jogi Mahal in Ranthambhor the alarm calls of sambar and langurs coming from the slopes of the fort in late evenings and early mornings indicate the movement of a predator. This happens daily, and pug marks on the road confirm the presence of a leopard.

The leopard generally lives near villages in abandoned houses and forts, or in caves, quarries and rocky crevices. Tigers and leopards are found in such close proximity that in many forests they have been driven out in the same beat and shot one after the other. During his visit to Gwalior the Prince of Wales (the late Duke of Windsor) shot a tiger and two leopards in the same beat, and many such cases are recorded in the hunting history of India and Nepal.

I have often found leopards using the same track as tigers. While I was in my hide at Jharokha in the Kachida valley on 9 February 1974 a leopard killed the bait but as it was firmly tied he could not carry it away. While he was struggling to open the carcass and finding it tough he was forced away by a tigress, who fed on the kill for four hours. After she left the leopard returned and had to make do with the remains. On several other occasions a leopard and a tiger were seen feeding on the same kill, one after the other, at this very place. In June 1973 I was in my hide at Kalighati when a leopardess came to drink at the waterhole while a tiger sat in the bush about 100 feet away waiting for darkness to fall. The leopardess finished her drink and went away, and the tiger then took the bait.

The association of an adult leopardess and a young tigress was observed by Abdul Shakur Khan in the Sawai Madhopur forests of Ranthambhor in 1928. The two came together to the waterhole and the kill, and he shot them both on the kill within two hours of each other. Most likely the leopard was in the habit of poaching the tigress's kills, and this is not unusual.

When an unusually large leopard is reported as creating havoc in a village the general belief is that the animal is a cross between a leopard and a tigress. They call it *adhbaghera*, meaning "bastard". Hicks describes an animal he shot which had the head and neck of a leopard and the body of a tiger, with stripes breaking into rosettes here and there. Such a specimen has not been recorded in any natural history museum, and there is no evidence of interbreeding. Iftikhar Ali Khan observed a big leopard and a well-grown tigress preying together for several nights: the leopard used to make a kill with the help of the tigress and both would enjoy the dinner, until finally both were shot in a beat. This unusual

Common leopard

behaviour of the pair living together was thought to be a sex partnership, but in the absence of any evidence of love-play it is more likely that they were just hunting partners.

A leopard feeds on smaller animals such as hares, chinkara, and four-horned antelopes which are generally ignored by the tiger. He does not mind small birds, partridges, porcupines, jackals and even rats. His ability to climb trees with ease provides access to arboreal animals like langurs and other monkeys, and big birds like peafowl, which are beyond the reach of the tiger. He also feeds on sick animals, and the fawns of sambar, chital and nilgai, as well as piglets. Does, apart from chital, are beyond his scope. Even so the presence of a leopard creates far greater tension among prey animals than that of a tiger. Once I watched a leopardess with two cubs coming to the waterhole at Kalighati. Three fully-grown nilgai were in a terrible state of nervousness and bellowed continuously. The chital and sambar also gave terrified alarm calls. I have never experienced such a commotion even when a tigress with cubs appeared on the scene. While in the hide I never normally keep my flash unit attached to the camera but that day, in an effort to get the right illumination, I did so; the flash head scratched against the frame of the window and the leopard jumped away. I shall never forget my bad luck.

All my records of killing by leopards show that the method is by strangulation after biting through the victim's throat. A film sequence made by His Highness of Jodhpur, and pictures taken by S. P. Shahi, support this conclusion. The leopard attacks from an ambush; he does not have the power to break the bones of the neck as does the tiger, so he depends on the throat bite. Due to the lack of powerful jaw muscles, he starts his dinner through the soft skin of the belly, unlike the lion or tiger who open up the haunches. This results in "mixing the dirt with the flesh" and the dinner becomes a messy affair, in complete contrast to the clean feeding of the tiger and the lion who meticulously remove the rumen without even puncturing it. These habits help to identify the predator.

The leopard does not hesitate to enter cattle pens to pick up calves or goats, an offence that a tiger never commits. A leopard will also prowl in villages to kill stray dogs, and risk entering houses to pick up chained dogs, or even children. During my visit to Bastar I was told horrifying tales of the lifting of babies sleeping with their mothers. In one case the father and mother were asleep near the fire with the baby between them; a leopard made off with the infant without rousing the sleeping parents. After such tragedies the people start believing in ghosts who become men during the day and leopards at night. In contrast the tiger has never been known to enter a house and even in the open he will ignore children.

In the Gir forests the leopard shares his hunting range with lions in much the same way as he does elsewhere with tigers. The evidence amply disproves

George Schaller's conclusions that leopards tend to be scarce when tigers abound and *vice versa*; according to my studies they coexist, for their prey range and feeding habits are different. The leopard is a solitary animal, like the tiger, and does not like to share his meal except with a female in heat. He is a nocturnal predator, more difficult to photograph or study than even the tiger.

Other co-predators with the tiger are the clouded leopards and golden cats in Assam. They too feed on small mammals, rodents and birds and, leading a mostly arboreal life, hardly cross the tiger's hunting horizon. The snow leopard, the most handsome of the family, probably never meets a tiger although they have overlapping habitats in the western Himalayas. Snow leopards prey on marmots, musk deer, hares, and also sheep and goats.

A chital doe running at top speed crossed a small stream and entered the rest house compound at Kanha; her belly was torn and her intestines were hanging out. She came close to the men working in the compound and fell while her pursuers, two wild dogs (*Cuon alpinus*), stopped near the fence, impatiently watching the dying chital. A similar situation occurred while I was camping in Periyar Sanctuary: a doe sambar, cornered by a pack of 18 wild dogs, crossed the water and approached the busy camping grounds while the dogs waited at a distance of 200 yards. That the fear of man is less than the terror of wild dogs is again illustrated by the behaviour of the chital who come to the forest rest house compound at Bandipur. Every night the whole campus is filled with the glittering eyes of chital, who are not in the least disturbed by the noise, honking cars, neon lights and men walking. By day-break they return to the forest. The explanation is not far to seek: their fear of the wild dogs in the Tiger Reserve. For once man can take the credit of being trusted: in no case have chital been seen running from man to dogs.

The teamwork, tenacity and savagery exhibited by a pack of hunting dogs is unparalleled in nature. Their mere appearance causes panic, and once a target is fixed the victim is doomed. Wild dogs are intelligent and plan their attack with full knowledge of the terrain and of the prey they have selected.

One cool and sunny morning I was camping at Periyar to study how best to conduct tiger census operations in the evergreen forests of the Western Ghats. I was told about a pack of wild dogs chasing two sambar fawns and rushed to the scene. There were 21 dogs, with bright red winter coats, black muzzles and black, bushy tails. One of the fawns was a yearling, the other hardly four months old, and clearly they had become separated from their mother. The terrified animals were being directed towards a deep channel where one of the dogs was swimming and waiting for them. The yearling turned and broke the ring of attackers, but the younger fawn fell into the water. The dog rushed at it and after a scuffle lasting only a couple of minutes the water became red with blood. The fawn breathed its last and its body drifted on to the shore, where two other dogs joined the killer in dragging it out. The dogs took turns to feed and the feast was quiet as everyone was busy, and in less than an hour there was nothing left except a few bones and the skull.

This is a regular drama that takes place along the shores of the Periyar lake almost every day when dogs are in the vicinity. The members of the pack separate one of a sambar herd and force it to enter the water, then one dog swims to hold it by the nose and it is led helplessly as if muzzled. "Operation drowning", which is conducted with the least effort on the part of the predator and performed with great precision, is a highly perfected means of predation which can be considered an evolutionary process. The predator has no risk of attacks by antlers or hooves, and it meets its prey at the same level on the surface of the water. If the victim does manage to escape, the other members of the pack are waiting on the shore. They attack on all fronts: belly, neck, head and even back. A frontal attack invariably blinds the victim and the killing is then easy. The whole process involves a division of labour and individual responsibility. Communal hunting ensures tolerance, and communal feeding is obligatory.

Wild dogs have been castigated for their cruel habits of eating the prey alive and are hated by everyone. But are they really so cruel? Death by drowning is not painful, nor is a multiple attack on an excited animal. The action is so fast that the victim hardly has time to suffer before it is paralysed and eaten. In the case of an unsuccessful attack by a tiger the prey bleats for half an hour or more; whereas a pack of wild dogs will finish everything, including eating the entire animal, in less than an hour, and no bleating is heard.

Ecologically the wild dog enjoys a status of its own. It fears no other predator, not even the tiger – whose only competitor in fact is the wild dog. Dogs make up for their small size by hunting in packs and are thus able to compete in the food range of the tiger. Out of ten common species of prey of the tiger, the wild dog competes for six: sambar, chital, barking deer, hog deer, swamp deer and wild boar. The index of overlap of the tiger and wild dog is higher than that of the lion and the cheetah.

Whenever a pack of wild dogs came to Kanha meadows the chances of seeing tigers were bleak, and I had to wait for weeks until they left. Although the tiger is more than a match for wild dogs, it yields to them and leaves them the whole field of operation. The reason is the tiger's wish to avoid their nuisance value, since they disturb the whole prey population by their long chase. Their heavy predation and the panic they create in the area reduce the tiger's chances of ambush attacks. At times wild dogs will also chase a tiger away from his kill and sometimes send him up a tree in fright. Dogs have even been known to kill and eat tigers and leopards; this is supported by some early-twentieth-century paintings and by recent observations.

Wild dogs are useful in culling overpopulation of deer and boars, helping to keep the habitat at a natural level. Also their nomadic habits cause the pressure of predation to be spread over large areas, and the tigers can return to their home range after the dogs have left.

However, no predator keeps the population of wild dogs in check. When their number swells beyond the carrying capacity of the area a few dogs and bitches separate and form their own pack to break new ground. This happens in winter when the bitches come in heat. If such spacing fails to occur due to ecological barriers, the inadequate food supply results in a starvation diet and low vitality, leading to virus diseases such as distemper in pups and rabies in adults. Epidemics will wipe out nearly the whole pack, then gradually it is rebuilt from the few survivors.

During my study tour to Serengeti in East Africa in October 1968 I photographed wild dogs, but when I revisited the area in September 1975 there was not one to be seen. In Africa the wild dog (*Lycaon pictus*) has always been considered vermin, to be shot at sight. In India the production of its black tail ensured bounty even in our national parks and sanctuaries; but with the new concept of total environmental preservation the wild dog at last enjoys a well-deserved status as a protected species.

In the Ramnagar Division of Uttar Pradesh bears have been found poaching tiger kills. Smythies records a pair of bears chasing a tigress in an elephant ring in the Nepal Terai; and Corbett mentions an incident where a bear attacked and killed a tiger. Although bears can escape from tigers by climbing trees, their clumsy run is slow enough for the tiger sometimes to catch one. During my wanderings in Karnataka while preparing the management plans for Bandipur I was shown the spoor of a tiger which contained also the nail of a bear, which presumably it had dragged; and Campbell also records the killing of a bear by a tiger. In the Himalayas, Burton considered bears to be normal food for tigers, but there has been no evidence of this in recent years.

Bears feed on fruits, termites, beehives and even carcasses, but when the Himalayan bear comes out of hibernation in the spring it kills calves and at times even attacks men. The sloth bear (*Melursus ursinus*), on the other hand, is not known to kill for food.

The Asiatic lion (*Panthera leo*) is not unlike the African lion in appearance except that it has a scantier mane and longer tail tassel, a more pronounced belly fringe, and more prominent tufts of hair on the elbow.

The relationship between the lion and the tiger has been a subject for speculation, and which of the two came to India first is still an open question. One school of thought is of the opinion that lions were the original inhabitants, and the tiger entered through the forests of Burma, driving the lions of the open country into the furthest western corner in the Gir forests of Gujarat. However, history does not support this view. The tiger was certainly in India by 4500 BC, whereas the lion was apparently unknown to the Indus Valley civilizations. Evidence of the lion in India dates only from the period of Ashoka and through the Hindu and Mughal periods, but this may be due to their bias towards the lion. I am not taking into account the reference to lions in the Vedas, since their dating is the subject of great controversy.

The Asiatic lion was well known to the Persians, in fact its scientific name is *Panthera leo persica*. Lions might have migrated to India from there after the Indus Valley civilizations perished, during a period of aridity which forced the tiger to move further east and south. There is no evidence of any interaction between the two species, although records show that the Gupta kings (Samudra Gupta) and Mughals hunted both lions and tigers. The location of the Guptas' lion hunts is not known, but beyond any doubt the Mughals hunted near Agra in Uttar Pradesh and Malwa where tigers are still found today. The presence of lions in these areas is difficult to explain, but presumably they occupied different ecosystems from the tiger. Probably they were confined to the uncultivated Gangetic plains, the last vestiges of which I saw in Bharatpur and Alwar during the early 1950s when they were teeming with blackbuck and wild boars. The tiger was conspicuous by its absence in these open plains, although he was to be found on the nearest hill less than five miles away. I am therefore not too surprised that a lion and a tiger could both feature in a day's shoot of a medieval maharaja.

But how is it that the lion has been forced to retreat from the game-rich

Asiatic lion, from Gir forests

areas of Malwa as early as the eighteenth century to the small patch of Gir forests in Gujarat? Did tigers drive them out? There is no direct evidence, but if we examine the probabilities in the case of a confrontation between the two some inferences may be drawn. In a fight a tiger would be unable to get close to the vital joint of a lion's neck because of his thick mane, but the tiger is vulnerable to the lion. Once a crazed prince who shall be nameless organized a fight between a lion and a tiger in a deep pit in his palace compound, and filmed the whole encounter. The result supports this theory: the tiger was killed.

In any inter-species confrontation lions would also have the advantage of support from members of the whole pride. But in my opinion a tiger is no match even for a single lion of equal strength. Moreover, tigers would tend to avoid confrontation by withdrawing from the area, and lions might have found an easy walk over tigerland by forcing the retreat of the tiger from the dry plains at least.

I have studied the lion's habitat in the Gir forests, which is quite unlike the African savannas. In these woodlands hunting strategy by more than one predator is not useful. The habitat, in fact, resembles that of the tiger, especially the topography of the dry deciduous Aravali region of Sariska in Rajasthan. Even the lion's prey consists of sambar, chital, wild boar, nilgai and cattle, exactly the same as that of the other great predator in a different habitat.

The absence of lions in the Gir forests in the historic past and their present confinement there has added to the confusion about their ecological status in India. All I can say is that it is not the tiger who should be held responsible for their withdrawal, nor can the tiger be considered ever to have confronted the lion in any of its prey ranges. It seems to be purely a case of geographical separation of the two predators to avoid competition. Their index of prey overlap is nearly 100%, but their distribution is so wide apart that overlapping does not actually occur. The lions of the Gir forests have an exclusive range.

Since the occurrence of the two predators in one niche is supported neither by evidence nor any natural law, any attempt to find an alternative home for the lion in India would be an example of man's interference with nature and an ecological blunder. I pleaded with the "Lion Committee" to drop the idea of searching for a place to rehabilitate the lion unless vast savannas teeming with blackbuck and boars could be restored, and I have my doubts about such a luxury being possible. Rightly, the plan for an alternative home for lions has at present been abandoned.

There are other predators besides mammals, notably crocodiles and snakes. Once I was fortunate enough to witness an encounter between a tiger and a crocodile. Ruined forts being my well-known weakness, I had gone to investigate the fort of Utgir in the Karoli forests when I was Divisional Officer of Bharatpur in 1954. I was sitting on the ramparts to recover from the long walk and climb at midday when I saw a tiger crossing the Chambal River which forms the boundary between the States of Rajasthan and Madhya Pradesh. A crocodile (*Crocodilus palustris*) saw him, got into the water and met him half-way in the river. The crocodile swam parallel to him for some time, then began to thrash with his long corrugated tail. The tiger lost his balance and got a ducking, after which he got another thrashing which made him nervous and caused him to swim faster. The crocodile managed to give him a hard hit on the back, but this time the tiger had his feet on the ground and with a great roar rushed towards the crocodile, gripped it in his mouth, dragged it ashore, and threw it about four metres away. In a few minutes he killed it, snarled at the carcass and went away. I regret those days when I had no telephoto lens and all I could record was a dead crocodile.

A similar incident was witnessed by a forest guard in the Kali Sindgh River of Kotah a decade ago. The shikar officer Tulsinath Singh told me that in 1932 he saw a crocodile approach a tiger's kill on an island in Kuwakhera, Rajasthan. The tiger, who was watching from a bush, caught it as it began to eat. The crocodile tried to bite the tiger, then to escape, but all in vain and in a few minutes it was killed. Burton also tells of a tiger gripped and killed by a crocodile and narrates their fearful struggle in his book (1933). His Highness of Kotah, who filmed all his tiger shoots, showed me a short film of a crocodile appropriating a tiger's kill in the forests of Shahabad; as soon as the owner arrived the poacher ran for the nearest pool in the river.

At one time crocodiles lived in almost all Indian rivers, lakes and estuaries, but most of them have been killed for their skins and now very few waters hold crocodiles. The only place where the salt-water crocodile (*Crocodilus porosus*) shares a habitat with the tiger is the Sundarbans. These were once famous crocodile hunting reserves, but today it is difficult to get even a glimpse of one. Only once did I manage to photograph a basking crocodile.

Crocodiles like to bask during the winter and they do not mind crowding on small islands, where their telescopic eyes help them to see any approaching danger or prey. They feed mainly on fish, but do not hesitate to catch and drown a deer or antelope, or cattle coming down to drink. While photographing a crocodile I tried to change my angle by moving on my back in a caterpillar action. This attracted the attention of the basking monster, who made a beeline for me and stopped only ten feet away. In a split second he would have been on the shore to lunge at me with his saw-like tail, but I quietly raised myself up and by resuming the appearance of a man scared him away.

Sometimes crocs become man-eaters and look for bathers, and they also leave the water and go hunting on land. They hide themselves in the grass beside a game path, rush out to grip the prey and drag it to the water to drown it. Fateh Singh, game warden of Ranthambhor, told me that one moonlit night he heard the distress call of a sambar and soon the whole lake and its

A cobra plunders a parakeet nest.
The birds are defenceless, and
their loss is total.

surroundings were echoing to the alarm cries of sambar and chital. He found a
sambar doe caught by a crocodile, which was pulling her towards the lake
shore about 400 metres away. Yet in spite of this danger sambar do not hesitate
to enter the water. The tanks of Ranthambhor Reserve have a sizeable population of crocodiles and I have always found it a challenge to approach them
closely to get good photographs.

The crocodile is the only aquatic predator in tigerland except for the fish-
eating gavial in the Ganges, Brahmaputra and Chambal. With aid from the
Food and Agriculture Organization of the UN (FAO), waters are now
being restocked and a few centres have been selected for crocodile farming. The
reptiles grow so slowly it will be some time before we know if it is going to be
an economic proposition, but at least it will be a conservation project which
should be able to save the species from extinction. Ecologically – in their role of
efficient predators – crocodiles play an important part in maintaining the
balance in aquatic ecosystems.

Apart from crocodiles, the only other reptiles that the tiger may confront
are snakes. Burton found a python which had been partly eaten by a tiger. In
the Kotah forests in 1964 a bus load of passengers witnessed a battle between a

python and a tiger which resulted in the death of both. I heard of it through the local paper, but by the time I arrived the villagers had taken the skins and there was nothing to be seen except trampled grass. My friend Bassia informed me that he saw a python gripping a yearling tiger, which it consumed in the course of a night; this happened in the Golpara forests of Assam.

Pythons feed mainly on rodents, small fawns and birds. Their excreta have been found to contain porcupine quills, but how they manage to catch and gulp the spiny creature is difficult to imagine.

Python

When a tiger encounters a cobra he is so frightened that he appears to be stunned, merely snarling and hissing. Tigers know by instinct that a bite is fatal and always try to avoid snakes; at my house the tiger known as Jim used to shy away from curved sticks or even a hosepipe.

The tiger also shares his habitat with smaller carnivores such as the mongoose, hyena, jackal, ratel, wild cats and civets, as well as other camp followers such as the varanus lizard, vultures and tree-pies. He helps to maintain them by leaving his half-eaten kills, but they also perform a very important service in disposing of animals which have died a natural death. Thus they keep the environment clean, and I protest at the term "scavengers" to describe such valuable members of the community.

Whatever is finally left after the camp followers have done their job is disposed of by white ants, larvae, maggots and bacteria. The strong tropical sun bleaches the bones, which eventually return to the soil to enrich the vegetation. By the end of a week there is no sign of a kill except for trampled grass, which soon stands erect again.

To understand nature's cleaning service we should examine the life-style of some of these creatures. They seldom poach before a tiger has quite finished with his kill, but if they do they are so cautious that they spend more time looking out for the owner than on feeding. The practice, in fact, is unremunerative.

One day at Sariska an excited group of tourists woke me to tell me about a big tiger that they had sighted at the entrance of the Pandupole valley. Since a bus load had been there, I did not think much of the idea of visiting the area, but I did so next day. The area is rocky and there was no sign of a tiger, but after searching round I discovered a sambar doe lying under a culvert. There were three tooth marks on her neck, but she had not been eaten – probably because the tiger had been disturbed by the tourists. There was no chance of the tiger staying near the kill as the road to the famous Hanuman temple gets busy even before sunrise. I decided to sit on a ledge and spend the day on the kill, accompanied by Sikand, the Divisional Forest Officer. I do not like company on such occasions, but his small size and khaki clothing helped to merge him into the rock and in fact he was more silent than I was. Nothing happened for two hours, and then appeared a mongoose, fat and furry with a black-tipped tail. He surveyed the carcass and climbed upon it, reassuring himself by retreat and reappearance. This time he landed near the sambar's snout, but seemed to have difficulty in tackling it. At each attempt the exposed patch of flesh became wider and he managed to gobble a few mouthfuls. He was then joined by two others, probably a female and her young one. The movement of the mongooses attracted the attention of a vulture, but he was not allowed to land until the family had had their fill. Within an hour they had lost interest and the vultures started landing. A pair of jackals joined in, and the dead sambar became a centre of activity.

The mongoose is always the first to approach a dead animal. Its powerful incisors help it to cut through the skin, whereas other camp followers do not have strong enough teeth or claws to open a carcass. Vultures sometimes make unsuccessful attempts through the eye holes or rectum, but mostly they wait until the carcass putrefies and the skin disintegrates. The small patch made by the mongoose is usually the beginning of the process leading to the final disposal of the carcass in the shortest time. But for the mongoose, the jungle would be littered with putrefying and stinking bodies.

The mongoose does not hesitate to take up a challenge with snakes, even cobras, but its agility is really tested when it confronts a hooded cobra. Once it has managed to grip the snake's snout its victory is assured, and the mongoose carries the body home for a meal. The mongoose also plunders nests and destroys both eggs and chicks, a natural predation to balance the population of birds, and it also looks for wounded or sick birds. The mongoose, in fact, is important in tigerland not only in its role of camp follower but also as a biological control.

The hyena (*Hyena hyena*) is rarely known by its proper name to the local people, who call it by a variety of names associated with death. One of these is the "horse of the ghost", who eats the soul of a man and leaves the body for his horse to feed upon.

The striped hyenas of India, unlike the spotted hyenas of Africa, do not live in packs and feed mostly on dead animals and left-overs from the kills of big predators, but at times they prey on cows, donkeys and even humans. The Indian hyena is a silent animal which rarely calls while hunting and lives mostly alone. Its burrows are in the banks of ravines, or it may drive the porcupine from its hole and shelter there during the day.

I have heard of how a hyena coming on to a tiger's kill encountered the owner and itself got killed, but the tiger made no attempt to eat the carcass or even drag it away. In Ranthambhor I usually found hyenas following up leopards' kills, probably because they can drive away the owner more easily. In the vicinity of Kalighati watch-tower I found a hyena on a tiger's kill and the returning tiger charged and killed the poacher; next morning I photographed the carcass, which was irregularly eaten here and there – perhaps less for food than out of rage.

Hyena

Since the numbers of tigers have diminished there are fewer left-overs, and even those that remain have very little for the hyena by the time it arrives. The hyena used to search for dry carcasses in the jungle and open countryside, but with the coming of the new trade in bone meal, man collects every bone to despatch in truck loads to bone factories in the cities: man is disputing even the scavengers' livelihood. Hardly anything is left for the poor hyena, who is probably in greater danger than even the leopard or the wild dog. His loss would be tragic, as he has just as important a part to play as them.

Once in Sawai Madhopur I watched three jackals (*Canis aureus*) on a kill busy removing the entrails, which they seem to prefer to the flesh. An abandoned kill provides the choicest meal for jackals, and usually all members of the pack assemble to feed on it.

On a cold January day at Rajbag, Ranthambhor, I discovered a fully grown buffalo left partially eaten by a tigress. I made an improvised hide of green branches and for fear of losing the early morning sun I endured the discomfort of this incomplete shelter. The first to arrive were some crows, whose noisy feeding attracted the nearest jackal. Soon two more members of his family joined him; they were highly resented, but after they had made one or two attempts he allowed them to share his prize. Within a few minutes 42 vultures had landed, but lacked the courage to approach the kill since every attempt they made was foiled by the angry jackals. Finally they settled in a flock, like mourners, 15 metres away from the carcass. The jackals worked only intermittently, enjoying their feed, then resting but guarding the kill by sitting round it in a formation that would make it easy to chase any intruder away. They continued in this way the whole day long, and when some intruding jackals carefully approached they gave up when the owners made the slightest protest. The intruder makes his hair stand on end to appear larger, and he also bares his canines to try and scare the owner: Indian jackals are particularly intolerant, and their numbers never exceed the family unit.

On another occasion at Mirag Talab the resident jackal arrived as soon as the tiger left the kill. It was early morning in the middle of May and the jackal was extremely cautious, watching, approaching, retreating, finally taking a piece of the entrails and making off. Again and again he came for more, until the swarming vultures made it impossible for him to continue. He had obviously been carrying pieces of meat to his partner or perhaps to store them under the earth for a later meal, so I tracked him and found four tiny pups waiting with their mother. When the father arrived she went to the kill herself and fifteen minutes later reappeared with a piece of meat.

Only one species of jackal is found from the foothills of the Himalayas to the Cape of Comorin, and it lives in forested regions as well as open grasslands and scrub jungles. Only in the delta region is it absent, and there are fewer jackals in the evergreen forests. Apart from scavenging, they also prey independently on birds, particularly sick or wounded peafowl and partridges, as well as hares, rats, chinkara fawns or disabled does. When the chital population increases jackals help to control the numbers by preying on fawns; killing is by strangulation. I observed two jackal kills, once in Kanha and once in Corbett Park. Reports are also coming in of increased killing by jackals of chital fawns. I once saw a jackal pick up a piglet which had strayed hardly five metres away from its mother. The predator used all his force to crush it between his jaws, but it took more than fifteen minutes to silence the squealing piglet.

Jackals are often found visiting burnt areas on the second day after the fire to search for animals and birds which have been roasted. But the cry of the jackal is becoming rare near villages, and they are disappearing from large areas because they are being persecuted by hunters for their meat and skins. After the ban on the export of leopard skins, traders mark leopard spots on jackal skins – perhaps more to bluff the customs officials than in a serious attempt to meet the market. And so even the jackal now needs protection.

During the day-time vultures often completely finish off a tiger's kill – if he has not dragged it under a bush. If he catches them at it the tiger will rush at them and if he succeeds in catching a vulture he tears it to pieces. But sometimes when a tiger is disturbed on a kill he abandons it, leaving it nicely carved for his camp followers. Then, taking the hint from the morning crow, the vultures land and within five minutes the whole carcass is swarming with them. Unless disturbed by jackals their feeding is continuous, and vultures can finish off a fully-grown buffalo in half an hour. I once watched two tiger cubs kill and partially eat a full-grown sambar; when they abandoned it 32 vultures finished the remains in ten minutes.

In areas disturbed by man and his cattle the tiger is unable to guard his kill and therefore has to kill more often, leaving more for the vultures. There are three main types: the common vulture (*Gyps bengalensis*), the king vulture (*Torgos calvus*), and the scavenging vulture (*Neophron percnopterus*). Once I watched a king vulture at Jharokha which within a minute of its landing had cut the ear off a carcass and gulped it down. This is not a common bird, and it lives either singly or in pairs. Its big black body, determined hooked beak and strong claws give it superior power among vultures. Its blood-red head and hanging red wattles lend it a certain regality, hence its name. Also, it is able to drive away any other vulture: after it has landed on a kill with a sound like a thud none of the others dare claim a share. Even so, it has not the power or the instruments to open up a carcass. The king is still a vulture.

The common vulture is a long-necked, ugly bird and a dirty feeder, putting its neck and often its entire body inside a carcass. These vultures live in flocks and have a rank order, the stronger ones getting a better feeding place. Sometimes the Griffon vulture (*Gyps fulvus*) also shares in the orgies.

The Egyptian or scavenging vulture is the last of the three to get its chance on a kill though it is the first to locate any carcass and land. Why it should be known as a scavenging vulture is not clear, since it is cleaner than the others and is often seen on bleached bones. Like the king vulture, it lives in pairs.

My common associates in the dry, drab summer days are the tree-pies (*Dendrocitta vagabunda*) – what an uncharitable specific name! – whose melodious calls are a welcome note in tigerland. The tree-pies pick fragments of flesh from the bones of abandoned kills, and they too have their preferred places for feeding and sometimes fight for their choice. They also help to remove parasites and are commonly seen on the backs of sambar, chital and nilgai. They are also favoured by chausingha. Tree-pies even enjoy the company of the tiger without fear. The confidence that these animals repose in the birds is remarkable – even allowing them access to their eyelids and nostrils. Yet it is a relationship where both benefit: the birds get food and the animals relief from parasites.

Nature has so arranged her creatures by area, size, movements and food habits that whatever is produced is fully utilized, whether in the trees, on land or in water. All enjoy their lives in their own particular horizon, and there is always a helping hand in procuring food. But at the same time nature has ensured controls to avoid over-use of the habitat, either by natural culling or by changes in climate which force consumers to search for food in new areas. Under-use is similarly avoided by increasing the population in years of bounty.

At first sight the life of animals equipped with tooth and claw appears to be competitive, consuming, cruel and bloodthirsty, but the study of the tiger and his co-predators and camp followers has shown that our anthropomorphic standards of judgement are wrong. We have observed the fine balance between prey and predators, and the grand understanding of living in their own orbit. Rigid observance of the law is the rule of nature, where indiscipline is not tolerated and punishment for its breach is death. Crimes like killing for the sake of killing, ill-treatment or criminal assault on the female of the species or intraspecies aggression for the sake of territorial expansion, are found only in human society and are unknown in nature. Under the law of the jungle everyone minds his own business. The larger predators keep the bigger prey species under control, the smaller predators see to those ignored by the others. The camp followers manage with the left-overs and do an excellent job in garbage disposal.

Nature, left to itself, will ensure the survival of life, but not necessarily of all species at all times. There are occasions when a species is made to die out as part of the evolutionary process. Any effort to save the doomed species is futile, and we should allow nature to take its course.

I have attempted to illustrate a cross-section of a typical ecosystem of tigerland. The animals have been placed according to their preferential habitat, and lines indicate their food preferences. The tiger is at the apex of the biomass and his role in environmental preservation is distinct. Any disturbance in the biomass is reflected in his behaviour and he may be considered, therefore, to be an index of environmental quality.

At one time in this world of prey, predators, co-predators and camp followers there was a perfect balance, without conflict. Even man was in tune with nature, hunting with his crude weapons and also feeding on the left-overs which he shared with jackals and vultures. He was part of the ecology of tigerland. But now, with his population explosion, technical achievements and greed in storing for the future, he has become not only the dominant predator in tigerland but a consumer of the actual habitat. From his position it is obvious that he is no more a part of the ecology of tigerland but a defier of natural laws. The result is clear: his own position is in peril.

Energy stored in the ground is transmitted to plants, which are eaten by a host of herbivores, and the energy is transferred to them. These are the primary consumers. They are preyed upon by carnivores to effect control, and the energy is shifted to this next level. These are the secondary consumers, or the topmost level of the biological horizon. Each horizon transfers back energy into the soil by the process of death and decay, and the energy is then recycled once more. Nothing is lost and nothing is gained in nature's cycle. This is also the Gospel of Truth of the Gita: "All life is His part, it emerges out of Him and finally merges in Him."

Langur, chital and peacock

above: *This drawing shows clerks of the East India Company, or 'writers' as they were called, on holiday hunting tigers. The tiger depicted has already been wounded and is springing on the elephant in self-defence.* below: *A day's shoot, showing the sikar camp of Col William Rice as it appeared in the mid-19th century. One tiger skin is shown, salted and stretched on nails, while another tiger is being skinned by 'expert' hands, and yet a third can be seen in the distance on its way to the camp.*

The Tiger in Indian Mythology

above left: '*Durga Saptsati*' *is a book in praise of the Goddess of Power and this illustration from it shows Durga riding a tiger and fully armed – a formidable force for the destruction of evil. Simply to touch a copy of this book was said to be enough to guarantee the Goddess's protection.*

above right: *An official seal of the Indus Valley Civilisation (2500 B.C.). Even then the tiger was India's chosen national animal.*

centre left: *An illustration of a tale from Panchtantra, again showing how in Indian mythology the tiger was seen as the major predator of its environment.*

centre right: *A mural in stone at Humpi depicting valiant Indian in confrontation with a tiger (14th century A.D.).*

below left: *A love legend from Madu Malti – rather different from the previous depictions of the tiger! A tigress courts young buck which, not surprisingly, is horrified and runs away. The story ends with the death of the buck and the tigress crucifying herself by falling on the pointed horns of the buck, and in her repentance gaining eternal peace.*

below right: *In this commemorative medallion the British lion overpowers the Indian tiger. The medal was awarded to celebrate the fall of Tipu Sultan in the battle of Seringapatam.*

Tracking a Tiger

1. *Disturbed grass will often show quite clearly the path a tiger has taken.*
2. *Pugmarks will help to judge a tiger's sex and age – even their weight and mood.*
3. *The tiger which killed this sambar can be identified from the space, size and position of its tooth marks. In this case the sambar was killed by two young cubs.*
4. *The height of claw marks on trees is a useful indication of a tiger's size.*

in softer conditions a tiger's pugmarks
erfectly distinguishable and census figures
tter climates are just as accurate as those
elsewhere.

trails of the tiger's victim, by the
in which they clot, are a useful sign of
a tiger has killed its prey and thus of a
s movements.

er's faeces are always dropped away from
ack. Analysing them will provide a clue to
rticular animal's feeding habits.

: I found this tigress with her three
the Kanha Reserve and immediately
their position. (PHOTO BY CHARLES
UGAL)

My hide at Sariska: I always try to make
sy and comfortable as possible.

right: Of all means of transport a jeep
nost stable for photography as well as
ependable across country and enabling
et closest to wild animals.

above left: *Project Tiger in action* staff officer in the Kanha Tiger Re explains how tigers may be counte

above right: *My wife and my da Pratibha with four cubs I found either neglected by their mothers or orphaned by poachers.*

below left: *The poacher's haul. large suitcases, containing tiger an leopard skins, were found abandon a car park at Delhi airport. At a conservative estimate they would fetched £20,000 on the black ma*

below right: *Delhi Zoo. A whit had died and at its autopsy I was discussing with Janak Desai, one zoo's doctors, the exact cause of de In fact excessive in-breeding had high infant mortality rate in white*

Jim, watchman at my zoo residence.

Part Two

CHAPTER 7

Myths and man-eaters

So far the emphasis has been on natural history; in this chapter we switch to history, and in the rest of the book I shall describe various aspects of man's relationship with tigers. As my obsession with these animals grew I resolved to trace the myths that man built up around them down the ages. Actually, my curiosity about their role in ancient history was aroused as the result of a curious coincidence. I met a man called Bhagwan S. Gidwani who was connected with civil aviation and tourism. (He has since become Director General of Civil Aviation in India.) When he heard my name he told me he was studying the eighteenth-century Sultan Tipu, whose awareness of water pollution caused him to change the site of his ammunition factory from the banks of the Kaveri – and the name of the Sultan's chief wildlife officer was Sankhala!

So I too began to look into Tipu's history. In the museum at his summer palace at Srirangapatam I discovered medallions recording the fall of the sultan, who was known as "The Tiger of India", and the victory of the British lion on 4 May 1779. On one side is engraved a lion overpowering a tiger and on the reverse is the scene of the battle. These medals were distributed to all soldiers who fought on the side of the British.

From then on I haunted museums and learnt a lot of disjointed facts about man's attitudes towards tigers in ancient times, some of which are worth recording. For example, in the National Museum in Delhi (where, however, there is no natural history section) I found a gold mine of information about tigers. Ancient seals showed that they were well known before 2500 BC to the Indus Valley civilizations of Mohenjodaro and Harappa. Men were depicted with tigers more frequently than with any other animal. Sometimes the tiger was shown as a creature to be avoided, or one to be kept captive; but he was also shown as an animal to be worshipped. Finally he was symbolized as the embodiment of power leading to the development of the cult of Durga, destroyer of evil. I was amazed at the accuracy of the design of the stripes and proportions of the body, even the characteristic loop of the tail.

Just as the lion was dignified in Europe and the Middle East with the title of the "King of Beasts", and today holds that title in Africa, there can be no doubt that the tiger has always occupied the throne in the Far East.

In the West, the Greeks saw their first live tiger in Athens during the third century BC after Alexander's return from India; it was a present from his governor in the Punjab, Selukas I. The Romans first saw one in the first century BC during the reign of Augustus. A cart drawn by tigers is depicted in a carving dating from about AD 220, during the time of the Emperor Heliogabalus. In Scythian art (fourth to fifth centuries BC) Siberian tigers with long hair are well-known motifs, for example on a golden plate.

The Koreans had known the tiger from remote times; and in Chinese mythology it is often depicted as the destroyer of evil spirits, while Hsuan Tan, god of riches, is sometimes represented riding a tiger. The tiger was painted on walls as the guardian of magistrates' courts and private houses, being held as a symbol of strength and courage. Its claws and the ashes of its burnt hair are considered to be potent in costly charms even today. Tiger bones are the most powerful ingredients of Chinese medicines, and wine made from the bones is said to cure rheumatic ailments. The Chinese represented the tiger in their paintings, sculpture, wood carvings and toys; and it features prominently in innumerable myths and legends, not only in China but all over central and south-east Asia.

Japanese artists in their Nara paintings depicted tigers without ever having seen one, and the tiger occupies an important place in the calendar: 1974 was the "year of the tiger". It also features in the coat of arms of Malaysia and Singapore, and a division of the Indonesian army, the Siliwangi, uses a tiger's head as its badge.

In the Khudabux Library at Patna there is an interesting manuscript containing a collection of pictures of 132 Hindu gods and goddesses. The author of the Puranas (a book of Vedic myths) is shown sitting on a tiger skin; Jolishmatic, goddess of miraculous drugs, rides a tiger, as does Aurkah, commander of the thirty-third cycle year. Sukra, priest of demons, is similarly shown.

The tiger has always occupied an important place in Indian mythology; Durga, for example, rides a tiger, and in Shivaite mythology Shiva wears a tiger skin. The association of the tiger with religion persists even today, and tiger skins are in demand for sitting upon during meditation. Its whiskers are much sought after as love charms; and some think that by burning a tiger's whiskers one does not become a tiger in rebirth, thus shortening the cycle of reincarnation at least by one stage. (In certain faiths it is necessary to pass through *all* stages of animal life before becoming a man again.)

After about 1500 BC the tiger seems to have lost its supremacy in India for a time. The lion takes over, and is mentioned over and over again in such religious works as the *Rig Veda* and in Sanskrit literature in general. Lions guard the gates of all temples of the early medieval period. After independence the lion capital of the Ashoka pillar of Patna (300 BC) was adopted as the emblem of India and later as its national animal. Only in 1972 was the tiger declared India's national animal, at last replacing the lion that had ruled so meaninglessly for more than 2000 years.

Tiger hunting has always been the pastime of kings. Six gold coins of Samudra Gupta (AD 335–80) show the king hunting the tiger with bow and arrow with the inscription *Vyagra-parakrama* ("slayer of tigers") on the reverse. But above all tiger hunting was paramount at the time of the great Mughals, the first of whom, Babar, was known as "The Tiger"; he hunted tigers near Peshawar on the banks of the Indus. The Emperor Akbar hunted both lions and tigers, and in one of his hunts 50,000 men worked for one month to round up all the wild animals in an area of ten square miles. When Akbar started the hunt, "charging like a fierce tiger", with the first stroke of his sword he felled a tigress; she was depicted in a Mughal painting *c.* AD 1570 lying on a heap of chital carcasses. In another scene three tigers are being hunted with arrows and spears; there is much frenzied activity, as a tiger has caught one of the hunters. The Emperor had a large menagerie which included tigers, and at one time he is said to have kept 1000 hunting cheetahs.

The Mughal Emperor Jahangir was a great naturalist. In his autobiography *Jahangir Nama* we are told of captive tigers roaming in his palace grounds without chains and of his attempts to milk a tigress. When he failed he concluded that milk production is the result of the mother's affection for her cubs, and that only when the young suckle is the blood in the teats converted into milk. Jahangir records that animals seldom breed in captivity, although one of the tigers which he kept free did mate with a tigress who gave birth to three cubs "after three months". Another story describes a tiger pulling down a fakir and attempting to copulate with him, but apparently the holy man was not harmed. I have not been able to trace any painting of a tiger by Jehangir's famous court painter Mansur, whose pictures of birds are so outstanding. But in *Jahangir Nama* there is an illustration by Forruk Chela of a royal lion hunt. In Persian culture the lion, unlike the tiger, was widely honoured and is often illustrated in miniatures.

In the Madari Bari shikar *gah* (hunting reserve) about 40 miles south-east of Agra (I was in charge of this area in 1954) Jahangir once missed his mark while out hunting and the tiger attacked Prince Khurum (later Shahjahan). Courageously a Rajput raja, Anoop Singh Rao, saved the prince's life by forcing his hand into the tiger's mouth, and Khurum managed to swing his sword and cut the tiger in two. There is a two-page illustration of this episode in the Badshah Nama in the Khudabux Library.

The first important record I could trace showing the superiority of the tiger over the lion in the Mughal period is on the royal sword of the Emperor Aurangzeb's collection (late seventeenth century). The sword bears the emperor's name and carries a holy verse from the Koran with the names of Allah Mohammed and Allai in high relief; near the edge of the hilt appears the figure of a tiger.

Hunting was the favourite recreation of the Rajput kings of Rajputana and Kanauj. A monolith describes a tiger hunt of Maharaja Ramsinghji of Kotah in March 1771 in Darrah forest. Evidently every tiger hunt of that time was celebrated with feasting, dancing and music; even the royal horses were included in the lavish feast given by the Maharaja celebrating the killing of a tiger. James Todd in his book *Annals of Rajputana* (1832) curiously enough makes no mention of princely tiger hunts although he mentions the presence of tigers in the forests of Udaipur, Kotah, Bundi and Ranthambhor. But that such hunts did take place is amply demonstrated by contemporary paintings from the princely States, in which the lion is featured far less than the tiger.

I have not been able to locate records of tiger kills of the eighteenth century, but in the nineteenth century, when there was a positive war on tigers, there is no lack of evidence. One George Udney Yule of the Bengal Civil Service killed 400 tigers in 25 years in Bengal after which, although he continued to shoot, he did not think it worth while to continue recording them. In 1830 groups of British soldiers on foot shot 17 tigers during a short summer leave near Booranpur. Colonel Rice, during summer vacations 1850–4, killed and wounded 93 tigers in open forests near Nimach Cantonment. Colonel Nightingale shot nearly 300 tigers up to 1868. A young cavalry officer of the 7th Hussars shot 42 tigers in two summer vacations. Gordon Cumming shot 73 tigers in one district of Narbada in two years (1863–4), sometimes killing two in one day over a period of five days. Montague Gerard had accounted for 227 tigers in Central India and Hyderabad by 1903.

This slaughter, though undeniably done for "sport", was justified in the murderers' eyes since the tiger had been declared vermin. A bounty was paid and the "pariah" people of the hill tribes of Bengal took up tiger killing as a profession. In Bombay Presidency (Maharashtra) 1053 tigers were killed by villagers between 1821–8. These claimed their reward, but there must have been as many tigers killed in remote places where it was impossible to claim the bounty.

Even poison was resorted to, and in 1874 no less than 93 tigers died in this way under an operation conducted by the official tiger-slayer Captain Caulfield and approved by the British Government. Captain Caulfield's job was to locate and poison the tiger's own kills, but he also resorted to poisoning baits which not only killed tigers and tigresses but cubs as well. It was a war waged on the species as a whole.

In Mysore State the bounty paid for killing a tiger was Rs 60, which was twelve times higher than the monthly salary of a forest guard. The incentive to kill can be imagined, and any lethal method likely to gain results was promptly adopted.

The traditional Mughal type of hunting was replaced by the Western style during the time of the British Raj, and the wealthy nawabs, rajas and maharajas joined with the British in the slaughter. Each one of them wanted the status symbol of scoring a century, and then to repeat it as many times as possible.

The late Maharaja of Surguja killed 1707 tigers during his lifetime (up till 1958), and held the record for the "highest score". In the small States of Bundi and Kotah the slaughter between the late twenties and early sixties was appalling. Only in the Alwar forests was tiger hunting limited to the killing of four to six per year because the Maharaja appears to have known the principles of harvesting and replacement. He was declared insane (for other reasons also!) by the British Government and removed from power, whereupon the regency government started killing tigers with a vengeance.

Maharaja Ganga Singh shot 104 tigers, of which 17 were killed in ten days in March 1920, in the Terai forests of Nepal. The former Prime Minister of Nepal shot 295 tigers in seven years (1933–9). Others who scored a century include the late Maharana of Udaipur, the Maharajas of Kotah, Jaipur and Vijanagaram, and the Nawab of Tonk. Tiger hunting in Rewa deserves special mention: in three years (1924–6) 163 tigers were shot, and over the period 1923–69 the total was 364. This also includes the hunting of white tigers. Maharaja Scindia of Gwalior bagged more than 700 tigers with his own rifle, and his guests accounted for a further 200. In the east, the Raja of Cooch Behar shot more than a dozen tigers of record size (over ten feet); and in the adjoining region the Raja of Gauripur claimed one 11-foot tiger and more than a dozen over ten feet in length out of the 500 tigers he shot between 1884 and 1940. In the south, in 1935, Prince Azam Jah Bahadur shot 35 tigers in 33 days in Adilabad alone, and such a score was not unusual in this district and in Warangal in Hyderabad.

Tiger shikar was the favourite pastime of every viceroy and governor and was always on the itinerary when they visited the princely States. Governors had their own hunting blocks where they used to celebrate Christmas by bagging a tiger. In Uttar Pradesh it was the tradition that the governor should shoot a tiger during his first year of office. Fortunately neither the presidents nor prime ministers of India have ever killed any tigers.

Royalty, too, enjoyed the sport. King Edward VII when he was Prince of Wales shot a tiger in Purnea (now in Bihar) in 1857, after which the Indian tiger came to be known as the "Royal Bengal Tiger". His grandson the Prince of Wales (the late Duke of Windsor) visited Nepal in 1921 and 17 tigers were shot in the week of 14–21 December, a shoot which was apparently organized at short notice. Continuing his tour to Gwalior, the Prince shot seven tigers in four days in February 1922. A tiger shoot also featured in the tour of Queen Elizabeth and Prince Philip in January 1961, when two tigers were killed at Ranthambhor (now a tiger reserve) in Rajasthan. Tiger shikar, in fact, was on the itinerary of every visiting dignitary who was at all interested in hunting.

*

The "sport" of pursuing so-called man-eaters has an added thrill, and no one pursued them more relentlessly than the late Jim Corbett, who described his experiences so vividly in *The Man-Eaters of Kumaon*. Corbett was a celebrated hunter of tigers in the heyday of the British Raj, and this book was a textbook in high schools, catching that particular generation at the most impressionable age. He enjoyed the Viceroy's patronage and therefore what he said was the last word. If he called a tiger a man-eater who was there to dispute it? Every person missing for reasons unknown, including those killed by leopards or humans, could conveniently be accounted for as tiger-kills and were entered in the district records as such.

I read and re-read his book and visited some of the tigerlands he described, and I found it difficult to agree with many of his observations. For one thing, it is certainly not old age that turns a tiger into a man-eater; all tigers become old (barring accidents) but all do not turn into man-eaters. A bullet or a porcupine quill in the mouth or forepaw is regarded as another cause of a tiger becoming a man-eater. This is also doubtful, because the wound that prevents the tiger from stalking and killing game can be an equally strong impediment to killing a man. In fact a tiger has to cover even longer distances if it turns man-eater because when someone is killed in a village everyone for miles around becomes alarmed and vigilant. What is a man-eater supposed to eat between one man-killing opportunity and the next? Does he go hungry for months or does he struggle to obtain normal rations? And if he can kill game in the ordinary way between incidents of man-eating then what is one to make of the excuse of broken teeth or disabling wounds?

Corbett's blood-curdling tales were of course by no means the only ones. Colonel Keshari Singh, known as the "Tiger of Rajasthan", also tells many stories about man-eaters. One such was the case of a tiger carrying off a newly-wed village girl while she was sleeping beside her husband in a locked hut at Ganwari, 96 km from Jaipur. I cannot myself believe any tiger would enter a hut to stalk a prey. Such accounts naturally tended to remove the last trace of sympathy for the tiger from the heart of civilized man. But were all these stories true? I determined to investigate cases of man-eating.

During the last thirty years in the States of Kerala, Tamil Nadu, Rajasthan, Assam and Bihar, all excellent tiger habitats, there have been no reports of man-eating tigers. There has been only one report from Andhra Pradesh; this happened some sixteen years ago and no details of the incident are available. In Karnataka the last record of a man-eating tiger was in December 1959, when an old woman was dragged away by a tiger while she was collecting myrobalan fruits. In April 1970 while I was travelling in Taroba National Park in Maharashtra I was told about a recent case of man-eating and I went to the Chandrapur Hospital to talk to the victim. It seems that the woodcutter must have approached too close to a tigress with two cubs and she jumped on the man, catching him by the arm. He tried to hit her with his axe but missed and overbalanced. Perhaps the tigress was frightened when the man fell; in any case, she left him and went back to her cubs. The tigress was duly declared a "man-eater", but luckily she was not shot.

My study of the habitat of Bastar revealed that there is very little food for predators in the forests, and the tribal people are not stockmen so the tigers have no alternative food in the form of cattle. Normally tigers would abandon such a place, but sometimes they arrive from adjoining areas and, finding no food, they feel trapped. Forced by hunger, they at times take to man-killing. This creates havoc and villages become deserted. I met a schoolmaster who described his plight when all the inhabitants of a small village in Abujmar fled one night and he was the only person left. There have been instances in Bastar where a tiger has quietly picked up the last man of a single file of people walking through the forest, and there have been occasions when tigers boldly attacked a group of women bathing in a pool. Then there was the case of a tiger making off with postmen in the forests of Hyderabad; the facts came to light when a couple of mail bags with the letters all intact were found alongside human skulls.

Are these not man-eaters? Yes, of course they are. They are animals that have lost their fear of man, perhaps during some accidental confrontation which resulted in the predator's easy victory. Many incidents like these have taken place when a tiger saw women bending down to cut grass; in such a position they would resemble a herd of deer rather than the upright being recognized by the tiger as human. This was supported by my experiments at Delhi Zoo where I found that tigers start stalking as soon as they find a man in a bent position, but when he stands up they lose interest. Similar observations are reported by Eaton (1972) in the case of the cheetah.

I came across an interesting story in Bastar where a European had gone to hunt a man-eater. The shikar company produced some silver bangles said to have been found in the stomach of the tiger shot by their client, which of course gave him a sense of heroic achievement. I saw the bangles which had been deposited in the forest office; they were perfectly round, and alleged to have been swallowed with the limbs of the victim. The man who invented this story obviously knew nothing about the feeding habits of tigers, which do not gulp their meat as does a crocodile. The tiger chews his meat, and is so particular that the smallest foreign body is rejected. The idea of his swallowing the bangles with the bony hands or feet of the woman of Bastar is a piece of pure fiction.

On another occasion when a woman was reported as having been killed by a man-eater police investigations proved that her husband had killed her in order to marry another woman. Quite a few cases of murder have taken place with the blame put on the tiger. In the end a police party set out to liquidate the man-eaters of Bastar, killing many innocent tigers and not even sparing the cubs – declared to be "potential man-eaters".

N. N. Sen, who was my immediate boss in the Forest Service and virtually brought me up in the profession, had shot 17 tigers during the heyday of shikar in United Provinces (now Uttar Pradesh) while Corbett was hunting in the same area. He also claimed to have killed a man-eater in 1944 in the Haldwani forests, but the only evidence he could put forward that this particular tiger was a man-eater was shaky. Some tiger had killed a man who was cutting grass and only one leg was recovered, but just who ate the body was not known. Since that event six tigers of different sex, age and size were shot within an area of 12 sq km in ten days. Which, if any, of them was the man-eater is anybody's guess. Each of the hunters claimed that it was his, thus getting a free permit not only for the tiger he shot but for free hunting for another year.

In recent years cases of man-eaters have also been reported from Uttar Pradesh. The last record of a tigress killing a man in Corbett National Park was in February 1967. The man was a member of a team of fourteen who were marking trees, and he was seized and dragged into a bush. Shikaris who found the body removed it to open ground and set up a *machan*, and when the tigress returned to it in the evening she was shot. A post-mortem revealed that two of her canine teeth were broken off to one-third of the normal size, an upper molar was loose, and four incisors were missing. This would seem to have been an old tigress, although age should not necessarily have caused her to kill a man for food, and this was her first victim.

Until recently almost every tiger living in the Sundarbans of Bengal was known as a man-eater! No one had the patience, or even cared to investigate the circumstances to verify whether a person's death was by accident or deliberate murder, but everyone added to the horrifying tales of man-eaters. One told of how a man dreamed of a tiger and at the same moment a tiger jumped into the channel and picked up the man from beneath the wooden cover of his boat. Just how anyone would know about the dream if the man was killed is not told, but the story caught the fancy of an artist who portrayed the horrifying scene. A. B. Choudhari reports that at the beginning of the present century 100 to 150 people used to be killed by tigers every year as against approximately 38 annually in more recent years in the Sundarbans, most of the victims being honey-collectors.

I went to the Sundarbans to study the habitat and behaviour of the man-eaters and I found that honey-collectors disturb the entire forest. In their search for bees they often almost bump into sleeping tigers in the dense cover – the men are either looking up into the trees or down at their feet to avoid stumbling – and the surprised animals attack the intruders out of fear and in self-defence. Also, the honey-collecting season coincides with the breeding season, and a tigress will naturally attack a man who comes too close to her cubs. My investigations showed that many tigers seen by woodcutters, fishermen, boatmen, and lately the Reserve officers (who have even photographed tigers at close quarters) showed no interest in men, and in some encounters with honey-collectors the tigers just snarled and walked away.

In the Sundarbans there is a narrow range of prey species, mainly chital and wild boars, and even these are diminished when there are high tides or typhoons, leaving the tigers starving. Forced by circumstances, the tigers take to a semi-aquatic life and feed on fish. They wait for the tide to recede and then raid the fishermen's nets. If the fisherman accidentally encounters the tiger in the early hours while the animal is feeding he is apt to be killed. Due to the particular circumstances – the tide, the crocodiles, and the wild boars who also feed on the dead – the bodies of the victims are not found and every disappearance is attributed to tigers. Fishermen store their catch under the planks in their *dingi*, and tigers in search of fish may well encounter a sleeping man mixed with their food. No tiger is going to ignore a living creature for the "ethical" reason that it is a human! I have also heard that in the past when a man owed a large debt to money-lenders and could not repay it he left his village and was declared "eaten by tigers". He reappeared after the death of the money-lender.

Recent work by H. Henrich in the Sundarbans of Bangladesh under an IUCN and WWF grant suggests that the salinity of the water has something to do with the man-eating habits of tigers, though how salt concentration should induce man-eating is hard to understand. This conclusion is not supported by Choudhari's investigations, for he has recorded more man-eaters in areas where the concentration of salt in water is *less*. From my own observations I agree with Choudhari.

Let us examine the man-eating situation more closely. The estimated tiger population of the Sundarbans is about 180 (the official record of 1976 is 181); if they kill 36 men in 365 days (as indicated by recent data), and allowing for the circumstances described above, can they be branded as man-eaters? All those killed do not form even 4% of the annual food requirement of the tiger population of the area; the total meat value of all the victims is not enough to sustain one tiger for more than two to three months. Man, therefore, could not be on the regular menu of the tigers of the Sundarbans.

In 1971 a tiger cub just separated from its mother entered a field near a village in Ranthambhor and was killed by a volley of police fire because of the fear that it might become a man-eater. How could an innocent cub be taken for a potential man-eater? The authorities decided that because of a wound in its fore-foot it was likely to become one. A very similar case occurred in December 1975 when a cub from Sariska Sanctuary approached a village in Sikar district. It was the first to be seen for 40 years and the present generation had never encoun-tered a tiger in their lives. In panic the whole village got up on the roofs of their houses and in the hullabaloo the cub took refuge in a shed for safety. Eventually a police party killed it with a volley of light machine-gun fire and took the corpse in procession through the streets. This action was sharply condemned by the then Chairman of Project Tiger, but before that project came into being any tiger could be shot as a man-eater and there would be no protest, no inquiry, no call for a shred of evidence.

Although during the last decade there have been no man-eating tigers in Rajasthan quite a few permits were issued for shooting tigers who killed people by accident. Sometimes man-eaters were "created" in a summary court inquiry in order to prevent payment of a hunting fee and to claim benefits for free shooting. Unfortunately a close analysis of the permits issued shows that the recipients were the friends of influential people. One officer was always preceded in his district posting by reports of man-eaters! He used to enjoy free tiger shikar in the course of his duties. I had to take up the issue with the State Government, which was pleased to order that no government officer was to issue a permit for shooting man-eaters or cattle-lifters in his own name, and that particular official never came across another man-eater for the rest of his life.

Corbett, who gave such horrifying accounts of man-eaters, also described the tiger as a "gentleman". He pleaded for its conservation yet he himself became the director of a hunting safari company in Kenya. I am unable to understand such contradictions. If the tigers of Corbett Park had the franchise I feel sure they would have voted for the Park to be associated with the man with the old plate camera, F. W. Champion, who inspired so many to give up the gun for the camera, including myself. It cannot be denied that Corbett's stories attracted many people to the jungle, but unfortunately it was not always for the love of nature but with the hope of bagging a "man-eater". The man-eating tiger is mostly the creation of the human mind as a result of man's intolerance of a co-predator.

Throughout history man has been unable to accept the tiger or any other predatory competitor. His aim has always been to eliminate rivals so that he himself might have the area exclusively to himself or graze his domestic stock without fear of attack. The wolf in Europe, the puma, bobcat, bears and coyote in America, the lion and leopard in Africa, and the tiger and leopard in India have all been persecuted relentlessly. In 1960 when I was travelling in the interior of the USA, freshly-killed bobcats were seen hanging on fences, and the shooting of coyotes from aircraft was a common practice. In India the war waged on tigers dates back over two hundred years. In North Bengal a tribe called the Parih used to produce tigers' tails to one district officer and the heads to another in order to claim a double reward. And I have mentioned already the poisoning of 93 tigers in the year 1874.

Yet there have always been some far-sighted individuals who have realized that man cannot survive indefinitely as a consumer of natural resources. There seems to be something about India's soil that inspires conservation and humbles man as only one thin thread in the web of the grand process of nature. Even some of those who devastated the wildlife of their own home country when they came to India jealously preserved its forests and animals. The pastoral Aryans who burnt the land of their origin to obtain better grazing preached about the preservation of life, and this philosophy is now impregnated in Indian culture. The first conservation edict was that of Ashoka the Great in the third century BC, and even those great hunters the Mughals followed the best traditions of hunting on foot. British foresters were conservators. In the past few centuries India has lost only two species of mammals, the cheetah from the Deccan plateau and the Sumatran rhino from the swamps of the Sundarbans. Even today, when the world is in an economic crisis and India with its huge population – denser than in any other country – is worst hit of all, priority is being given to environmental preservation.

CHAPTER 8

Circus or zoo?

Before the affluence of recent years began to attract large numbers of tourists to national parks and "safari parks", the only way for most people to see wildlife was in zoos. It must be allowed that these institutions played their part in conservation, but when I became involved in one myself I began to see that its main role was entertainment. Nevertheless, my five years as Director of Delhi Zoo (1965–70) were both fascinating and satisfying. Once you are part of a biological institute, whether national park or a zoological park, you become deeply involved and develop a wonderful family relationship with its inhabitants.

When I took up my appointment the foundations had been laid and a few enclosures built. The lay-out was designed by Carl Heiginbeg, the famous "zoo man" of Germany who revolutionized the concept of managing wild animals in captivity without bars. His design was partially modified to include an oriental backdrop of the medieval fort of Delhi, seat of the great Hindu kings and Mughal emperors. The zoo spreads over 100 acres where once the cavalry of the Pathans and the Mughals was housed. Odd relics of milestones, stables and monuments still stand, and it is not uncommon to dig up skeletons of men who might have lost their lives fighting or defending the fort.

When I arrived hoolock gibbons, riding elephants, begging bears, performing otters, smoking chimps and talking parrots were the main attractions. Rabbits, rats, guinea pigs, fawns, chained pups and cubs in the "Children's Corner" were loved both by the children and their parents. On Sundays the Corner was packed, and the queue for elephant rides was always long. Most visitors to the zoo saw little else.

For the first three months I watched. The more I saw of the performing animals the more horrified I became. The animals were presented in an un-natural way, both psychologically and ecologically; they were, in fact, an entertainment. A zoo is not a circus and a zoo director has no business to be a ringmaster; but if that is what the public wants the solution is not easy, and I did not find it at once.

One morning I received a call from Miss Padmaja Naidu. I had known her mother Sarojini Naidu, the nightingale of India (whose poems were in my school textbook) and the first woman President of the All India Congress the year I was born. Her daughter Padmaja had just relinquished her office as Governor of West Bengal after serving for more than two terms of five years each, and had come to find peace in Delhi after her hectic political life; she had been one of the most successful Governors of turbulent West Bengal, and now she wanted my help in planting trees in front of her house. I was amazed by her knowledge of plants, and subsequently whenever I met her I used to brush up my botany in advance. The next day was 1 July 1966, the first day of ceremonial tree planting in India. Mrs Indira Gandhi had planted the first cherry tree and afterwards we celebrated in Miss Naidu's small drawing-room. As well as Mrs Gandhi herself, among the guests were her aunt, Mrs Vijay Laksmi Pandit, who once adorned the UN as its President, other members of her family, and Dr Karan Singh and his wife. Mrs Gandhi had just taken over as Prime Minister then, but there was no formality and she was often addressed as "Indu".

After the guests had left I asked Miss Naidu if she would care to pay a visit to the zoo, and she accepted. Next day the roads were cleaned, animals were not given food so that they should be active, the men were asked to wear uniform, and the elephants were decorated. This was the routine for every VIP's visit. Immediately on arrival Miss Naidu asked for "Urvashi", a baby elephant presented by the late Jawaharlal Nehru; she had looked after it while it was at the Prime Minister's house. I presented Urvashi who, as usual, was dancing and playing a mouth organ. "Should Urvashi dance to earn her living in your zoo?" asked Miss Naidu. "Keeping her in captivity is enough punishment." I was tongue-tied with shame, but her remark kindled a ray of hope for developing my own philosophy of what a modern zoo should be.

Immediately I cancelled the performances, but when it came to stopping the elephant rides and abolishing the Children's Corner there were protests in the local papers. The subject came up for discussion in the zoo council meeting presided over by the Union Minister Mr Jaggivan Ram, a clear-headed statesman. I explained my philosophy of presenting animals in their natural habitat so that people could learn about the way they live. The Minister listened to my argument that animals should have priority over man, at least in the zoo, and that riding them shatters even the concept of equality. The decision was in my favour, and the elephant rides were stopped.

The next item on the agenda was the Children's Corner. It had been planned to enable children to fondle baby animals and identify with them. The idea was sound, but in practice it was a toy house where the excited children sometimes dropped animals like rabbits or cubs, or held them so firmly that they were maimed or even squeezed to death. Again the decision went in my favour, and of course I became very unpopular with the children and their parents. From then on Delhi Zoo became free from circus acrobats and monkey tricks. The long Sunday queues for joy rides disappeared and people began to spend more time enjoying other features of the zoo.

My next battle concerned the animals' surroundings, and here my problem was the zoo vet. He was an expert on cows and buffaloes, but when it came to lions and tigers it was a matter of trial and error. One of the white tigers, Raja, was taken seriously ill and was passing blood in his urine. We found that he was suffering from a disease caused by a tick which affects the blood. I had to admire the vet who worked day and night until all the affected blood was drained and the tiger was saved. But he then wrote a long report advising that to stop a recurrence of the disease the enclosures should be cleared of all vegetation and floored with cement, like cowsheds on a dairy farm. I quietly turned this down, explaining my concept of Delhi Zoo. We embarked on a massive programme of planting so that the enclosures should be made into woodlands. The tiger enclosure became an ideal one and attracted all the wildlife photographers and film makers who had failed to get a glimpse of tigers in the wild. The lion enclosures, and islands planted with natural vegetation for monkeys, otters, crocodiles, bears, zebras and chinkara became especially popular. Shallow water features, with duck-weed and a few pinioned birds, attracted migratory ducks. The water birds found the zoo ponds safe in spite of the thousands of visitors surrounding them. Not much food is available, but the birds arrive to rest during the day and make off at dawn and dusk to feed in the adjoining fields. The congregation is so dense that at times birds find it difficult to land.

With the planting programme, and allowing jungle growth to spread wherever it appeared, the zoo became an ideal nesting place for weaver birds, moorhens, tailor birds, shrikes, partridges and bush quails. But the most spectacular feature that developed was the Audubon maternity ward of egrets, cormorants, herons, and especially painted storks. Even Saras cranes nested.

Saras cranes

During October the zoo becomes a miniature Bharatpur, the famous paradise of bird lovers.

A proper environment, as close as possible to their natural habitat, inspired animals like the otter and brown bear to tunnel deep into the ground and bring up their young there after a long period of hibernation. They needed no care from us; in fact they appreciated our neglect. Others who enjoyed their bushy enclosures were the various kinds of deer, who found secluded corners to deposit their fawns. Manipur deer, rare by all estimates, flourished more at Delhi Zoo than even in their home of floating swamps at Keibul in Manipur. Although I am against cross-breeding in zoos with the production of "tigons" or "ligers" – we are already interfering with nature and in the zoo we should maintain the purity of the race – we did have an extraordinary record of inter-generic breeding. The most spectacular success was not planned but was more of a double accident. The first cross occurred on the President's estate where a chital and a sika deer got mixed up. The second cross happened when we lost all hope of getting a pure-bred swamp deer as a mate for a lonely stag, so the chital-sika doe was provided for company. Their offspring, a female fawn, grew up to resemble a swamp deer.

All the time the breeding records of tigers and leopards escalated to new heights until it became a problem to dispose of the surplus. At one time I had 40 tigers on my hands. We sold leopard cubs for less than £10 each, and found no buyers for lion cubs. Of course we were not prepared to sell to circuses or small menageries lest free-living animals should be subjected to hard training.

Many times my mornings began with news of the escape of a tiger or bear, or of a fatal accident resulting from a fight between the inmates of one of the enclosures. The sad reports of the death of rare animals were even more disturbing. But the sun used to shine more brightly if a rare animal, or an animal difficult to breed from, gave birth in captivity. When a Nilgiri langur produced a baby it was the first time in the history of zoos; and when the white tigress Rani delivered all-white cubs my happiness had no limits.

At such times I was proud of my success and was convinced of the importance of zoos in conservation. Yet at other times I felt I had more blood on my hands than the most hardened poacher. No one understands death better than a biologist, for death is a biological process; but separation by this process brings its own pangs. There were some animals who died of old age, others due to prolonged illness. Such shocks were mild, for the mind was prepared for them; but this was not always so. Wild animals have great powers of resistance and may look in perfect condition even when they are sick, then suddenly they are found dead. Such shocks were brutal. Moti, the snow leopard, seemed to be in good health and was playful one evening; the next morning he dropped dead. His whole chest cavity was full of blood, a parasitic worm having entered a blood vessel and made its way out through the aorta. An even worse shock was the death of Raj Kumari, the white tigress, which was equally sudden. The only satisfaction I had was sometimes to be present by their side during their last hour, a helpless witness like a priest without a Bible.

After death the animals were not simply thrown over the wall for scavengers but were ceremoniously taken to graveyards and lowered to rest with dignity. This helped to build up the concept of equality of the zoo inmates with man. The men working for them began to regard their charges as part of their family. When sick, the hoolock gibbon Renu would accept food from no one except her keeper Bhagwana. The tigress Asharfi while in labour pains liked me to caress her to give her confidence, and I was always by her side when she produced her three litters. My wife's annoyance is justified because when our own children were born I was nowhere near her for days.

The tigers that you see walking up and down in the zoo are the fortunate ones. Many of their brothers and sisters who have escaped the nets and traps of poachers have lost their lives suffering horrible injuries. Some were speared and skinned and their carcasses thrown to the vultures, others who were in good condition died of neglect at an airport or railway station on their way to a zoo. The worst sufferers are leopards, who fetch more money dead than alive for the sake of their skins. My experience has been that for every wild cat that comes to a zoo another nine are lost.

Perhaps the saddest case is that of the apes, who are allowed no peace after capture. Because apes are closest to man, people like to see them perform tricks, like tricycle rides or the famous chimpanzee tea party at London Zoo. As they are such intelligent animals the only way to capture them is to kill the mothers and collect the young. I purchased three hoolock babies to try to establish a gibbon island at the zoo, but even with extra care they died one after the other. Infant mortality is highest of all in apes, and I am sure that for every wild ape caught 100 others are killed.

Nukul Sarkar, an animal dealer and expert in rearing rare species, once brought me 19 Kalij pheasants, which had been marriage presents to his bride, a Naga girl. All were adult and freshly netted, but they could not stand the stress and strain of captivity and all died within a week. The fate of deer and antelopes is similar unless they are caught young and acclimatized gradually. We think of reptiles as a very hardy group which has survived long geological changes, but when it comes to captivity even pythons go on hunger strike for months and crocodiles may die rather than eat.

There are many problems, too, even for those animals who can stand the arrest and imprisonment. Often partners of the right age are not available and they suffer from loneliness and sex starvation. When transplanted into an entirely different environment their vitality drops and they become susceptible to disease. In some zoos there is even no vet available, no post-mortem is conducted, and the death certificate records "natural causes". Many we kill due to our ignorance, with a wrong dose or an incorrect diagnosis.

My morning walk round the zoo generally started in the hospital. Although I know little about animal diseases I rarely failed to spot a sick creature because of some sixth sense developed by my close association with them, and by experience of their ways in the wild. My next stop was usually the zoo kitchen; though I had never even peeped into our house kitchen, I was always anxious to know what was being cooked for my wards. A double check had to be kept on items like fruit, milk and eggs to prevent pilfering. Some food had to be mixed in a way unfit for human consumption to ensure that it reached the animals. A zoo kitchen is a most complicated unit, having to provide vegetable foods for the ungulates, and beef, mutton, eggs and chickens for the carnivores.

I once visited the National Zoological Park in Washington DC and was surprised at the way the big cats were fed. They got minced meat packed in gelatine bags, the reason being that splinters of bone might otherwise stick in their throats. I prefer to give full meat with bones so that the lions and tigers can have the satisfaction of tearing and chewing. Sometimes I used to provide a whole carcass with hair and skin intact. A few snakes, particularly pythons, need live rats, and of course there are also exclusive fish-eaters like otters.

On most days after my rounds of the hospital and kitchen I would walk from enclosure to enclosure seeing frolicking fawns and suckling cubs, some coming up to me, others running away to hide behind their mothers. It was a happy family, and I was part of it. But not all days were such smooth sailing. Escapes, especially of the big cats, created commotion and confusion. Once the tigress Ratna walked out of her cage through the front door which had been left open by the keeper and the news spread like wildfire. By the time I arrived she was sitting in a bush surrounded by a few hundred spectators and keepers armed with sticks and stones. Driving tigers in the required direction was nothing new to me after my field experience, and I soon arranged the beaters on three sides allowing one free for the tigress to escape. After leaving her to rest for over an hour I started the beat all of a sudden with the banging of tins and shouting, having given the beaters strict instructions not to throw stones or get too close. Ratna got up and walked casually away from the noise towards the place where I had posted myself, my son Pradeep and a friend, Juny. We were hidden behind trees, and when the tigress came near to the cage with its open door I suddenly appeared, spreading my arms and shouting. Ratna was hardly 20 feet away, and she got such a fright that she ran straight into the cage for safety.

In some ways the escape of chimps was even more hectic because of their intelligence. They would pick up the unattended keys to open the lock and climb to the topmost branch of the nearest tree. Neither the banana trick nor any amount of shouting would work, and I was always afraid that these acrobats would swing on the wires and get electrocuted. But the chimps were terrified of the trumpeting of Gopal, our bull elephant, and it was his mahout who would bring them back. Trembling, they would enter their cage like disciplined school-boys. Unfortunately, not all these recapturing attempts were successful, and some chimps died or had to be killed.

Some escapes I encouraged: these were wild birds, caged for a few weeks to make them used to humans and then released by opening their doors. Finding an ideal habitat in the unclipped hedges and wild bushes, they established themselves as residents and so increased the zoo's natural fauna. It was a pleasure to see the ibis settle down in the moats, and Saras cranes and peafowl flying from enclosure to enclosure and nesting – all our "deliberate escapes". Best of all was to watch the francolins bringing up their chicks and calling from their roost in front of my zoo residence.

We had planted some fruit trees and when they started bearing the zoo started to auction the fruit while still on the trees; it was then up to the con-tractor to keep the parakeets, bulbuls, mynahs and crows away. When I challenged this system I was shown the relevant paragraph which was to appear in the next audit sheet. I explained that the fruit trees had been grown for the benefit of the free-living birds in the zoo, the objection was dropped, and the birds continued to enjoy the peaches, mangoes and guavas.

The objectives of Delhi Zoo were clear to me. The animals were to be exhibited in habitats as close as possible to their natural ones to avoid subjecting them to unnecessary physical or psychological stresses. The zoo is also com-mitted to the conservation of wildlife through the education of the people, encouraging them to appreciate nature's gift to mankind, to share the planet with the other animals and to learn the natural laws which govern all life. With a natural habitat the animals are able to avoid the visitors when they want to, which of course runs against the visitors' interests. A person may come to the zoo only once in his lifetime and he does not want to see a sleeping lion hidden under a bush. He wants to see a tiger walking, or even better roaring or charging, and every visitor desires the same. When this does not happen they throw stones to provoke the animal. I did my best to remove all stones from the surroundings, but some visitors were found bringing stones from their homes – as part of their lunch. Our losses were substantial owing to this chronic disease of throwing stones. Once a group of boys aimed at the lanky legs of flamingos to make them take off and we lost five birds. Mute swans were hit, and even to-day it is not unusual to find heaps of stones near basking crocodiles and in the tiger enclosure. Luckily the deer enclosures are large enough and there is sufficient vegetation to allow the animals to escape.

Another problem developed as a result of this habit. A few miscreants would throw stones in our duck pond, causing the ducks to fly over guns waiting outside the zoo compound. Their low flight provided the "sportsmen" with an easy target, but since they were outside the premises and had a valid duck shooting licence I could not stop them. The solution was to get the area within a five-mile radius proclaimed a sanctuary where all shooting was prohibited.

During my years as Zoo Director I did not try to be a "stamp collector" aiming to keep everything under the sun. I fought against this temptation, concentrating on displaying a few animals in the best possible way according to their natural surroundings. They are not arranged as if in a textbook, with all bears together, or all cats in one series, as is done in many zoos including famous ones like San Diego or even the Bronx Zoo of New York. Our system is arranged on an ecological basis and according to zoo-geographical zones: Eurasian, African, the Americas and Australasian.

The zoo has been developed as a wilderness, with minimum signboards and direction indicators. By having to search for the enclosures the public get a thrill of discovery and a feeling of nature in the wild. I really enjoyed it when people lost their way, feeling I had succeeded in making a natural wilderness in the heart of the metropolis.

A walk round the whole zoo covers more than 10 km and it is tiring, but I always opposed any move to provide any form of mechanical transport. In modern life there is little opportunity for people to use their legs, and in my view a walk round the zoo is good for their health. My heart sank when a train was introduced in 1976. The zoo is now part of the life of the city of Delhi. The lawns, flowers and hidden hedges attract young couples and courtship continues outside as well as inside the enclosures. Grandparents bring their grandchildren, family groups and school parties throng there in thousands. We have not even provided shelter from the rain because the weather is predictable and the showers few. And in a climate like ours a sudden drenching is a thrill which is actually enjoyed by the visitors. The only concession I made was to provide a courier service for the old and infirm, and for mothers with infants in arms.

The zoo is always in the news because editors like to train their reporters there, especially on days when nothing much seems to be happening elsewhere. They can rely on picking up some story from the zoo, which can take the credit of bringing up almost the whole school of creative journalists in the city. Two of them are now special correspondents of a leading daily, two others are in senior positions in the press, and a talented animal story writer, Prem Kumar, is a senior resident reporter. All made their start at the zoo. There are also the celebrated photo-journalist brothers S. Pal and Raghu Rai who have made the zoo their second home, and Raghu even met his life partner, Usha, also a journalist from the zoo school, on the zoo lawns.

I followed a definite policy of public relations, believing that people had a right to know about the zoo, good or bad. In earlier days the reporters had to use their "secret service" to get news of losses or accidents, the reports were not always correct, and the zoo was becoming unpopular with the press and the public. One day Captain Arjun, chief photographer of Delhi's leading morning paper, told me that he had been asked to photograph a white tiger which had been bitten by a stray rabid dog. The patient, Govind, was in hospital under-going treatment with antibiotics and I hesitated for a moment. At first I said "yes", but then I added: "Captain Arjun, I have already given the news to the press, but a photograph of the tiger would give undue importance to the event, and we would get a bad name through no fault of our own." I asked him if he could avoid taking a picture, and he telephoned his editor and obtained his consent. He told me that this was the first time in his 30 years of photo-journalism that he had returned without accomplishing his object.

The involvement of the press and its constant reporting of zoo stories, from the birth of babies to petty domestic quarrels, paved the way for developing a favourable climate of opinion towards wildlife. People became concerned about its loss, and began to understand its role in the balance of nature. Recently a district magistrate and a police party got their photograph published with a tiger they had killed; the press was indignant and the act was condemned by one and all.

The zoo was on the itinerary of almost every VIP who visited India. Lord Mountbatten of Burma, the last Viceroy and first Governor General of inde-pendent India, came with his daughter; their schedule allowed only half an hour, but the First Sea Lord cancelled his other engagements and stayed for three hours. The zoo always took more time than anticipated because every visitor

Hoolock, or flying ape

found it to be something different from the usual meaning of the word.

Delhi Zoo is a regular place to hold receptions connected with wildlife because of the atmosphere of the wilderness it provides. The reception of the IUCN General Assembly was held near the waterfowl resort, and the lawns were full of leading figures in nature conservation from all over the world. Sir Peter Scott asked if the ducks were wild. Dr Harold Coolidge, who was then President of IUCN, tapped the microphone three times – a signal which triggers flight from the pond – and the whole sky was filled with wild ducks hovering before landing again. Sir Peter must have been reminded of his home at Slimbridge. Sir Hugh Elliott also paid us the compliment of saying that Delhi Zoo is one of the three best zoos in the world.

Running a zoo is a strange business in this money-orientated world. Money cannot be spent to produce animals, and we relied on the ancient system of barter and exchange. There is no standard price for any animal, and a zoo director may exchange an elephant for an antelope if he so wishes. The auditors do not understand the logic, and people sometimes misunderstand the Director. For example, if he finds a sex-starved individual his conscience pricks him; his feeling of responsibility is much the same as that of a father who has to marry off his daughter, and the cost becomes irrelevant. On other occasions it is essential to get rid of young animals produced in a zoo when their living quarters become too cramped. It is not easy to appreciate these problems unless one is a zoo director.

Unfortunately a great deal of illicit dealing goes on in the zoo market. Many a time dealers, or even colleagues, would try to pass on a sterile or problem animal, or one with a chronic disease. But with the help of the International Zoo Directors' Union it has been possible to keep up the best traditions of the trade by international co-operation. This institution has reduced the cut-throat competition and has eliminated the trade in endangered species. Zoos are no longer interested in obtaining a mountain gorilla or an orangutan. The code of conduct does not allow any member to purchase a tiger unless its origin is known. I have always tried to comply by sending a complete history of the animals exchanged, and it is always a pleasure to receive a letter from a colleague telling me of the successful breeding of an animal I have sent. It is like the birth of a grandchild in the family.

In April 1970 I left the zoo to take up my new assignment to work exclusively on tigers for two years, but I retain sweet memories of my association. I still return from time to time as a visitor, and a few animals still respond to my calls. Of course I keep records of all the tigers, with cards giving up-to-date information of what is happening in their lives. Raja and Rani, once the stars of the zoo, are now on pension; the elephants Gopal and Raj Laxmi are dead; and Ravi the chimp has become too old to scale the walls. And the uncut bushes continue to harbour many escapers.

In the year that I left the zoo I took a short holiday to visit the "city of flamingos", a spectacle that made such an impression on me that I cannot resist describing it for the benefit of those who may not be so fortunate as to see it. In the Rann of Kutch, a hostile and treacherous land, a million pink legs perform a highly organized mass ballet with a bedlam symphony as background music. I was privileged to attend this unforgettable performance in October 1970, with the help of the Border Security Force of Bhuj. After a jeep ride of about 100 km over rough roads and a camel ride of more than six miles we reached the shore of the Greater Rann of Kutch, which is just south-east of the Pakistan border. Then began a long journey through the marshes, with no path and apparently no direction. Our young camel driver, Sale Mohammed, broke the monotony with his witticisms, but otherwise there was no life except the occasional dragonfly.

At first the water was four feet deep and the poor camels with their flat foot-pads – which enable them to run swiftly on sand – were finding it hard going. A camel walks with the two legs on one side lifted simultaneously, but on this slippery surface they had to walk like elephants, lifting only one foot at a time.

Gradually the water began to get shallower and I became more hopeful, but on the contrary the camels started losing ground, slipping, slithering and skidding through the mud. Sometimes they fell, endangering our food and photographic equipment in the dangerously corrosive brackish water. The water of the Rann is even more saline than that of the Arabian Sea and becomes more so every year.

The whole day the sun burnt our faces and the exposed parts of our limbs, and by 5 p.m. when the camel driver told me we were near the shore I was convinced it was another mirage. The land seemed to be moving under water as if there were an earthquake, an illusion created by gazing for long hours at the water. But at last the struggling camels set foot on the island of the "city of flamingos". What a setting! Everywhere there was space, the sky turbid on the horizon, changing to light blue and then deep oceanic blue overhead, finally fading into turbidity near the horizon on the other side.

I approached the "city". The birds rose and stood in silence, a few occasionally honking. Slowly they left their nests and started walking away from the colony, parading their pink stockings, white bodies and graceful necks. Eventually I must have crossed their line of tolerance and they took off, at first bird by bird and then flock after flock. In a couple of minutes the whole sky was covered with birds, streamlined with extended necks and fully stretched legs in all types of formation, flapping their wide wings, displaying patches of pink against a snow-white background, honking in despair. When I approached even closer the chicks began to run here and there, whistling for others to join them and leave the colony. There must have been several thousand who walked towards the shore to join their parents. All that remained was a deserted city of adobe houses with thousands and thousands of eggs yet to be hatched lying on the roof tops. A few minutes earlier the city was bubbling and gaggling with life; now there was not a single soul.

To study the city planning I walked down one of their main highways, but I had hardly gone a few steps when I felt the ground giving way. Mohammed shouted to me to lie flat and I obeyed in a reflex action. Evidently I had stepped on a patch of quicksand. Mohammed led me through the mounds, avoiding the open ground which can be so treacherous that a camel would sink without hope of recovery.

I counted about 20,400 nests but there were thousands more. They were of varying heights. The well-formed ones were truncated mounds 60 cm in height, the average circumference at the base being 4 metres, tapering to one metre at the top. In the top was a slight depression and generally there was only one egg in each. The mounds look like miniature volcanic craters. The nests were in groups of eight to twelve, almost touching each other, then there would be a corridor or "street". Sometimes these open spaces are used as runways for take-off. The planning of the streets and nests is such that the movements of thousands of long-legged birds do not crush the eggs lying in the open or trample the helpless fledglings. The chicks are real ugly ducklings whose woolly body and black legs give no clue to their future grace. How the parents identify their chicks or the chicks their parents is an unsolved mystery. Ornithologists are inclined to think that chicks are raised irrespective of ownership; they belong to the community as a whole and are a joint responsibility of the city commune. I did in fact see a parent bird acting as kindergarten teacher taking the whole school for an outing to the sea shore.

There were a few broken eggs, their contents spilt into the depression of the nest, and some dead half-developed chicks. In the absence of crows or vultures they just stayed there. The only means of disposal is the highly saline soil, desiccating winds laden with salt particles, and the scorching sun, dazzling beyond description.

Suddenly I heard a noise and looked round for a chick. There was none. Again a cheep came from a near-by mound and I realized it was a chick in an egg which had a slight crack. After a short interval another call confirmed the latent life. Probably the chick was calling to its mother for help. I could not resist the appeal and at once offered my services as midwife. I was confident of my skill as I had acted in that capacity on several occasions as Zoo Director. With infinite care I removed the shell piece by piece and there emerged the baby with neck, head and little beak folded between its wings, its legs curiously coiled – a masterpiece of packing done by God. The chick continued calling for its mother and I did not know the next step the flamingo takes in the way of nursing. Probably I was the first to be a flamingo midwife, and I felt it was best to leave well alone. Presently I looked back and to my happiness I saw the mother and chick reunited. I had a wonderful feeling of achievement.

CHAPTER 9

The white tigers of Rewa

"How is Rani?" someone would enquire, but they did not mean my wife. They were asking about the health of the white tigress of Delhi Zoo, who had just delivered three cubs.

Ever since white tigers were discovered people have been fascinated by them, and scientific opinion has differed as to whether they are a separate race, complete or partial albinos, or merely mutants. Lyddeker (1907) doubted if there were any albino tigers, but he was wrong. Old records of Cooch Behar mention that a normal-coloured tigress was shot along with two coloured and two white cubs, which were sickly-looking with extended necks and pink eyes. Obviously these were albinos, as was a white tigress described by Cuvier in his *Animal Kingdom* whose stripes were visible only at certain angles of reflection. True white tigers, which are rare mutants, have dark brown stripes visible at all angles against the white background; the nose and lips are mottled grey-pink and the eyes are ice-blue.

When people express interest in white tigers, as frequently happens, social conversation turns into a zoology class. I begin by explaining that parrots are green to merge with the foliage, butterflies are multicoloured to mix with the flowers; the chital's white spots on a rufous background blend with patchy light falling on dried leaves, and the tiger's markings merge into half-burnt reeds and tall grasses. Some colours change seasonally, as in the case of the snow hare, snow fox and snow partridge. When I talk of abnormalities people listen attentively because of the fear of finding them in their own offspring, but I find that when I get on to deficiencies of colouring matter in the skin, hair and eyes my audience becomes uncomfortable and some melt away.

Although most people regard albinos with pity and repugnance, in some Indian societies an albino girl is thought to be so exotic that she receives better marriage proposals than her normal sisters. And zoo directors will go to seemingly any lengths to obtain an albino: a white python was bought from India by an American zoo for a fabulous price, and the white gorilla of Barcelona Zoo is considered to be beyond price.

From time immemorial white elephants have been known in the East and are still believed to be an incarnation of the Lord Buddha. In spite of this, the kings of Burma, Thailand and Cambodia used to present white elephants to people who had incurred the king's displeasure as a mark of punishment. Their owners were obliged to maintain them without giving them any work to do and the drain on family resources often led to starvation and death; that is why a "white elephant" came to mean economic ruin. Innumerable stories are told about white animals and birds: for example, that on the day of judgement all crows will become white. In Assam it is believed that anyone who kills a white tiger will die within a short time.

One of the earliest records of a white tiger was of a specimen exhibited at Exeter Change in 1820. White tigers were reported from Burma and the Jynteah hills of Meghalaya by Pollock (1900). Other authentic records tell of the shooting of white tigers from 1892 to 1922 in Poona, Upper Assam, Orissa, Bilaspur and Cooch Behar. In the 1920s and '30s several were killed in various districts, and fifteen white tigers were shot in Bihar alone. Some of these trophies are exhibited in Calcutta Museum and at Mica Camp, Tisri, in Bihar. On 22 January 1939 a white tiger was killed by the Prime Minister of Nepal at Barda camp in Terai Nepal.

The famous white tigers of Rewa, now known only in captivity, are sold for the fabulous price of $16,000 a pair compared with $1000 for a pair of ordinary tigers. Rewa was the capital of the erstwhile princely State of that name in central India, now included in Madhya Pradesh. In December 1915 the late Maharaja Gulab Singh of Rewa captured a two-year-old white tiger cub near Sohagpur which he exhibited at his summer palace of Govindgarh. The tiger lived for five years and was then stuffed and presented to King George V (novelties from India were customarily presented to show loyalty). Eight more white tigers were shot in the forests of Rewa, and the very last to be known in the wild state was shot in the Hazaribagh forests of Bihar in 1958. Since then there have been rumours of other white tigers in Hazaribagh, in the Tora forests of Rewa, and in Kanha National Park; but the reports are unreliable and were probably spread to cater for news reporters.

The most famous white tiger of all and the last to be captured was the one obtained in 1951 by his ex-Highness of Rewa, Shri Martand Singh. In the feudal State of Rewa tiger shooting was the main entertainment that the Maharaja could provide for his guests, who included viceroys and governor generals. In the last week of May 1951 the Maharaja was camping at a place called Deva to hunt tigers. Deva is 70 miles from Rewa, a small village surrounded by the dry deciduous forests of the Vindhyan range. At that time of the year when the temperature soars to 108°F (46°C) the entire forest is leafless. Tigers retreat to evergreen glades and there the shikaris were busy tying their baits. One afternoon the Maharaja was told that a tigress with four cubs, one of which was white, had made a kill in the forest of Bagri.

The next day two machans were prepared for the Maharaja and his guests. The beat started with trumpet blasts, the beating of drums and cans, and blank shots mixed with human shouts. Within a few minutes a tigress walked slowly towards the first machan where the Maharaja and his guest Swarap Singh were sitting. Swarap Singh fired and the tigress dropped dead. Soon afterwards the four cubs followed, with the white cub leading. The first to spot it was Maharaja Ajit Singh of Jodhpur, who was on the second machan; but in spite of excited prompting by his assistant, who had never seen a tiger in his life, the Maharaja spared it. But tigers are not found in his arid country of Jodhpur and it was too much to expect him to resist his itching finger altogether. Three shots rang out in quick succession, the first two by Maharaja Ajit Singh, the third by the shikar officer. Two cubs fell dead, but mercifully the white cub was not one of them.

The beat was called off and the hunters proudly gathered round their trophies, which were taken to the base camp with mixed feelings of joy at the successful hunt and frustration at missing the white cub. At that time it was within the rules to shoot a mother with cubs and no one felt the slightest regret. The shikar officer took the measurements and entered them in the register – a routine job in case at any time the Maharaja should shoot a specimen large enough to be eligible for Rowland Ward's hunting records. For me these meticulously kept shikar records were more valuable that King Solomon's mines.

At dinner the talk was all about the white tiger. Some argued that the cub was too young to survive without its mother, that it was bound to starve to death or fall prey to a bigger cat or poachers – a lame excuse always put forward by the trigger-happy. But both the Maharajas were glad that the cub had been spared, particularly the Maharaja of Jodhpur, who had held his fire.

Next morning the shikaris went in search of the cub but could find no trace. At last the cub, forced by hunger, returned to the kill his mother had made and the next morning, 27 May, fresh pug marks were found there. They were traced to a crevice in a projecting rock where the cub was hiding, and the opening was quickly closed with a net. There was no time to get a proper cage from Rewa as the cub might have died of thirst in the meantime, so a carpenter from a near-by village was commissioned to make one. Since he had only made doors and window-frames all his life it took him some time to understand the principles of a drop gate, but by the end of the day a rough cage of round timber had been constructed. The cage was taken to the opening of the cave, the net removed, and a water pot was placed inside. A shikari was posted to drop the gate at the right moment and everybody else was told to go away.

Evening fell, and only the lonely last calls of the grey partridges and the "jing-jing, jing-jing" song of the crickets were heard in the jungle. At last the cub, whose thirst was further increased by the heat and desiccating winds of May, could not resist the water any longer. It walked quickly into the cage, the shikari heard the "flip flip" sound of lapping and dropped the gate with a bang. The white tiger was trapped.

Next morning the cub was transported to Govindgarh, a small village dominated by the Maharaja's multi-arched 150-room palace. One of the rooms with an open courtyard was allocated to the cub. It was more than 30 years since the palace had resounded to the growls of another white tiger. The cub ate and drank, but mostly it remained withdrawn in a corner.

On the morning of 30 May, a day after its arrival, an attendant was surprised to see the fresh pug marks of a tiger cub in front of the palace gate. This created some excitement, as a tiger had never been known to come so near the palace. But soon it was discovered that the white cub had escaped. The news had to be conveyed to the Maharaja at his shikar camp, and an experienced shikar officer, Lal Sahib, was given the task of "Operation Recapture".

The pug marks were traced to a small patch of forest and a shikari tried to throw a net over the cub but missed. The cub attacked the man with an angry growl and managed to maul him. It then went for another man standing by who was armed with a club, and, out of fear, he gave the animal a hard blow on the head and it fell down unconscious. The shikari tied its legs and put it inside a portable cage. Everyone prayed for its recovery and special offerings were promised to the local goddess. After a few hours the cub regained consciousness and was reintroduced to its repaired enclosure at the palace. There it lived for the rest of its life.

The cub must have been destined to live to make an outstanding contribution to the breeding of white tigers, for he had escaped death three times: first from the Maharaja of Jodhpur's bullet, next from starvation and dehydration after his mother's death, and lastly from the head injury caused by the club.

Mohan, as he was named, grew up in a princely atmosphere with personal care, good food and no work, and he turned into a handsome Prince Charming. The Maharaja was interested not only in exhibiting a live white tiger but he also wanted to breed them and establish them as a race. When Mohan became adult a normal coloured tigress of the same age was trapped in the forests of Rewa and introduced to him. He soon settled down to family life and on 7 September 1953 two cubs were born to his wife Begum. Both were of normal colour. In her second and third litters of April 1955 and July 1956 she produced four cubs each time and all were coloured. These breeding experiments were frustrating to the Maharaja, who sold Begum to the Ahmedabad Zoo where she lived as a retired old lady until 1969 – the oldest captive tigress in India at that time.

By the time Radha, a female cub from Begum's second litter, was four years old she was introduced to her father. On 20 October 1958 the success of the experiment, and a sound vindication of the principles of genetics, was triumphantly announced: Radha produced four cubs, Raja, Rani, Sukeshi and Mohini, and all were white. All four were brought up by their mother and there were no casualties. Raja, the only male of the litter, and Rani are in Delhi Zoo, now retired from exhibition. Sukeshi continued to live at Govindgarh as a mate for Mohan, and after his death she too came to Delhi where she died in 1974. Mohini is in Washington Zoo and is probably on the US pensioners' list.

In 1960 Radha gave birth to Malini, a normal coloured tigress, and two white males, Niladari and Himadri. Both were purchased by Alipore Zoological Gardens in Calcutta for Rs 94,000 ($10,000) – a sum which the zoo authorities recovered in six months by charging extra to see the white tigers. Malini, who was to go to Delhi Zoo, was exchanged with Alipore Zoo for two pairs of mute swans and a promise to share her future progeny. The mute swans did not mate, and no litter of Malini's has been shared with Delhi Zoo so far. She and Niladari produced a white female cub, Ravi, in 1965, and the pair again produced one coloured male in April 1967, but it did not survive. In their third litter in September of that year there were two normal coloured cubs, a female, Sashi, and a male which had to be destroyed. At last, in May 1969, Niladari and Malini were the parents of four white cubs: Arun, Barun, an unnamed male, and a female, Kiranmala. Three more litters have since been produced by the pair, but out of five cubs only two are white: the female, Rupa, is at Calcutta, and Subhas who was sent to Gauhati died there.

Himadri and the female Chandani were established as a new breeding pair who produced six litters of 20 cubs, all white. Six cubs of the first two litters died due to neglect by the mother. Three out of the four cubs from the third litter were stillborn, and the fourth died after a year. From the other three litters only four survive: Sefali, Tara, Hira and Himadri Junior. Sefali was sold to Gauhati Zoo.

In 1962 the original pair at Govindgarh, Mohan and Radha, produced four white cubs. Two were infant casualties but the other two, Champak, a male, and Chameli, a female, were sold by the Maharaja to the Bristol Zoo in England for Rs 94,000. This pair produced three litters, all white. In the first, three were stillborn and the fourth died within ten days. Their second and third litters of July 1968 and May 1970 consisted of five cubs each, and only two were males. One cub, whose sex could not be identified, was said to have been eaten by the tigress. Only four of the females, Sumuti, Nirmala, Chandra and Shubra, are progressing well. The father, Champak, died on 22 August 1970 after an illness lasting several weeks, and in the absence of a mature male Bristol Zoo retired from the breeding programme until a white male from Delhi Zoo, Roop, was acquired. A litter of Roop and Sumuti, consisting of three white cubs, two male and one female, was born in May 1975, but all died within six days. Sumuti's second litter of four cubs, two male and two female, all white, was born after a year, in the same month. One cub was stillborn but three survived – Akber II, Jehan and Chandra. Roop also courted Nirmala, and she produced two males. One cub died within ten days, the other, Shiva, survived. Both Sumuti and Nirmala have also had abortions.

Sukeshi mated with her father Mohan in Rewa and gave birth to two white cubs on 17 July 1963, but both died after three days. In their second litter of 22 November 1964 a male and a female white cub were born, and this happened also in the third litter of 26 March 1966. On 6 September 1967 Sukeshi delivered two female white cubs; and in her fifth litter of 17 November 1968 there was one male and one female, both white, but the female was stillborn. In the following year Mohan retired from the breeding programme, as told later in this chapter. Sukeshi remained at Govindgarh without a sex partner for six years, as her son Virat showed no interest in mating with her. She was then brought to Delhi Zoo where she died on 2 February 1975. Out of her ten off-spring only one, Homa, survives; Virat died while his sale was being negotiated in 1976.

Sukeshi's sister Mohini was bought by the Radio Corporation of America from the Maharaja in 1960 for Rs 49,000 and presented to the National Zoological Gardens in Washington, DC. She was the first white tigress to leave India, and was a VIP in Washington, where she was visited by the late President Eisenhower. She mated with a normal coloured tiger, Sampson, from the second litter of Mohan and Begum and they produced two litters. The first was on 6 January 1964, when one white and two coloured cubs were born, but only the normal coloured male, Ramana, survived (he lived until 1974). In the second litter of February 1966 both cubs were normal; one was stillborn and the other, Kesari, survived.

Ramana was mated with Mohini and in May 1969 a white cub, Rawati, was born as well as a normal coloured male which died after two days. In March 1970 five cubs were produced, two white and three coloured; one was stillborn and three were crushed by the mother after three days. The remaining cub, Moni, lived until July 1971. Ramana also mated with the normal coloured Kesari and there was a throwback of three white cubs as well as one coloured; all are still alive. Kesari was then mated with Poona from outside the gene pool and produced six cubs, but only one female, Marvin, survives.

During my time at Delhi Zoo we established a breeding centre for white tigers and I was fortunate enough to be able to follow closely the life stories of the pair Raja and Rani. Originally the Maharaja had demanded Rs 100,000 for them, but an agreement was reached whereby the zoo should pay nothing at all. The arrangement was that Raja and Rani, as well as Mohan and Sukeshi at Govind-garh, should be maintained by the Government of India and that their progeny should be shared equally between the Government and the Maharaja of Rewa.

In May 1964, soon after her arrival in Delhi, Rani gave birth to two white cubs, a male and a female. But out of curiosity and apparently over-zealous licking she mauled them, with the result that the female cub died after two days. The male, Tippu the tail-less tiger – who is otherwise a handsome beast – was hand-reared with great difficulty. In August 1965 Rani again produced two white cubs but she neglected them and both died.

Rani soon became pregnant again and one cold night – 19 December 1965 –

my door bell rang; it was Ramrikh, keeper of the white-tiger house, who informed me of her condition. I rushed to her specially-designed maternity ward to find her in labour and moaning restlessly. As soon as the first bundle appeared wrapped up in its plastic sac she began licking, ruptured the sac, and a miniature white tiger was uncovered. It remained motionless for ten minutes while Rani continued to clean it, and five minutes later it gave its first cry. It began to search for food, but the mother was busy with her second cub and then a third. She reared them in a normal way for about 40 days when she suddenly lost interest in them and they had to be hand-reared. The two males were called Dalip and Ravi, and the female was called Raj Kumari. She died at the age of seventeen months, and Ravi went to the Maharaja of Rewa who sold him to Miami Zoo; but unfortunately he died at Kanpur railway station on 17 April 1967, on his way to be shipped to the United States. The third cub, Dalip, made history in two world exhibitions, as I shall relate.

Out of Rani's fourth litter of August 1967 all four were white, but one was stillborn; only one, Roma, is still alive. In her fifth, of May 1968, there were three white cubs, all males, and two of them, Rakesh and Hari, are still living. Rani delivered her sixth litter of two white cubs on 11 April 1970 and one, Ashima, is alive. Out of her seventh litter of four white cubs (one stillborn) of 27 August 1971 only one, Nandni, survives, and is at Hyderabad. Jayanti (white), born in her last litter on 14 July 1973 from Dalip, died after 8 days.

In all Rani gave birth to 20 cubs, all white. This is the highest record of reproduction of white cubs in a zoo tigress, equalled only by Chandani of Alipore Zoo. Only seven of Rani's offspring are alive today: Tippu, Dalip, Rakesh, Hari, Roma, Ashima and Nandni, of which the first four are males.

On three occasions I was present at the time of birth. I kept a close tag on Rani's movements for the first month after the cubs were born in order to find out how much time she spent with them and which of the cubs was neglected, with the result that infant mortalities were reduced. I also tried to photograph every aspect of her life from courtship to family-raising.

Returning now to Radha, the mother of Raja and Rani: when she arrived at Delhi she was pregnant and gave birth in August 1964 to three cubs, of which one was white, but it died at the age of 21 months. All five of her cubs born in July 1967 died, partly on account of her neglect and partly due to an outbreak of gastro-enteritis. She produced her sixth litter of four cubs, two white and two coloured, in June 1969. One of each colour died in their first week, again due to the mother's neglect, but the remaining two were saved by partial hand-rearing. The surviving offspring of Radha are Raja, Rani, Mohini, Niladari, Malini, Roop and Swarna.

Radha beat her daughter's record for reproduction, although unlike Rani not all her cubs were white. In all Radha produced thirteen white cubs and nine coloured. Even in her sixteenth year, an advanced age for a tigress, she mated again but no cubs were produced. Radha died on 2 May 1974, having established herself as the First Lady, with the largest family of white tigers in the world.

A record of white tigers has been carefully maintained and so far there have been 58 litters involving the Rewa lineage, consisting of 114 white and 56 normal coloured. Mohan, patriarch of the world's white tigers, was retired from the breeding experiment in September 1969 after completing eighteen years; his last son was born on 17 November 1968. Mohan died on 18 December 1969. He had been well looked after, with the best veterinarian to attend him. The Maharaja was so concerned about Mohan's health that he used to receive medical bulletins whenever he was away from Rewa. When Mohan was in his last days I was summoned many a time and there was regular communication about his condition between Rewa and Delhi. Probably no other animal ever received more care, and he deserved it. A plan was being prepared to celebrate his twentieth birthday in May 1970, but sadly he did not live to see it. He was laid to rest with Hindu rites in a courtyard of the palace. whose staff observed official mourning.

Mohan, the white tiger

Mohan's well-documented history helped me to understand the old age of tigers. When I first saw him in 1966 he was in his prime. He maintained his health and vigour until 1968, when suddenly he became old and saggy, with his hip bones sticking out, and he was unfit for exhibition. Then he became blind, and finally his hindquarters were paralysed. In his last months he was fed on milk and eggs. His age of 19 years and 7 months when he died, though great, was not the greatest ever recorded: an Australian zoo tiger is said to have lived for 26 years.

Radha lived for 19 years. Sukeshi died at the age of 17. Raja, Rani and Mohani are 19 years old. Chameli is in her sixteenth year and past her breeding age. The breeding records of these white tigers helps us to understand details of the reproductive biology of tigers in general. Out of 48 litters, beginning with Radha's first, 148 cubs were born; 105 of these died without reproducing, and even more shocking is the fact that among the dead are 72 cubs and adolescents who died of non-accidental causes (excluding seven stillbirths). In Washington, Ramani and Rajkumar died of feline enteritis at the age of ten months. Lakshmi succumbed to intestinal colic when she was eighteen months old. Sampson died of kidney malfunction at the age of eleven years. Govind, the newly-established breeding sire of the third generation, was found dead in his cell on the morning of 13 August 1971. The only breeding male remaining in the USA, Ramana, died on 18 June 1974; and more recently Champak died of an unknown disease at the age of eight.

Other non-accidental causes of death are stillbirths, congested lungs, trauma of the abdomen, loss of appetite and swelling of the abdomen, lumbar paralysis, pneumonia, trypanosomiasis, pernicious anaemia, feline enteritis and feline distemper. Infant mortality from unknown causes within a week of birth has also occurred. The death of Moni in Washington is attributed to a neurological phenomenon at the age of 16 months, and congenital deformities like shortened tendons of the forelegs have been reported from the same zoo. Bristol Zoo has recorded an underdeveloped kidney in a cub which had to be destroyed. Arching of the backbone, twisted neck, shortened legs and weak eyes are other manifestations which have been observed. Prolonged illness leading at times to conditions beyond recovery and the necessity to destroy the animal has also been reported.

I have noticed that grandchildren from the same parents, although they frequently mate, either do not produce a litter or the offspring do not survive. Miscarriages have been recorded on eight occasions. All this is presumably the result of inbreeding owing to the fanatical race by zoos to produce white tigers. To reduce the death rates we have recently introduced fresh blood at Delhi, and of the four normal coloured offspring of Moti and Homa (a white tigress) two survive. Poona was introduced to Washington Zoo but he was from the same gene pool and all except one of his offspring died within four months. It is amazing that by the end of 1976 there were still 40 living members – including 30 whites – of Mohan and Begum's family, even though the cubs suffered heavy casualties at the infant stage.

What are these white tigers? As already explained, they are mutants, not albinos, and we must now look a little more closly at their genetics. The tiger is a diploid animal producing haploid gametes, as in other cats, and the inheritance of the "white" character can be clearly explained. It is determined by a single autosomal recessive gene, w; its allele determining normal coloured coat, eyes and nose is designated W. All white tigers are of the gene type ww, and coloured tigers may be either WW or Ww. In crossing tigers of ww and ww genes we will always get white offspring, as in the case of Sukeshi and Mohan, Rani and

Raja, and Chameli and Champak. In the mating of ww and Ww there is a chance of both white and normal, depending on the segregation of the genes at the zygote stage. The result may be all whites, as happened in the case of Mohan and Radha in their first two litters, or a combination of whites and coloureds as in subsequent litters.

Where one parent is Ww and the other WW, as in the case of Vindhya and Suraj, none of the cubs is white. Normal coloured tigers with the genetic combination $Ww \times Ww$, however, may produce some white cubs: out of the 13 cubs of Sashi and Ravi, three were white (they were born in 1974 and 1975 at Alipore Zoo, Calcutta). About the same time at the National Zoological Park at Washington, DC, the tiger Ramana (Ww) and the tigress Kesari (also Ww) produced four cubs of which three were white and one coloured.

White tigers are larger and heavier than ordinary tigers. At birth the average length is 53 cm (normal cub 50 cm), shoulder height 17 cm (normal 12 cm), weight 1·37 kg (normal 1·25 kg). At two years the white tigers Dalip and Krishna weighed 139 kg and 120 kg respectively, compared with the normal coloured tigers Ram and Jim whose weight was 106 kg and 119 kg respectively at the same age. Raja at the age of ten years had a shoulder height of 100 cm, Suraj at twelve years was 90 cm. Even Ratna and Vindhya, normal coloured tigresses from the white race, are higher than the average for ordinary tigresses: 87 cm and 88 cm compared with, for example, Asharfi's height of 82 cm.

Mohan was by no means the first white mutant; as already mentioned, white tigers were shot on a number of occasions in Rewa before 1951 and others were shot in Cooch Behar, Upper Assam and Nepal. But it is certainly owing to Mohan that the white tigers of Rewa have achieved world-wide fame. Quite often a christening in the family takes place with ceremony: Bahadur and Roopa were named by Mrs Indira Gandhi, Swarna and Roop by U Nu of Burma, Kesari and Rawati by the Indian ambassador to the USA. At the end of 1976 there were 30 white tigers living in zoos: seven in Delhi, seven in Calcutta, one at Gauhati, one at Lucknow, one at Hyderabad, eight in Bristol and five in Washington, DC.

No description can convey the true image of a white tiger. One has to see them not behind bars or on a cement floor but in the deciduous forests, or at least in a semi-natural setting, to appreciate their enchanting beauty.

Although Delhi Zoo was the first to develop a breeding centre outside Rewa and the largest number of white cubs have been produced there, one fact intrigues me: their colour is always whiter at Rewa than anywhere else in the world. In spite of their living in a dusty courtyard they were always snow-white, perhaps because Rewa was their original home. Delhi Zoo has made it possible to return white tigers to Rewa out of its breeding stock, and it is hoped that one day some of them will be re-introduced into the wild. Our ambition is to make a White Tiger Reserve.

Perhaps the most exciting experience I had with white tigers involved a journey to Japan. A telephone enquiry from the Ministry of Foreign Trade regarding our white tigers at the zoo got a swift answer from me: "Eleven, but they are not for sale, especially to a foreign market." The conversation ended, but within an hour I found the enquirer in my office. "We are from External Trade," he said, "at present organizing the India Pavilion at Osaka for Expo Seventy. It has been decided that along with other exhibits from India we should display a white tiger." And before I could express an opinion he continued: "It will help our image, and attract Japanese to India to see our wildlife."

Normally no zoo director would agree to any of his animals being exhibited, especially the priceless rare ones, as they are exposed to hazards that might endanger their lives. Also, moving them round like circus animals is no part of our philosophy. I was determined to say "no", but I wanted to give a diplomatic "no". I tried to explain that tigers are moody, and if they were subjected to conditions they were not used to they might go on hunger strike. I pointed out that in Japan they feed their carnivores on seal meat (and in American and European zoos they use horse meat); in Delhi we feed them on fresh buffalo meat, and there was no possibility of getting buffaloes in Japan. A change in food and environment always causes difficulties, and these would be even worse at Expo 70, where the tiger would be constantly exposed to crowds and noise. I therefore made it clear to the officer that I would be most reluctant to risk the life of a white tiger, and in any case it would be impossible to hand him over to someone to whom he was not used. I prepared a rough estimate of the expenditure involved, which came to over $10,000. The officer merely said he would explain these points to the Committee, and I felt sure that nothing would come of this hazardous exercise.

For weeks I heard nothing and thought the proposal had been dropped. Then one day I got a frantic telephone call and was asked to meet my boss immediately. I usually received such calls only when something was seriously wrong, or when there was a parliamentary question on the management of the zoo, or adverse comments by the press and other complaints to which a zoo director is always exposed. In fact his question was "Can we exhibit a white tiger at Expo Seventy?" I meant to say "no" but the answer came out "yes". Yes, because of the tremendous opportunity to publicize the wildlife of India at a world fair, and so create international public support for the preservation cause.

So now I was to escort a white tiger to Japan. Being a member of the International Union of Zoo Directors I was no stranger to my counterparts Dr Tazumi Wada in Osaka and Mr Nobuyuki Ishiuchi in Tokyo. I made preliminary arrangements for stop-overs for food, preferably beef, and a stand-by vet at all transit stops.

My choice for the honour fell on Dalip, a handsome, well-developed white tiger who was not only friendly and docile but also one who was not likely to fuss over any change of place or food. While health certificates and other travel documents were being prepared, I "watched" the progress of the construction of the enclosure at Osaka via telex messages. The drawing prepared by the architect showed a pit ten feet deep and the visitors were to see the tiger from above. I reacted sharply as I did not want the tiger to be looked down upon in such an undignified manner. Finally a compromise plan was agreed on.

Early in the morning of 9 March 1970 Dalip was brought to the airport in his travelling cage. There were no customs formalities and no passport check. He was driven through the VIP gate to the aircraft and was given a traditional send-off, as is given to a member of the family proceeding on a long journey, with garlands, *tilak* and *arti** performed by my daughter Pratibha. Dalip was quiet except when the cameramen wanted him to pose for a photograph. In the plane, of course, there was some excitement among the passengers and crew, none of whom had travelled before with a white tiger, nor would be likely to do so again.

Later, while everyone was relaxing, I was passing through some anxious moments. Would a mail bag fall and block Dalip's cage and suffocate him? Would the noise of the take-off give him a heart attack? There was no way of knowing what was happening in his cabin. After six hours the plane landed at Bangkok at 2 p.m. local time. I was the first passenger to alight and waited anxiously for the opening of Dalip's cabin. The station officer of Air India was already there. When at last the door was opened I found Dalip relaxing with his head resting on his paws. Obviously he had enjoyed his first flight. During this first transit stop he was offered only water, which he refused.

Another live shipment was taken on board: two baskets of parakeets, each holding about 50 young birds. Dalip looked round in surprise at the commotion in his cabin, but perhaps he was glad to have company. The door was closed and the plane took off. Dalip's co-passengers were off-loaded at Hong Kong, bound for some bird dealer. The island is well-known for its animal and bird markets, and one could get anything from a bird of paradise to an orangutan, mostly procured illegally. Attempts are being made to control this unbridled trade in wildlife through the efforts of preservation societies and the Government.

The plane took off for Tokyo at 6.45 p.m. By now it was dark and Dalip enjoyed a quiet sleep except for occasional jolts in disturbances over the Pacific. When we landed at Tokyo at midnight it was raining, but this did not deter a large gathering of cameramen, press reporters and TV crews. They all rushed towards the plane before it had even come to a halt and by the time I could get out Dalip's cage was already floodlit. When I opened the cover a stream of

---

* *Tilak* is a red mark made on the nose as a symbol of honour; *arti* is a plate of burning camphor which is circled round the face three times to guard against evil.

camera flashes were on him, and he obligingly growled and posed. In spite of their drenching everyone wanted a better view. Dalip was the second Indian to receive such an ovation from the Japanese, the first being Mrs Indira Gandhi who had visited the country a few months earlier. At last I managed to close the cover of Dalip's cage and took him for quarantine and customs clearance.

Miss Nichi and other members of the UENO Zoo were at the airport to help, and Dalip was taken to the zoo in a heated bus. Housed in their invalids' cage, he was served with dinner and allowed to rest. His companions for the night were an old sick turtle and a dove. Next day Dalip was in good spirits and the whole of Japan saw him on TV and on the front page of their news-papers.

Having completed the first phase of the journey I felt relaxed, but my next worry was the enclosure for Dalip at Expo 70. When I examined the cage I found a severe technical hitch. Probably the designer had imagined that the tiger would alight from a car and be led into his chamber by his keeper; in any case he had failed to provide sliding doors or even an entrance gate. Thoroughly disgusted, I proceeded to get things put right as quickly as possible. Makeshift arrangements were made and the tiger put into his temporary home.

Now that the fanfare of the reception was over my work began. The night was becoming colder and colder, and the infra-red lamps were raising the tem-perature of the cell only up to 5°C. Dalip started shivering. I rushed to the pavilion and collected kerosene heaters from wherever I could, but there was a danger that the straw provided for Dalip's warmth might catch fire. I therefore decided to stay with him in an adjoining chamber which was meant to house his dinner. I kept watch for the whole night and acted as a thermostat.

Next morning the festivities of the opening ceremony started at 9 a.m., but I was too tired to watch. I brought Dalip out into the courtyard, where he strolled from side to side. Swarms of people came to see the "*sorai tora*" (white tiger), and by the end of the day Dalip had received half a million visitors. This continued every minute from morning till evening during the whole six months that Dalip was at the Expo. I am sure by then every Japanese house had a photograph of the white tiger and he acted as an excellent ambassador for the wildlife of India.

When an opportunity came for someone from Delhi Zoo to go to Budapest for the World Exhibition of Hunting there were protests from the other inmates of the tiger houses of the zoo, who pleaded with their keepers for "oppor-tunities for all". We decided to send Gautam, another white tiger, but destiny did not co-operate and he died a week before the scheduled departure. Once again Dalip represented the wildlife of India with the message "what not to hunt".

Dalip is the only tiger to return to India after foreign visits; he is really a gorgeous beast who performed his ambassadorial duties most efficiently.

CHAPTER 10

Tiger in the house

Killing tigresses and collecting the cubs, preferably those less than six months old, was a flourishing trade in India up till 1965. The cubs fetched $1000 apiece in the foreign market, being required by circus companies and zoos in order to introduce "new blood into their stock", as well as for personal pets. There are nearly 500 zoos in the world, all wanting tigers that have been caught in the wild, so the drain can be imagined. And all of them came from India.

I pleaded with the members of the Indian Board for Wildlife to introduce a system of providing a certificate of origin for the export of tiger cubs during the Fifth Session of the Board in June 1965. Every consignee would be required to produce evidence of the manner in which the cubs were obtained. My proposal was accepted, and soon the trade collapsed and the cubs and their mothers were saved. I feel sure that Jim Corbett, whose photograph was watching the deliberations of the Board at the Corbett Park, must have been comforted in his grave, for this was the first positive step towards tiger conservation.

Once when I was on my way to Kanha National Park I heard about some cubs in the care of the Divisional Forest Officer, Jabalpur. They had been collected by a brigadier, who had found three of them mewing over the body of their mother whom he had shot. (In those days there was no restriction on shooting during the breeding season.) One had already died and the others were not in a good condition, so I collected them to see what I could do.

It was the month of June, and the high temperature and hot winds, as well as the travelling in a small car, presented problems in keeping the fortnight-old cubs alive. I improvised air conditioning by providing a big slab of ice. At first the cubs made noisy protests, but soon the motion of the car lulled them to sleep. After a long journey of 1000 km they arrived safely at their new home. I put them into the zoo hospital where the tigress Asharfi was undergoing treatment, and the little cubs soon regarded her as their mother. But they were destined to be sent as a present from the President of India to Field Marshal Tito, and they are now living happily in the Belgrade Zoo.

Later on, another cub less than three weeks old was brought to the hospital. It had been given by some villagers to a local politician, who was camping in a forest in Madhya Pradesh and he named it "Jim" in memory of Jim Corbett. The story was that the villagers had found Jim in a bush, but it is not at all easy to pick up cubs of this age since the mother is always watchful, so I have my doubts about this story. More likely the mother was poisoned by the villagers or shot by hunters.

When Jim got to our zoo hospital he was suffering from acute gastro-enteritis, which is nearly always fatal in infants and my veterinary officer had little hope of saving the cub. But Jim survived, and he grew up in every comfort and luxury like a pampered child.

When Jim grew big he became rather rough with children and one day he caught a domestic cat and gulped it alive, without even tearing or chewing it. This incident scared the owner, and Jim was presented to the zoo on the condition that I personally was to look after him. I readily agreed as I knew that such a pampered pet would die for want of affection if left in a cage. Only a few days earlier we had lost a handsome leopard cub named Meena who had been reared by Meenaxi, a friend of mine, as her own child; she pined away simply because she could not get used to life in a cage with only straw as her bedding and nobody to play with her.

Frankly I am against keeping such pets in the house as it takes up too much of one's time and creates jealousy among one's children. Also, bringing up animals in an unnatural environment is cruel to the animal, and this holds good for all wild creatures from parrots to panthers. Ever since the story of Elsa of *Born Free* became famous more and more people have tried to copy it with all kinds of wild animals, including tigers. As a personal story it is dramatic, but depriving them of what nature has made them amounts to cruelty. Also, it has little scientific value and the ultimate fate of such animals is generally a sad one.

As a zoo director I tried not to give special treatment to any of my wards, but Jim became an exception. He started living with us. There was no special place for him, he had complete freedom of movement and the choice of sharing a bed with any of us was entirely his. For the first nine months he lived mostly in my bedroom or with my son in his bedroom-study. I could not spare much time for him except to say hullo and sometimes play with him – and Jim was very playful. He would attack only if someone got down on all fours or tried to run away. He used to jump at me and knock me down, trying to get hold of me by the neck, but he never used his claws, and when he held my arm or leg in his jaws his teeth never punctured my skin.

Jim enjoyed his morning walk, but it had to be outside the zoo where nothing would excite him. Walking in an area where most of the diplomats lived with a one-and-a-half-year-old tiger on a chain was quite an experience. People would open their windows to watch us, and early morning walkers would change their course or do an about-turn to avoid meeting us. I cut my sleep by two hours and started taking Jim out at 5.30 a.m., but even so I got a letter of protest claiming that the area was falling in its rental value due to the hazard of wild animals. That was the end of Jim's freedom outside the zoo compound, and instead I took him on my morning rounds in a jeep. This he enjoyed enormously and would always try to hold the steering wheel. When we passed the deer and antelope enclosures he would get excited, but the elephant house left him unmoved.

By now Jim was so big that we could no longer allow him to share our room, so he was given the garage with a special full-size bed. My *chowkidar* or night guard was in the habit of sleeping on duty, and he was warned that we would not be responsible if he became Jim's first victim. This kept him alert, and our security supervisor used to send us his chowkidars for training in how to remain awake when on watch.

Jim was the best sentinel I have ever had. He used to take up his position in the middle of our drive and put to flight most of the stray visitors. My guests would ring me first. I replaced my predecessor's warning "Beware of the dog" with one reading "Beware of the tiger", probably the first time such a sign had gone up outside a residential bungalow.

Any piece of rubber, the jeep seats or the cushions were Jim's weaknesses and he would never leave it until he had torn it to pieces. All our sofa seats still bear the signs of his treatment. One night he got hold of a rubber mattress which he tore to pieces, growling and chewing all night long until he was sick. After that I tried to prevent him coming in contact with rubber. He was as scared of hose pipes as he had been when once he saw a cobra. After that he started to develop a complex about possible snakes, and even moving branches on the trees would frighten him.

By February 1969 when Jim was two years old he was so strong that my son was forbidden to handle him. I still had confidence that I could do so myself until one day it was completely shaken. He dragged me by his chain for about 100 metres and I could well appreciate the sensation of those given the punishment of "dragging by horses" inflicted by the Mughals. Thereafter Jim was kept on two stout chains with three men to control him.

After eating his dinner Jim was a different animal. While feeding he was very possessive and would not allow anybody to come anywhere near, but when he had finished I could approach with confidence and he would allow me to pat him. Our friendship continued.

One day my friend Shanti Kothari, then a member of parliament, who always invited Jim to his house parties, came to see him, together with some officers of the Ford Foundation. They were introduced and Jim shook hands with the chief guest, but he then knocked him down and got hold of his throat like a tiger intent on making a kill. His friends had some anxious moments, but the chief guest got the thrill of being eaten by a tiger without so much as a scratch.

The time for the IUCN conference was approaching and as I was its organizing Secretary from September to December 1969 I was busy with the arrangements. I could no longer devote any time to Jim, and that was the end of his freedom. He became a member of the zoo like any other tiger. I had plans to settle him with Rosy, a wild tigress two years his senior. She had lost her mother to some shikari in the Dehra Dun forests when she was a month old, and grew up with human children in our zoo ranger's house. Jim and Rosy, in fact, had a similar early life and should have had much in common. They were kept looking at each other for over three months but when released together they fought and injured one another, so that was the end of that piece of match-making. I also failed to settle Rosy with the white tiger Krishna who did not get his mother's care in early life either. These animals, I realized, raised in association with humans and deprived of maternal contact, develop different reactions with members of their own species and take much longer to settle down to family life.

Vimla was a handsome tigress of the same age as Jim who was born in Delhi Zoo. She and Jim gave me a unique opportunity to record their growth almost from birth. Periodically I measured their length from nose to tip of the tail along the curves, their shoulder height, and weight. These measurements were compared with those of other tiger cubs growing up in the zoo. When they were babies I would compare their size also with a cat and a guinea pig to provide a visual comparison. At birth a tiger cub is about the size of a guinea pig; it weighs about 1·5 kg and measures about 15·4 cm at shoulder height and

RATE OF GROWTH OF TIGER

53·7 cm in length including the tail. By the time it is three months old its weight is 10 kg, shoulder height 37 cm, length 100 cm, or about the size of a medium-sized dog. The weight and measurements of male and female cubs show no differences up to the age of six months, after which the male begins to gain. Growth is rapid up to eighteen months, then it slows down and almost stops by the time the tiger is four years old.

I had seen a diagram illustrating the growth of horses projected against a graph board so I decided to do the same for tigers. Jim usually co-operated well, but occasionally he refused to stand close to the board. I took a set of photographs of him from the same angle and same distance at regular intervals, and I tried to do the same with Vimla, but she refused to co-operate. I was concluding my paper on the growth of tigers and taking the final measurements of Jim to present at the first Cat Conference at Lion Country Safari, Los Angeles, when I inadvertently put my hand on the bars of the adjoining cage. Suddenly I felt as though an axe had fallen on my fingers and a spurt of blood gushed out. Vimla had got the tips of my first two fingers. I had to go to the conference with my hand in a sling, which of course lent a certain aura to my role as a tiger man.

A question I am often asked is: how do you distinguish between a tiger and a tigress in the wild? In spite of the difference in size this is not so easy, mainly because one rarely gets a good sight of any tiger. It is very seldom that one sees a pair together for comparison. From my close association with Jim and other tigers at the zoo I developed an instinct so that I could usually identify them at first sight, but I admit that it is not easy when an animal is on the prowl at night, or running after being flushed from the jungle. Many a time a hunter has shot a tigress carrying cubs through ignorance of her sex and in the excitement of the moment, his finger resting on a cocked trigger.

According to Rowland Ward's hunting records the largest tiger and tigress shot in India were from the Duar forests of Bengal; they measured 11 ft 5½ in (349 cm) and 10 ft 4 in (315 cm) respectively and weighed 491 and 360 lb. My notes from the hunting records of Rajasthan show that the largest tiger shot there was 11 ft 2 in (342 cm) long and the largest tigress 330 cm. I doubt these figures!

Rowland Ward's maximum for the shoulder height of a tiger is 4 ft 2 in (127 cm) and for a tigress only 3 ft 1 in (94 cm), a difference of 13 inches (33 cm). I measured two pairs of the same age and brought up in the same environment in Delhi Zoo and their shoulder heights were as follows: tiger Raja 100 cm, tigress Rani 93 cm (both were white tigers – and were brother and sister); tiger Suraj 90 cm, tigress Asharfi 82 cm. The difference is 7 cm and 8 cm respectively.

Apart from differences in body size it may be possible to distinguish between tigers and tigresses in the wild by the size and contours of the head. In the '30s

HEADS OF A TIGRESS AND TIGER
(*top left*) *a tiger, aged ten, with larger head and conspicuous mane compared with*
(*top right*) *tigress of same age.* (*bottom*) *Tiger and tigress of four years old: the*
tigress too will have a small, mane-like ruff round her neck.

G. R. Burton compared the skulls of more than 70 animals and discovered that
the circumference of a tiger's skull averaged 83·8 cm while that of a tigress
averaged 64·8 cm, a difference of 19 cm – more than 25%. I have traced outlines
from photographs of tigers and tigresses of the same age, often of the same
litter, which show that the head of a tiger falls slightly outside the alignment
of the neck. The development of hair on the neck of a male is more pronounced and appears almost like a mane. The large head, heavy build and
prodigious body muscles even at adolescence are conspicuous features which
help one to identify a male tiger in the wild. Confusion can occur in the case of
an exceptionally big tigress, who may even have a ruff of hair on the neck like
a mane; but to a trained eye the identification of the male from the massive
formation of muscles and the large head should pose no problem.

Jim's vital statistics – length 282 cm (9 ft 3 in), shoulder height 93 cm (3 ft)
and weight 192 kg – are not much, compared with those mentioned in Rowland
Ward. However, he has a big head, broad shoulders, and tough muscles
rippling under a glossy skin. He shows an active interest in any passing animal,
more so than in the case of any of the other tigers. Given the opportunity he

could easily stalk and kill his prey and could be released in any tiger area, but the problem is his friendly nature towards man; if he saw a person in the wilds he might well come up for a pat. He and I do not meet as we used to do, though when I go to see him he will hold my hand in his mouth to remind me of the old days.

It would have been perfect if Jim and Vimla could have settled down together, but they did not. Another zoo-born tigress entered Jim's life: Ratna, who bore him seven cubs in three litters from 1972 to 1976, and who now happily shares the same enclosure with him.

What is the age of maturity of a tiger? Estimates vary from three years and nine months for a tiger (New York Zoo) to four years and six months (Basle Zoo). My own records show the minimum age of maturity to be 4 years and 3 months for a tiger and 3 years for a tigress.

The question of the sex ratio of tigers and tigresses is vital from the point of view of conservation and management as it indicates the reproductive potential. Valuable information may be obtained from the hunting records of ex-rulers who noted the sexes of the tigers they shot; but in studying them I found that the relative proportions differed considerably, from 131 males to 45 females (74:36) in Bundi to 25 males and 55 females (31:69) in Kishangarh. Perry (1964) mentions that out of 668 tigers shot in the former princely States in 1936-9 only 200 were females (70:30). But since these records are mostly of machan shooting, the comparative boldness of tigers in approaching baits must be taken into consideration.

The hunting records of Rewa are more valuable because there they used to flush out the forests from one end to the other, shooting or collecting all tigers irrespective of age or sex. During the periods 1923-7 and 1930-7, 154 tigers and male cubs were shot as against 166 tigresses and female cubs. If we assume a population of 100 tigers in the Rewa forests the ratio of male to female is 48:52, or a feminine preponderance of 4%.

My information on juvenile sex ratios in the field is scanty. Only nine records are available from the Jaipur forests, but these show a 24% majority of female cubs (13 males and 21 females). Out of three litters produced by a tigress in my study area in Kanha, and one litter each of tigresses in Ranthambhor and Sariska, there was a preponderance of male cubs which would work out at 54:46 in a population of 100.

Field observations of the sex ratio can never be reliable because of unrecorded casualties of cubs, and the data from zoos is therefore far more valuable. There the sexes of all cubs born, including those stillborn, are recorded accurately. From nine litters of Basle Zoo, eleven of New York Zoological Park, and fifteen of Lincoln Park (Schaller 1967), there were 56 males and 37 females (60:40). On the other hand, Zuckerman (1953) and Sadleir (1966) record 24 males and 37 females (39:61) from 25 litters.

In Jaipur Zoo, of which I was in charge for four years (from 1958 to 1962), out of a total of eight litters of four tigresses *all* 12 cubs were females in four cases, in three litters there were 8 more females and 4 males, and in only one litter were there two males to one female. Out of 24 litters at Delhi Zoo producing a total of 62 cubs, 26 were males and 36 females. All together, out of 32 well-recorded litters in zoos of which I have been in charge, the proportion is 30 males to 44 females, a preponderance of female cubs of about 20%.

My detailed study of the family history of the white tigers recording 37 litters shows a preponderance of females of 10%.

In assessing the value of figures of tigers and tigresses shot in the wild we must bear in mind that tigresses were sometimes spared. Tulsinath Singh of Udaipur informed me that it was taboo to shoot tigresses there, and my conversations with the ex-Princes of Bundi and Tonk also revealed that tigresses were generally spared. The figures from Udaipur, Bundi and Tonk must therefore be excluded from consideration. The total numbers of tigers and tigresses shot by the former rulers of Kotah, Alwar, Bikaner, Jaipur and Kishangarh – who generally did not spare tigresses – are 312 tigers and 374 tigresses, or 45:55. Once again this shows a 10% preponderance of females.

Although these data may not stand the strictest statistical analysis as there has been no uniformity in their compilation, they do seem to show that in a normal population there are at least 10% more tigresses than tigers. I feel that this has a biological advantage in maintaining the population of tigers in the wilds.

PUG MARKS OF TIGER (JIM ♂)   PUG MARKS OF TIGER (VIMLA ♀)

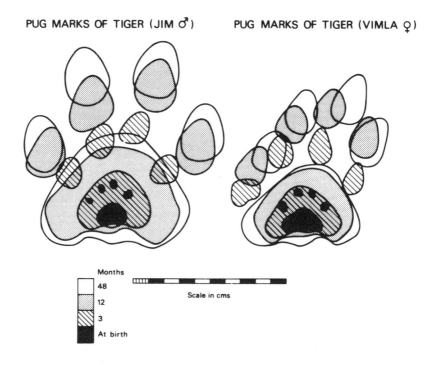

Months
48
12
3
At birth

Scale in cms

CHAPTER 11

Operation census

Speculation about the tiger population has always been rife among hunters in India, and my searches through the hunting diaries and other archives has at least provided some idea, however sketchy, of the populations at various times in the past. Some details have been given in chapter 3 concerning the different regions, but this very limited information lacks uniformity. I have therefore selected a few regions where the figures can be compared with those of the country-wide census conducted in 1972.

The results are shocking. Even in the Sundarbans, where the habitat has been disturbed least of all, the tiger population has dwindled from an "abundance with no chance of annihilation" to about 180. In the Narbada forests where 74 tigers were bagged in one year (1863–4) there are not even 70 tigers today (only 63 were reported in 1972). In the forests of Rewa, where as late as 1924 no less than 162 tigers were shot in one year, only 21 now remain. In one district of Coimbatore 93 tigers were poisoned in 1874; now there are only four surviving. The list is long and shocking.

The total number of tigers shot in 1938 as compiled by Prater and published in the *Journal of the Bombay Natural History Society* may be compared with the figures for 1967 compiled by me; the hunting records printed overleaf give a good indication of the situation of tigers throughout the Reserved forest areas of the country over an interval of 30 years.

To his figure of 540 Prater added another 20% for tigers wounded and not claimed, plus another 101 for those killed in Madras, U.P., Assam, and the District of Nagaland (51, 25, 18 and 7 respectively). By adding another 100 tigers shot outside the Reserved forests of Bihar, Orissa and small States in the Central Provinces like Panna and Chattarpur, as well as 42 shot in Rajasthan, the total for 1938 comes to 891. In the case of the 1967 record of 159 we can safely add another 100 tigers unreported, so the total comes to 259 – less than one-third of the 1938 figure.

The hunting situation in 1938 was by no means the same as in 1967. In 1938 hunting was a pastime, few forests were open, movement was slow, and the equipment was medieval. By 1967 hunting had become more of a commercial enterprise and most of the forests were accessible by jeep. The hunter was equipped with deadly accurate rifles with telescopic sights, powerful ammunition and spotlights. He was motivated by the intent to get his money's worth. Even so, the 1967 records show far less hunting success: 1730 permits were

STATES	1938 (Prater)	1967 (Sankhala)
Andhra Pradesh	18	3
Assam	18	19
Bihar	10	3
Madhya Pradesh	112	
Indore	14	
Gwalior	11	66
Surguja	18	
Rewa	39	
Maharashtra	34	16
Mysore	54	1
Orissa	19	—
Uttar Pradesh	116	57
Tamil Nadu (formerly Madras)	19	(tiger hunting banned)
Nilgiris	5	(tiger hunting banned)
West Bengal	51	3
Cooch Behar	2	
	540	168

issued in that year and only 159 tigers were shot throughout the country, a "success" of only about 10% compared with almost 100% in the nineteenth century.

Those concerned with tiger shikar always inflated the estimated figures of the population in order to enjoy unrestricted hunting. Jim Corbett estimated that there were 2000 tigers left in the early 1950s, a good guess considering that he had no basis for such an estimate and his knowledge was limited to part of the Himalayan foothills. E. P. Gee, the celebrated naturalist, roamed the jungles far and wide in pursuit of wildlife photography; according to him, about 50 years ago there were some 40,000 tigers, and by 1964 there were 4000. When I asked Gee about the basis for his estimates he replied: "Some estimate is better than none, and it should hold good until it is improved." Rather naturally, neither of these estimates were taken seriously and the tiger continued to be killed.

I too speculated when I began my search in 1969; but I proceeded forest division by forest division and collected information from every state of India. I admit the estimates were based on second-hand information, but I had the help of my Forest Department colleagues who were in a better position to know the true facts. According to my estimates there were nearly 2500 tigers in the forests of India. The estimate served its purpose most effectively, and within six months the Government had placed a complete ban on tiger hunting throughout the country. The cherished dream of conservationists suddenly came true. India's alarming situation also helped the tigers of Nepal, Bhutan and Bangladesh, as well as the few left in Java, Sumatra and Indochina, to find a place in the IUCN's *Red Data Book* as animals in need of protection.

Armed with the figures I had collected, in 1972 I went from area to area all over tigerland to check on their authenticity. At the same time a massive census operation was launched by the Indian Government. Under this programme nearly 5000 men went out to count tigers during two weeks in April 1972 in the eastern sector and in May in the rest of the country. The instructions were to collect every possible piece of information indicating the presence of tigers.

Because tigers operate as individuals, their presence is known by signs along regularly-used paths – footprints and droppings – as well as by their kills, roars and occasional encounters. By far the best method of distinguishing individual tigers is by their pug marks, but in the absence of comparative data it was impossible to assess a tiger's exact age. In my studies of the growth of Jim and Vimla I therefore prepared a special pug mark tracer board and recorded stencils of their footprints at various ages. I found that at birth the paws of males and females are of the same size, but at three months the area of the male's pad is double that of a female, a difference that is maintained throughout life.

Pugmarks of tiger (left) – conspicuously larger than that of tigress (right) of the same age.

In the field the pug marks were recorded through a glass plate on to tracing paper or else by pouring plaster of Paris into the footprint and obtaining a cast. With each sample we collected all possible information about location, direction of movement, date and approximate time of passing of the tiger whenever possible. The information was not always complete, and we also interviewed the local people to supplement the evidence we had managed to collect. The total population reported amounted to 1827.

I collected a few hundred prints, but many of them were just irregular circles from which nothing could be inferred. Sometimes the footprint recorded on one day was different the next day. The tiger walks a lot and in one night may cross the beat of three forest guards, each of whom recorded it and made three tigers out of one tiger.

After eliminating duplicates as best we could and correcting various errors, the figure we obtained for the grand total was 1863. On to this we may add the estimated populations of tigers as 200 in Nepal, 40 in Bhutan, and 350 in Bangladesh (an overestimate), a total of 590, plus a further 288, this being the known increase in the tiger population in the nine Reserves in India from 1972 to 1977. Thus the grand total of tigers throughout the continent comes to 2741, or say 2700 to be on the conservative side.

It is clear that the tiger population has dwindled to such an extent that it is not even as great as the numbers killed annually during the last century. Estimates of populations in the past are almost valueless, and the only record I have been able to find where tigers were actually counted was by the Maharaja of Bundi in his small State – with less than 300 square miles of tiger habitat – in 1941; the figure is 75, compared to 6 tigers today – a loss of 94%. The dry deciduous forests of Bundi are similar to those of Gwalior, where Ellison's 1925 estimate of 400–500 tigers may be compared with 26 today, a loss of 93%. This kind of habitat, which forms 45% of the forested areas of India, was rich in tigers; both Gwalior and Bundi were maharajas' shikar preserves and represented an optimum tiger population. The enormously high losses are despite the fact that the old-time forest guards continued to sustain a high level of interest in wildlife preservation. As Bundi was my first posting I was able to see the habitat in all its glory as long ago as 1953, and I have followed the fate of the tigers there regularly for nearly 25 years. We may take it, then, that the overall loss of tigers throughout India is no less than it is in Bundi or Gwalior, about 93% in 50 years. Gee's estimate of 40,000 tigers early in this century was therefore not far wrong: according to my study based on hunting records, the population of 50 years ago was about 30,000.

Comparison of the sizes of tigers from different parts of India shows that those of the northern region – the Duars of Bengal, Assam and the Himalayan Terai – are decidedly larger than the peninsular form. Rowland Ward's hunting records (1922) list more than 20 large tigers from the north, the biggest being from the Duars (length 10 ft 7 in); those from peninsular India hardly exceeded 10 ft and only two from the central provinces measured 10 ft 5 in and 10 ft 4 in. Purnea district, now in north Bihar, was once famed for its giant tigers, and two shot in the 1870s measures "11 ft 5 in and 12 ft 4 in"; even after allowing for the fact that they were measured round the curves they are still giants. (Standard measurements of a dead tiger are taken in a straight line between two pegs fixed at the tip of the nose and the tip of the tail, and the difference between the two methods is about 7–8 inches). Extensive urbanization in the Indo-Gangetic plains has completely separated the northern and the peninsular tigers and there is now no chance of interbreeding.

Ecologically the tigers of the Sundarbans are also separated from the rest of tigerland. I found that their footprints are smaller than those of other tigers, and I was amazed to see how shallow the prints are in the mud of the delta, indicating the light build of these tigers. It may not be too long before they develop into a distinct race, characterized by short fur, a light and lanky body, and a relatively small, elongated skull. The peninsular form may also become racially distinct from the type species of the north. Even within these areas there are some tigers marooned on landlocked islands who have no hope of survival beyond a few generations. Groups like the 86 tigers of the Vindhyan region of Rajasthan are in genetically non-viable numbers. Irrigation in the Chambal command area has recently split the 26 tigers of Madhya Pradesh from a group of 60 tigers in Rajasthan; and the gap of Palghat has now separated the population of the Western Ghats into two units, 127 in the north and 64 in the south.

All this is bad enough, but an even more urgent concern must be for tigers marooned as individuals or in very small numbers. There is only one tiger in the forests of Poona and one in Jalgaon, two in Abu, three in Dhar and Indore and another three in Bhadrachellum, and so on. These have no hope of survival, particularly where the proportions of the sexes are unbalanced, and they should be evacuated unless a few more tigers can be released in these areas.

Our main hopes lie in the 615 tigers of the central peninsula, 530 in the Sundarbans (combined), 476 in the eastern region, and 481 of the northern foothills and Terai belt. There the habitat is more or less continuous, and the tigers have freedom of movement to mix their gene pools. It is essential to keep the corridors intact, at least in these major ecosystems of tigerland.

The 1972 tiger census if not 100% reliable was at least based on the best available facts rather than guesswork, as in all previous estimates. But some doubts were expressed about the methods used and arguments centred on the "pug mark controversy". Dr Dillon Ripley, Secretary of the Smithsonian Institution of Washington, said in a press interview in India in March 1976: "I cannot believe that tigers can be counted by pug marks." To a certain extent his doubts are justified, because the pug marks of the same tiger differ when they are in soft ground or hard, and the forest staff have to memorize the individuality of pug marks in order to count tigers. However, Dr Ripley was probably not aware of the methods we used to overcome these problems.

The practice of tracking tigers by their footprints must be as old as Indian shikar itself. Experts could identify sex, age and physical conditions like size and weight from the impressions. Some of these gifted trackers received court honours: the Maharana of Udaipur gave a *jaghir* (a large tract of land with revenue rights) to a family of trackers for their services to the royal shikar. Of course it was not a science: it was an art perfected by long practice. Those who had this knowledge guarded it as a trade secret which passed from father to son, and if the family link was broken the expertise died out, as was the fate of many other Indian arts.

During the days of the British Raj many noted hunters and naturalists relied a good deal on the study of pug marks. F. C. Hicks, the son of an army officer who joined the forestry department as Assistant Conservator, describes the identification of tigers in his book *Forty Years Among the Wild Animals of India* (1910). He distinguishes the pug marks of a male as being much rounder than those of a female. He says that the pug marks of a tigress are ugly and mis-shapen, and her forepaw resembles the hind paw marks of a male tiger. I completely agree with his observations, the only change I would like to make being one of nomenclature. I would describe the front pug mark of a tiger as *regular* (a term used in taxonomy for describing a flower) and that of a tigress as *zygomorphic* or *irregular*. But Hicks made a wrong observation concerning the cross-wise movement of a tiger's limbs, which was challenged by F. W. Champion, also a forest officer and a noted naturalist. After much hard labour Champion tracked a tiger over a long distance and found that 25% of the fore pug marks were covered by those of the hind feet. In the other 75% the hind foot mark was 2–4 inches in front of the forefoot. Champion was supported by Dunbar Brander, who concluded that the overlap occurs when the tiger is cautious and attempting to stalk his prey; but in a normal walk the gap some-times exceeds six inches. Brander observed tartly of Hicks that his "opinions on the natural history of the game he hunted have never carried much weight amongst those capable of verifying them". Harish Chandra, writing in *The Cheetal* in 1969, explained the impression of the hind foot falling ahead of the forefoot as being due to the longer length of the hind legs.

Of all the various ways of counting tigers there can be no doubt that the evidence of pug marks is the most reliable. It is the approved method of counting Siberian tigers, and K. G. Abramov has described how the age and sex composition of a population is determined by studying footprints along trails. He classifies four age groups according to the width of the heel print, and the impressions are also indicative of the nutritional state of the animal. Those of

leisurely stroll

fast walk

*running, with
three legs in the air*

*the spring, launched
from hind feet*

fully airborne

landing to spring again

well-fed tigers, he says, are well defined, while those of ill-fed tigers are shallow and may show wrinkles.

In order to make full use of this system we need to understand thoroughly the stride and gait, which differ from individual to individual but which involve basic principles common to all tigers. Although earlier workers had made it amply clear that a tiger walks with both side limbs lifted together, like a camel but unlike a horse, the issue was still confused when the 1972 census was conducted. It was assumed that it was impossible to record forefeet impressions because those of the hind feet were superimposed on those of the forefeet. (No note appears to have been taken of Hicks's observation, with which I am in full agreement, that a tiger's hind pug marks are similar to the front pug marks of a tigress.) When I told my friend Bharat Singh, a conservator of forests in Rajasthan, that a tiger walks like a camel he obviously did not believe me, although too polite to say so. Next day his daughter told me about her father's efforts to understand the walk of a tiger by practising on all fours! The wildlife wardens who were conducting the census just laughed until I made one of them, Fateh Singh, walk on all fours along the pug marks of a tigress in the Kachida valley of Ranthambhor. The late Sir Billy Collins and Lady Collins were surprised at the locomotory movement of the tiger when I demonstrated it to Fatch Singh, and the doubt lingered in the latter's mind until I could produce an actual photograph of a tigress with the two limbs on one side lifted together. A similar photograph was taken by Panwar, Field Director of the Kanha Tiger Reserve.

Having proved my point, I pressed for the recording of the front pug mark because it is used in killing and eating, and these operations are likely to differ more from one individual to another. There are also greater chances of sustaining injuries and deformities in the front feet as compared to the hind feet which are used only for walking.

Let us consider the limbs as 1, 2, 3 and 4, the first two being the forelimbs. When in a stationary position they are marked on the ground as 1 and 4 on the left, 2 and 3 on the right, and the distance between front and hind pug marks gives an indication of the size of the animal. In a walking tiger the impressions left on the ground are 4/1, 4/1 (left side) and 3/2, 3/2 (right side), the hind marks 4 and 3 preceeding the front ones 1 and 2. The distance between 1 and 1, or any of the other similar numbers, is a stride, which gives a more accurate idea of the size of the animal. A small variation occurs between the spacing of 4 and 1, and 3 and 2, as pointed out by Champion. With a little effort these individualities can be identified in the field, and we are helped by the fact that tigers are spaced out anyway and that they normally stay in an area for some time, especially after making a kill.

Obviously it is not difficult to distinguish between the pug marks of young adults and adults, or of adults in their prime and very old tigers. Nor is it

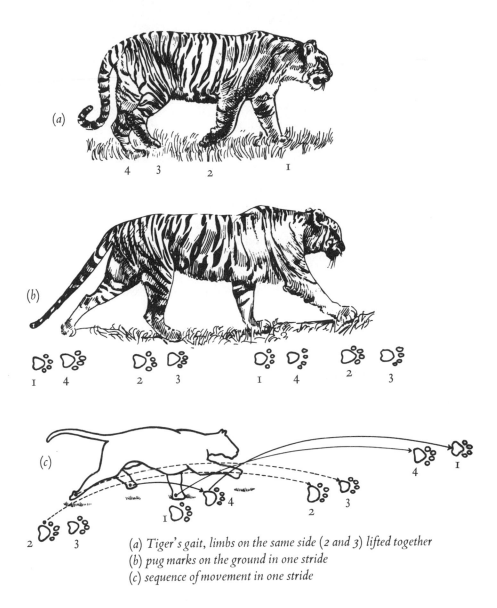

(a) *Tiger's gait, limbs on the same side (2 and 3) lifted together*
(b) *pug marks on the ground in one stride*
(c) *sequence of movement in one stride*

difficult to follow the footprints of a tigress with cubs up till the time when the cubs separate. Confusion between the pug marks of a leopard and a tiger does not occur because the impressions of even a six-months-old tiger cub are much larger than those of an adult leopard; and cubs of this age are still with their mother, so the presence of her footprints should clear any doubts.

Problems can and do occur on the rare occasions when tigers of the same age and sex happen to cross each other's path, or in the case of a tigress with several grown-up cubs. Then one must depend on other corroborative evidence like kills, fresh droppings, claw marks, roars and, if one is fortunate, sightings. In such situations it is justified to provide a bait and actually see the tigers concerned.

Measurements of pug marks taken with the help of sticks or fingers was a primitive method; even the taking of plaster casts is cumbersome, but it sometimes helps in discovering individualities from the contours. My "pug mark tracer" was based on the principle of the "Cavalry Board", an old-time instrument used for measuring distance while the horse is galloping. It has overcome all the difficulties and defects of the plaster cast and tracing through a glass plate, the only snag being that it is more expensive. If one rewinds the spool, a mark traced earlier can be brought back to be superimposed on a later one for comparison. The instrument also has the ability to record a series of impressions on the ground with accurate spacings, which helps to work out gait and stride. There is also enough space on the tracing to record soil conditions, direction of movement and probable time of passing of the tiger, and other relevant information.

After field tests the instrument was first introduced by me to the international cat symposium at Lion Country Safari in March 1971. I am told that the tracer is in use in South Africa for counting the Kalahari lions, although this is more difficult than in the case of tigers: members of the pride disturb the individual pug marks. I wished that Dr Ripley, who had expressed his doubts about the method of counting tigers by pug marks, could at least have seen the instrument first. His objection that pug marks in soft soil are different from those on compact ground is justified, but for all practical purposes we do not depend on impressions in soft soil, and in comparing pug marks the similarity of the ground is taken into consideration. And, in the absence of any other evidence, even footprints in soft soil do at least indicate the presence of a tiger.

There are far more serious problems, however. Sometimes we get no impressions at all, as in evergreen forests with thick ground cover, or hard black cotton soil, or rocky topography. It is also difficult to find pug marks in the season when leaves fall so thickly that the ground is covered with litter; or in the Sundarbans where tides wash out any impressions twice every 24 hours. The only chance of finding tracks is along river banks or paths. Even estimates given by local people are better than nothing, and after all, people living in the jungle do not tell lies. All census figures are, by and large, estimates, and a tiger census is no exception.

For any census operation to have meaning one needs to have a knowledge of the behaviour of the species being counted, and this applies also in the case of human beings. In the past all tiger censuses (J. W. Nicholson in Bihar 1934 and the usual Forest Department counts) were made by counting pug marks at waterholes during the summer. These cannot be taken seriously as they were based on the false premise that a tiger visits no more than one waterhole in a night, and that he does so only once in 24 hours. Neither of these conditions necessarily applies, especially in summer.

Limitations are unavoidable in an operation so vast as attempting to count tigers over the whole of the sub-continent, and they must be tolerated. A census helps in the conservation of the species by mobilizing public opinion; it certainly drew attention to the plight of the Indian tiger and for that alone, although scientifically unreliable, the operation was worth while. The 1972 figures for Kerala, Mysore, Arunachal, West Bengal and Assam were based on interviews and estimates only, and will have to be rechecked. It will not be necessary to conduct a completely new survey of the whole of tigerland, however; rather, a survey in carefully chosen areas will indicate how the population is changing. This is what we need: "total surveys" are generally erroneous, and should be avoided. But before describing the encouraging results of the 1972 survey we must look more closely at some of the reasons why the tiger population was reduced to the precarious position revealed by the census.

How the Indian tiger might develop. (top) the Assam tiger, broadhead, conspicuous mane, a large and heavy body, stout limbs and minimally tapering tail. (bottom) The Sundarban or Bengal tiger, with a light body, small to longish head, scanty fur and mane and a conspicuously tapering tail.

CHAPTER 12

The skin trade

Over 100 years ago, in 1872, Captain J. Forsyth, Settlement Officer and Deputy Commissioner of Nimar in what was then the Central Province, was one of the first to express concern at the losses in tiger population. He mentions particularly the Narbada valley of Madhya Pradesh, and in 1882 Captain J. H. Baldwin of the Bengal Staff Corps supported him. Baldwin spoke of the good old days when one could bag a dozen tigers in a fortnight, whereas in his time only two or three could be obtained in the same period. What a wonderful way of monitoring populations!

In 1900 Russell recorded his objection to the reward being offered for every tiger killed in Mysore (Karnataka) as he feared it might lead to the destruction of the tigers there. It did.

In 1930 A. I. R. Glasford drew attention to the commercialization of tiger trophies; at that time the price of a skin was 200 rupees and a rug with mounted head cost Rs 300. The trophies were collected by local dealers and resold to co-operative societies in big cities like Bombay and Calcutta where Europeans returning home bought them as souvenirs.

Also in the early '30s R. G. Burton in *The Book of the Tiger* (1933) gave a warning that in Hyderabad the habitat was deteriorating and the number of tigers rapidly decreasing; but he came to the entirely false conclusion that after the withdrawal of British rule in India anarchy would prevail, agriculture and population would be reduced, and that tigers would once more be able to flourish. Quite to the contrary, as we know, peace prevailed, agriculture and the human population increased, and tigers dwindled.

His brother, R. W. Burton, was more perceptive. In 1952 he wrote in a history of Indian shikar that the tiger population was wasting away; it was, he said, a national asset and he pleaded strongly for its preservation. Jim Corbett also felt that the tiger was on the way out. His contemporary M. D. Chaturvedi, a retired Inspector General of Forests, who had witnessed the death of over 250 tigers and had himself shot more than 50, mentioned that the tiger was still holding its own but needed protection; however, he still continued to bag his tiger each year till he retired in 1954. When I met Chaturvedi on my arrival in Delhi in 1965 I reminded him of the advice he had given to us in the Forest Service: that we should ask our fathers-in-law to give us a pair of guns instead of ear-rings for our wives. Chaturvedi was crestfallen.

Such pious statements about the need to protect tigers coming from those who were still associated with hunting were naturally not taken seriously. In 1956 I circulated a letter to the members of the Wildlife Board of Rajasthan appealing to them to stop the shooting of tigers at least in the hot months of May and June. Unfortunately most of the members of the Board were those who were used to easy shooting, and my suggestion was overruled. Again in 1958 when I was drafting shooting rules for Rajasthan I pleaded for a close season for tigers from November to June. My boss did in fact declare July–October a close season, more for the convenience of the hunters than the tigers, as one would hardly go into the malarious rain forests at that time of the year anyway. This was in line with the regulations in other states. Tigresses are usually either pregnant or with cubs in spring and summer, and this was the open season for shooting, with the result that many pregnant mothers or others with cubs at heel were killed. Sometimes the cubs were collected as a bonus by the hunters, but many died of starvation or were killed by other predators. The fortunate ones were those who came into our hands like Jim, Rosy and Ratna. An excited hunter would pull his trigger on any tiger whatever the size, and even some forest officers who ought to have known better did not spare cubs. I wish I could name them here.

In June 1954 when I was camping at Dholpur I received a message that a tiger had been killed in the Banvihar forests. I rushed to the scene in my old loading truck, and to my surprise found a police party in a jeep with the Superintendent of Police at the wheel. In the police truck that was following was a tigress with a cub about six months old, both dead. I asked the Superintendent to unload the bodies of my wards, and was told that the action had been taken in self-defence in the course of anti-dacoit operations. This explanation could hardly have applied to the cub, whether or not it was true in the case of the mother.

Even as late as 1968 there were no restrictions on shooting tigers in Orissa and West Bengal, and even after the introduction of a fee for a hunting licence it was nominal. Nowhere, except on paper, were any restrictions imposed on the shooting of tigresses; the pretext was that a hunter cannot identify the sex of a tiger in the jungle.

Every year more tigers were killed than were replaced by the process of reproduction. Tiger economics based on wrong assumptions led to depreciation of the capital as well as the interest. Yet in 1969–70, when a ban on tiger hunting was in the air, even more licences than usual were issued.

The tiger had withstood the onslaught for decades, and he might have been able to stand it for another decade were it not for the predation by man. He began to destroy the home of the tiger and at the same time to kill the animals on which it preyed. The loss was greatest immediately after India became independent, when a few greedy and short-sighted citizens organized large-scale hunting campaigns for personal gain. Nets were spread, pits were dug, traps were laid, forests were burnt. No animal was spared, mostly to cater for city restaurants where venison suddenly became popular. Soon block after block of forest became a storehouse for timber and a wildlife desert. One has not to go far to see our actions at that time; they are reflected in the nearest hill.

The cattle population of India is far more than the human population and is one-fifth of the total cattle population of the world. Although less than 11% graze in tiger habitats, the grazing pressure is still intense in the deciduous forests, which produce excellent fodder. Cattle are competing with the wild ungulates, and in recent years there is a new threat to the wildlife due to the large influx of migratory cattle. Coming from distant non-forested lands, they are exerting unprecedented pressure on tigerland, especially in Rajasthan, Madhya Pradesh, Bihar and Maharashtra. The pastures and forage available for the tiger's prey have started to disappear. The meandering herds of cattle are eating the last straw of food, drinking the last drop from the waterholes, and spreading uncontrollable diseases like foot-and-mouth and rinderpest.

The pastoralists build camps, *bhattan* or *gwaras*, inside the forests and constantly disturb the habitat. The man guarding his cattle sings to break the monotony, keeping the wild animals in a state of tension and forcing them to go to more vulnerable areas where they are killed. Pastoralists enjoyed legal protection before the ban on tiger killing; in "defence of their property" they killed tigers by any means, even poisoning and employing professional hunters to eradicate the predator.

The tiger's perfect prey – two chital

The uncontrolled extension of agriculture is another cause of the destruction of wildlife. Areas like "Tiger Haven" in Dudwa, once the best area of tigerland in the Terai region, have been released for agriculture. Pockets of open areas inside the forests have been allocated to forest labourers for growing food, wild animals are attracted by the crops and are killed as a matter of right with the crop protection guns.

Farming communities newly settled near forests acquired the rights to remove firewood, charcoal, thatching grass, bark, bamboos, timber and fruits for "domestic use", as well as having the right to kill wild animals for crop protection. When the population was limited and the demands were local the forests could sustain this pressure, but the introduction of fast mechanized modes of transport meant that supplies could be sent to distant places for commercial use, thus further accelerating the destruction of the forests.

When the population was limited, the *jhoom* method of shifting cultivation in the evergreen hills provided the wildlife with a better habitat by opening up the forests by felling and burning. Now the population in the hills is rising as everywhere else and pressure on the land is increasing, necessitating more intensive application of the *jhoom* method. When carried beyond a certain point, i.e. with a shorter rotation period, shifting agriculture upsets the ecological balance. Thus in the eastern hills we have the spectacle of a dwindling habitat and wildlife in the face of an explosion in human population. A visit to the area in March is revealing: the burnt hillsides are a potential danger for soil erosion.

Because he was not in his division when it was on fire, a forest officer was summarily dismissed in the Boat Club of Nainital and ordered to take the first ship back to England. This story is told to the trainees of the Indian Forest College year in and year out. The forest fire is the forester's nightmare. I saw my father fighting fires in the Aravali hills and I myself spent days and nights doing the same in the forests of Udaipur. It was a losing battle, as most of these fires were started deliberately. It should not be forgotten that *controlled* fires bring back nutrients to the soil much faster than the normal processes of decay; but quite obviously undesirable are the fires started by tribal people to drive wild animals into their nets; or ritualistic fires to propitiate the gods or to ask for favours such as the birth of a son or the cure of an ailment. Patches of forest are also burnt to beseech the gods for a good harvest, and the more effective the burning the better the gods are pleased. Some fires are started – at the wrong time, at the height of summer – by pastoralists to get a new flush of grass for their cattle. Others again are started to take revenge or to victimize the fire protection staff, and forests are even burnt when some VIP visits the block.

A forest burnt without thought or planning will remain a desert for at least a month, and wild animals will either leave the area or die of starvation. A repeatedly burnt forest deteriorates very fast. No watch-towers or walkie-talkie sets can prevent these deliberate fires; only better public relations can do it, and this is a slow process.

With a rapidly-growing demand for forest products men and their machines leave hardly any area of tigerland undisturbed. For at least six weeks a tigress needs a secluded lair in which to bring up her cubs; where now can she find one? Unfortunately the season of forestry operations, when almost every corner is visited by man, coincides with the tigresses' breeding period. Often the cubs are abandoned, to get killed or picked up by poachers. This has acted as a further limiting factor on the enhancement of the tiger population.

The foresters' folly of felling trees that had no chance of regeneration because of heavy grazing or soil erosion paved the way to total destruction. These homes of tigers and their prey have been lost for ever, as the ghastly sights of the forests of Gwalior, Alwar, Bundi, Udaipur and Jaipur make only too clear.

Natural forests are also being replaced by "man-made" forests for the production of paper, plywood, coffee, tea, rubber, cinchona (for quinine) and eucalyptus. Regions that had remained for so long more or less undisturbed were exploited, the victims of affluence and the attitude of foresters who wanted to "squeeze the last rupee from the forests". This was a complete contrast to the outlook even a decade ago when the old guards were conservators in the real sense.

The construction of irrigation and power dams also introduced a large influx of labourers into the forests. They thinned out the trees to meet their fuel demands and heavy machines operated round the clock, disturbing the habitat. Men working on the dams found shikar the only diversion and destroyed the wildlife recklessly.

Tiger hunting was always a tradition among tribal societies like the Nagas and those living in Manipur and Arunachal. There were tiger clubs called *keirups*, and any tiger coming to the knowledge of members was doomed. It was surrounded on all sides and as the circle closed it was killed by spears and axes. Originally it was a sport, but with the passage of time it became a profession to sell tiger skins. The population of tigers in the tribal areas began to decline very fast, but even as late as March 1972 tiger killing had not stopped in the Khasi hills.

During the festive season in Delhi in December 1968 I conducted a survey in the central fashion market and posh hotels. It was in its way one of the most interesting assignments I ever had, watching women dressed in their best for ten days between 7 and 9 p.m. What a contrast to studying deer and ducks! As my sample each day I took the first hundred women, and out of the total of one thousand there were fifty ladies wearing spotted or striped fur coats. Most of them were foreigners. I interviewed a few Indian ladies on the matter. "It was given to me by my mother," said one. "My husband gave it to me as a wedding present; he is a forest officer," explained another. They also informed me that they were only wearing them because they had them and had no desire to acquire a new one. The fault, they declared, was not theirs: the animals were killed long before the ladies got their coats . . .

Delhi becomes very cold in December–January when there is a snow fall in the Himalayas and temperatures below zero are recorded. Indian women put on woollen capes, but, being largely vegetarian, they do not like the thought of skins being ripped to decorate themselves. Spotted and striped skins, therefore, were almost entirely exported to the West and to the East.

Once I was deputed to conduct a Canadian minister and his wife to the wild-life sanctuaries of Rajasthan. At Jaisamand they watched a pair of leopards for nearly an hour. When I went to the airport to see them off although it was a cold January night I found the lady carrying her leopard coat over her arm. "Believe me," she said, "I will not put this coat on again."

The pace of the person-to-person campaign to stop the heavy drain on our leopards and tigers was too slow for me, and I decided to raise the tempo. But how? I talked it over with my friend Razia, a charming lady on one of the national newspapers, and we devised a plan. She was to pose as a lady shortly to be married who was to be given a choice fur coat as a present from her brother in England. A photographer would take a picture of her in the coat in order to get it approved by her brother before he bought it. And so we went from shop to shop, taking stock of the pelts and having a perfect excuse to photograph them.

One shopkeeper informed us he had a regular supply of 1000 snow leopard skins a year. Another specialized in clouded leopard skins and his annual supply was nearly 2000. Countless leopard skins were neatly piled up in his shop: he said he had nearly 3000 on view and double that number in his warehouse. An interesting piece of information came to light: most of the exports were to East Africa. I could not understand this carrying of coals to Newcastle, for Africa has far more leopards than we have in India. I was told that in Kenya leopard skins could be sold at a much higher price because of the numerous tourists who went there; also, the local traders could obtain a certificate of origin for these imports which came in handy for smuggling Kenyan leopard skins. The illegal killings of Indian leopards were being utilized to legalize the killing of leopards in Kenya. The vicious circle had no end, and the leopards of both countries were losing ground.

I counted 22 tiger heads and all seemed to be laughing at us; probably they were mocking at our mission. There were hundreds of tiger rugs, and I pulled out four and spread them out on the floor. The trader immediately offered me a 30×40 ft carpet for $10,000. I asked if one was readily available. "Yes," said he, "but you will have to place a firm order as I have to bring it from a palace." I found a ready excuse to decline the offer.

The next shop had just as many skins. "The fur of cubs is softer," said the shopkeeper, adding that it required nearly 80 skins of leopard cubs to make a coat. After taking photographs of the lady wearing various coats and counting the stock we concluded our investigations.

The soft pelts of snow leopards, which the ladies love best and from which the shopkeepers earn a substantial profit, came in a steady flow of 600–800 skins per year in the fashion market. Snow leopards are so rare that even people living in the Himalayan regions hardly ever see them. They live at an altitude of about 12,000 feet where they prey on marmots, musk deer and snow hares. Occasionally they come down to the lower pastures but hardly ever have a chance to attack the sheep of the ever-vigilant Gujars. But some of the graziers, renowned as tough walkers and climbers, who for the six summer months live above 8000 feet, are tempted by the lucrative offers of the valleys. Equipped with firearms and living in rugged mountainous areas where there is little chance of the civil law being enforced, these men become poachers and soon run amok, endangering the whole wildlife of the Himalayas. They chase the snow leopard relentlessly, showing no mercy to pregnant females or mothers with suckling cubs. Abandoning their sheep, they go all out to stalk snow leopards, leopards, lynx and martens for their pelts and musk deer for their musk pods. Down the valley they go to the emporiums, where they get their loans paid off quickly and even obtain the lure of extra money.

The story of the striped skins is equally pathetic. In the Dehra Dun forests I heard of a tiger held up in a snare for two painful days. When the Wildlife Officer came to dispatch the beast it broke its paw and ran off into the jungle to die an agonizing death. Another tiger was stoned to death in the Umariya forests of Madhya Pradesh in 1970. Sometimes villagers trap tigers and invite influential persons to shoot them at point-blank range.

In my study area of Rajasthan I came across a special class of professional shikaris known as the Bavariyas who are expert burglars. After committing a crime a Bavariya could walk more than 8 km backwards, with his feet pointing in the opposite direction to his movement, to deceive police trackers. In March 1960 while I was camping at Ramgarh in Jaipur I received information that a tigress had been making regular kills so I went to investigate. While the forest guards were busy searching for the pug marks I sat quietly near the village well. Presently a man came towards the well with his clothes stained with blood. I thought he had committed a murder and was about to clean himself, so I loaded my gun and told him to stay where he was. He took me for a police officer but having committed no murder he made no attempt to run away. I told my driver to tie his hands with his turban. The man informed me that he had shot a tiger, not a man. Meanwhile the forest guards had found another man running up the slope of a hill, but being no match for a Bavariya they had abandoned the chase. My captive Bavariya was fined Rs 500 (then $100), but the skin had already gone to market where he made good his loss.

In order to kill a tiger with a low-powered muzzle-loading gun the Bavariya has to hit a vital part from close range. Such country-made guns produce a large hole which reduces the value of the pelt, so they do not use this risky, noisy and uneconomic method of poaching. Instead they obtain free from the villagers a supply of Folidol, DDT or any other poisonous insecticide and smear it on kills made by tigers. After even one gulp the tiger is hardly able to walk away from the carcass, and sometimes a whole family of mother and cubs falls victim in this way. The poacher gets a skin free of holes, readily acceptable in the hungry foreign markets.

This large-scale poaching, especially by poisoning, has proved fatal to the big cats of India. I put most blame on the traders who purchase the pelts and are quite unconcerned how they were obtained. The price of a tiger skin in the later '50s was hardly $50; ten years later it had risen to $500. This was too much of a temptation for habitual poachers to resist, particularly when the average annual income of a man working in the forests is less than what he could make by selling one raw uncured tiger skin.

The results of my investigation with my lady accomplice were published on the front page of the *Indian Express* in 1967. It was followed by numerous letters to the Editor and led to questions in Parliament. A ban was immediately imposed on the export of all kinds of spotted skins, and the firms concerned raised a tremendous hue and cry, presenting their pre-ban commitments for not less than 20,000 skins. Many tigers and leopards not yet born were destined to honour these commitments. The case was presented to the Indian Board for Wildlife with a plea to the Grievances Committee of the Government. The Chairman of IBWL, a young and effective minister, Dr Karan Singh, reacted sharply: "In that case we have grievances against the Grievances Committee." The ban on the export of skins was imposed effectively in 1968.

Then of course the firms started to give wrong declarations, coining names of sources not to be found in any book. Skins started to come to me from the Customs Office for verification and I found most interesting cases of adulteration. Wild cat skins bearing the designs of leopard spots were printed with a special dye. My problem was whether I should call them the skins of a spotted cat, a banned item, or merely the skins of wild cats which were free of export control? To save the wild cats, whose pelts ran into a few thousands annually, I declared them to be adulterated skins which could not be identified for export.

Once the channel of commercial export had been stopped the skins started going out of the country as personal baggage, for which there were no restrictions. Also the cunning traders dispatched skins roughly stitched into the shape of pants and coats since the export of tailored pieces was not controlled. Traders and shikar companies formed a strong lobby, and the representatives of foreign trade argued against a total ban on the export of tiger skins on the grounds that these earned much-needed foreign exchange.

I waited for another opportunity and it was not long in coming. The Tenth General Assembly of the International Union for the Conservation of Nature and Natural Resources met in New Delhi in November 1969. In her inaugural speech the then Prime Minister, Mrs Indira Gandhi, to everyone's surprise declared: "We need foreign exchange, but not at the cost of the life and liberty of some of the most beautiful inhabitants of this continent." This silenced the foreign trade advocates and shikar outfitters once and for all.

Up till then one always had to contend with the indifference of the public who continued to admire photographs of hunters with one foot on a dead tiger, their deadly telescopic rifle resting on the trophy. Such pictures constantly appeared in popular magazines, and the image had to be destroyed. That is why I had concentrated on a publicity campaign giving glimpses of the personal lives of the tigers in Delhi Zoo to the press. Having created the right psychological climate, the time was ripe to tell the people that the Indian tiger was on its way out. The people were shocked. My friend Sunil Roy (the then Director

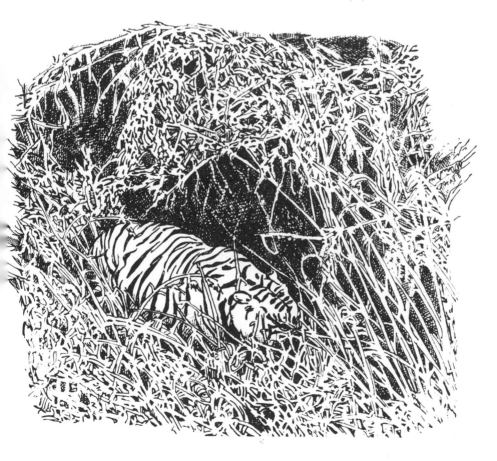

General of Tourism) and I pleaded before the Indian Board for Wildlife for
nothing less than a complete ban on tiger shikar. Various people opposed us on
the grounds of the rights of the "honest sportsman", but they were never that.

My paper entitled "The Vanishing Indian Tiger" was presented to the IUCN
meeting on 29 November 1969. This proved to be a red letter day for the tiger,
which was entered in the *Red Data Book* as an endangered species. The Report
of the Expert Committee, of which I was Secretary, criticized the Forest
Department for its neglect of the interests of wildlife. This enraged my colleagues in the Forest Service and I was declared a rebel. Though severely
criticized at the time, the Report was to become a landmark in the history of
nature conservation in India and a guide for all future measures, including the
Wildlife Protection Act of 1972 and the inauguration of Project Tiger.

Meanwhile, in 1970 India placed a total ban on tiger shooting and soon other
countries followed. Mrs Gandhi wrote personal letters to the heads of all the
States, but unfortunately the short period between the IUCN meeting and the
imposition of the ban proved to be the worst period yet for the tiger. Everybody
wanted to bag his tiger before the law became effective. Short-sighted self-
seekers distributed their last favours to friends, and more tigers were shot in
those few months than in any year of the preceding decade.

Many protests and appeals were made to the Government, shikar companies
pressed for last permits, fur traders pleaded for relaxation to enable them to
honour their commitments. One shikar operator named A. Imam, popularly
known as "Two Two", wrote an open letter to the Prime Minister implying
that she had been misguided. He quoted wrong figures, claimed the loss of
foreign exchange, and alleged the capital loss of over 60 million rupees as a
result of 50,000 cattle killed by tigers every year. In another letter, to Dr
Karan Singh, the writer, P. C. Barua Raja of Gauripur, claimed that the ban on
tiger shooting cost India Rs 30 million annually. In a letter to *The Cheetal* I
advised people to ignore these false claims. The claim of the shikar operators
was that as free citizens of India they should enjoy freedom of trade. The ban on
tiger hunting and the export of skins had, they said, deprived them of their
legitimate trade and livelihood. The case was argued on behalf of the Government, or rather I would say on behalf of the Indian tiger, by a learned government lawyer.

In February 1971 Delhi High Court was the scene of this significant event.
The hall was full to capacity with ex-maharajas, jagirdars and landlords who
had taken up tiger shikar as a business, as well as travel agents who had joined
them in their venture.

The judge read and reread passages from my paper on "The Vanishing
Indian Tiger" in which I had stressed that pregnant tigresses and tigresses with
cubs at heel were being killed. It appealed to his heart as well as his head on the
grounds of national interest and in the first hearing the tiger won the case. After

that most of the shikar companies pulled down their shutters or changed their signboards.

Unfortunately the lucrative trade in skins did not stop, and curio shops and fur traders continued to encourage poachers to poison tigers. The next step was to ban the export of skins even as personal baggage, but still the traders continued to collect and hoard in the hope of some relaxation in the export regulations.

Clearly, more effective methods were needed. The timely visit of Guy Mountfort, a trustee of the WWF, on 10 April 1972 was just what was required. He met our Prime Minister and promised one million dollars to go towards tiger conservation. Next day Dr Karan Singh was appointed Chairman of a task force to conduct a thorough Inquiry and work out a proposal while I was appointed Officer on Special Duty to prepare a plan of action; the minister presented the proposal to the Prime Minister in September 1972. This was the birth of Project Tiger.

CHAPTER 13

Project Tiger

It was my privilege to be a member of the task force for setting up Project Tiger and to prepare the draft plan. The proposals were based on the information I had collected in my field studies under the Jawaharlal Nehru Fellowship, as described in Part I of this book. These proposals detailed the need to eliminate all the many factors contributing to the tiger's decline: habitat destruction and disturbance caused by forestry operations and cattle grazing; the loss of prey populations by poaching and by competition with domestic stock; and the killing of wildlife in general for trophies and trade.

To re-emphasize a very important point: predators like the tiger are second-stage consumers which cannot be preserved in isolation. They require primary consumers (prey), which depend on producers (vegetation), which in turn depend on converters (micro-organisms in the soil). Any plan to preserve the tiger therefore requires a thorough knowledge of the whole range of prey populations and their habitat, including the socio-economic behaviour of humans. It is important to guard against certain fancy ideas of wildlife management whereby the habitat would be manipulated to increase the wildlife population to an artificially high level.

The broad concepts of Project Tiger were clear: it would be committed to the philosophy of total environmental preservation in selected areas and nature would be allowed to play its part fully. Management would be limited to eliminating or at least minimizing human disturbance and to repairing the damage already done by man.

We began cautiously. Instead of spreading our thin resources all over the country we decided to concentrate on nine specific areas in different ecosystems. We lost no time in producing well-documented "management plans", and Project Tiger was launched at the Corbett National Park on 1 April 1973 – by a curious coincidence exactly 20 years to the day since I started my career in the Forest Service. Some people called it a "quixotic project"; but at least their complacency helped us to work undisturbed.

For economic reasons alone it would have been impossible to preserve the whole of tigerland, as that would have meant the elimination, or at least the drastic alteration, of a number of forestry operations. That was neither necessary nor possible in a developing country like India. The criteria for selecting the nine areas as reserves were that each should be representative of a certain type of tiger habitat; that the habitat should be as undisturbed as possible; that the

population of wild animals including tigers should be adequate or their development potential high; and that there should be no competing factors like copper
or coal mining, the harvesting of valuable timber, or any other vital economic
or human consideration. As far as possible the reserves should be in different
States of the Union so that each State should be responsible for giving the tiger
reserve due priority in management.

Jon Tinker, who visited India when we were finalizing our plans, wrote an
article in *New Scientist* of 28 March 1974 entitled "Can India save the tiger?"
He remarked: "While India's plans to save the tiger are not scientifically perfect,
they are politically shrewd and realistic." Probably he had relied too much on
the census figures, which were only one of the factors we considered in selecting
an area as a reserve, or on Professor Leyhausen's arbitrary figure of 300 as a
viable population of tigers. I feel sure that with the ecological information
and biological studies of the tiger presented here, and the successes we have
already had, he and others will be convinced that the project is also scientifically
sound, even if there is always scope for improvement.

If the habitat is basically good and is given protection the reactions are bound
to be favourable. The tiger, who is only one part of it, will automatically
increase. In fact this has already happened in all the reserves. The latest count
in the reserves shows the following increases: 31 to 51 in Manas, 22 to 30 in
Palamau, 17 to 60 in Similipal, 44 to 73 in Corbett, 14 to 22 in Ranthambhor,
43 to 54 in Kanha, 27 to 57 in Melghat, 10 to 26 in Bandipur, and 50 to 181 in
the Sundarbans. (In the case of the Sundarbans the initial count could not cover
the whole area.) These increases have been compared with the figures from the
1972 census; the recent figures (556) are more dependable. Although this includes 55 cubs born this year, the figures are not all the result of reproduction;
some tigers came into the area and stayed on when they found it to their
liking.

The nine original tiger reserves (another, Periyar in the Western Ghats, is to
be added) are plotted on the map. We would have wished to add a few more to
the list, for example one on the Bastar plateau – notorious for man-eaters –
in Madhya Pradesh; another in Balfakram, in the evergreen forests of the Garo
hills in Meghalaya; still others in Dudwa in the Terai in Uttar Pradesh. Then
there are the famous foothills Terai forests of Cooch Behar in West Bengal;
and Sariska in Rajasthan. Due to limited financial resources and other practical
considerations they could not be included, but slowly they too are likely to be
brought under the umbrella of the Project.

India's tiger reserves are of course not as large as Wood Buffalo National
Park for bison in Canada, nor the Serengeti in Tanzania or the Tsavo National
Park in Kenya, famous for their lions and elephants respectively. Because of
India's high density of human population there are no large tigerlands com-
pletely free from human disturbance. But still, in spite of the heavy pressure

on land and forest produce, forests of 12,000 sq km have been set aside under
Project Tiger as reserves to be scientifically managed. The central funds
amount to nearly Rs 4 million, and the sacrifice by way of loss of timber and
other resources is substantial.

The wildlife of a country nowadays is of more than local interest. International concern was voiced over the dwindling of the tiger, the most magnificent of the world's predators, in its natural home. To save it is an international
responsibility, and the call to support Project Tiger through the World Wildlife
Fund received a prompt response from all over the world. The imaginative
publicity campaign, which included painting competitions for children and the
selling of special stamps to collect funds, reached almost every door. Small and
large donations in cash or kind poured in and the WWF collected more than
one million US dollars.

Project Tiger was piloted by its Chairman, the Federal cabinet minister Dr
Karan Singh, as his personal responsibility assigned to him by Mrs Gandhi
during the first four years of the Project. No conservation project is ever
popular to begin with because it imposes restrictions and even sacrifices, and
there are no immediate economic gains. This is especially so in the case of a
project which aims at total environmental preservation and where the guiding
principles are: "Do nothing and allow no one else to do anything." My task of
implementing the Project for its first three years was certainly challenging.
Experts wrote to tell me why it would fail, and even many wildlife enthusiasts
had doubts about its success. Some of my colleagues laughed at the idea of a
campaign to stop forestry fellings and the grazing of domestic cattle, even more
at the prospect of shifting villages. There was no precedent for such a programme; and perhaps their scepticism was justified.

The scheme depended for its implementation on the State governments,
who were in no mood to accept controls, particularly in the harvesting of
timber. But the Prime Minister's message clearly spelled out the policy, and
they accepted their responsibilities. The direction was that "Forestry practices,
designed to squeeze the last rupee out of our jungles, must be radically
reorientated at least within our national parks and sanctuaries, and pre-
eminently in the tiger reserves. The narrow outlook of the accountant must give
way to a wider vision of the recreational, educational and ecological value."
The query, "Is it beyond our administrative or political competence to achieve
this?" put us on our toes and we accepted the challenge. In the reserves felling
was stopped, cattle were removed, and villages were shifted.

I watched the people moving their belongings, and they did so not reluctantly
but enthusiastically, happy to start an easier life free from the problems of wild
animals destroying their crops. I asked one man, called Jagan, of Annantpura in
Ranthambhor, how he felt at leaving the home of his forefathers. He replied
that all their lives he and his family had spent cold winter nights scaring sambar

and wild boars away, and he was looking forward to an undisturbed life in their new home. Jagan's wife gave birth to a son – her first child after twelve years of marriage – soon after. Everyone was given a house, more land than he had had and community facilities far better than he had enjoyed before. They entered into the mainstream of the life of the country.

A prophet is without honour in his own land, and I was not sure how seriously the Project would be taken up in my home State of Rajasthan. I had my vehicle boldly painted with the tiger of the Project and the panda of the WWF and sent it to Ranthambhor. The villagers, and even the district authorities, had never seen such an impressive vehicle even in the times of the maharajas. It had the desired effect, and the people were convinced of our seriousness. I was told that they thought the vehicle had been specially sent by the Government!

Having enlisted the support of the district authorities we were able to make the necessary restrictions really effective, and the reserve took shape so quickly that it was the first of the few to be free from cattle. The others were not far behind. Generous donations of speed boats for the delta of the Sundarbans, elephants for the rain forests of Manas, camels for the arid land of Ranthambhor, and bullock carts for Melghat enabled our protection forces to move much faster than would otherwise have been possible. For the use of the flying squads each reserve has been provided with jeeps with diesel engines to save on running costs. The poachers were broken, physically and psychologically, both by these methods of apprehending them and by the weight of public opinion against them. Our use of radios further demoralized them and gave confidence to our own men in the interior where means of communication were poor.

All this has paid huge dividends. The habitat has improved in all the reserves and the population of tigers has increased – it was good to know the tigers themselves seemed to approve!

One of our main problems was to recruit the right people to implement Project Tiger. A scheme of this nature needs zeal, faith and dedication. How were we to find such committed personnel? After the inevitable teething troubles we acquired a dozen hand-picked officers, and I took them to East Africa to gain experience of national parks. This visit cemented their dedication. They have become involved in the Project not for promotion nor for extra money – which is hardly there – but for the sake of their convictions and the faith they have developed for the cause of conservation. I had my satisfaction when one of them, Sinha, said that the prospect of only eight years left to work for the service was far too short, and he wished he had become involved with wildlife earlier. Before, he had hardly handled a camera in his life, but soon he is to have a one-man show of his elephant pictures explaining their ecology.

In Kanha, Panwar is mad about his Minolta camera, capturing the ecological changes in the meadows and studying the causes of depletion of the vanishing swamp deer. C. B. Singh protests even about angling with line and rod in the

Ramganga River in Corbett Park; he is a purist. Debroy exchanges fire with poachers even at night in Manas and they know full well that he is a crack shot. Wesley's wife but for her age and the responsibility of grown-up children would have gone to the law court over his absences. Koppikar has lived most of his life as a married bachelor so his new life-style in the Project does not bother him; he prefers a bullock cart to a jeep. Fateh Singh's wife is a Rajput girl who is used to neglect as part of her traditions, so she is unlikely to protest. Saroj is virtually living with Khairi, a tigress in the Similipal hills. The commitment is total and the team is perfect.

Common palm civet

In India we who manage the reserves are all foresters. In forestry we are used to the slow growth of trees and do not expect to enjoy the fruits of our labour in our lifetime. But the success of Project Tiger in just two years has dazzled even the field directors. No axe falls on any tree, no saw moves on dead or fallen wood. Dead animals are left on the forest floor once again to become a part of nature with the help of scavengers and termites and bacterial converters. Even bleached bones and shed antlers are not allowed to be removed for what some people call "better economic use" because even dried meat fibre is somebody's food, and bones a source of calcium. Death and decay are part of nature's process and are allowed to proceed undisturbed. Our prescriptions of management are more rigid than in a national park, and this is one of the main reasons why we prefer to call them tiger reserves.

The springs have revived. The flowers bloom, no longer browsed by domestic stock. The ungulates have all the space they need and their population has increased. Tiger sightings are more frequent and there has been a baby boom. In Jaipur Zoo I failed to provide an environment for a tigress to rear her full litter of six cubs, and similarly with two tigresses, Radha and Vindhya, in Delhi Zoo, who gave birth to five cubs; but in Ranthambhor, in one of our reserves, a tigress has successfully brought up five cubs, thus creating a new record of success even in the wild.

You are sure to irritate a Bengali if you are undiplomatic enough to tell him that the Bengal Tiger is not the largest. Equally I will be unhappy if you say that Rajasthan is no place for the tiger to live. Nobody wants to admit that there are no tigers in his land, or that his tigers are smaller, less colourful or less ferocious than other people's. Now the tiger is claimed to be at his best everywhere. The concept of total environmental preservation has paid dividends, and the tiger has once again returned to these areas to the surprise of the new generation.

The enthusiasm of people from all over the world, especially the European children who saved their pocket money and sold tiger stamps, was so encouraging that we invited a few of them to come and see the results of their efforts. Particularly encouraging, too, was a note in *International Wildlife* (1975) from Hal H. Harrison and his father George who travelled extensively in the reserves under the sponsorship of the Wildlife Federation of America: "In spite of the cryptic criticism of the non-official wildlife enthusiasts the boys on the firing line are doing a heroic job", they wrote. I feel this compliment is a well-deserved reward.

The project has fully demonstrated that by tradition and training the Indian forester is much better equipped to administer a conservation project than anyone else; this view is shared by my friends the American foresters who manage wildlife habitats.

We must now look a little more closely at the ecology of the tiger reserves. The nine original reserves – Periyar in Kerala is to be added as a tenth – were based on the major ecosystems of tigerland outlined in chapter 4. The full utilization of these different habitats by the wild animals is effected by three natural processes: (1) by seasonal shifts from one habitat to the other according to the availability of water, food and shelter; (2) by adaptive physiological functions to ensure conservation of energy during a "pinch" period and the storage of energy in the form of fat during a time of plenty; (3) by individual selective feeding habits, as described in chapter 5.

The changing facets of the ecological units of tigerland depend on seasonal variations in temperature, moisture and soil which affect the vegetation.

Thus during the rains the luxuriant growth of grass and other vegetation

MOVEMENT OF ANIMALS
ACCORDING TO SEASON

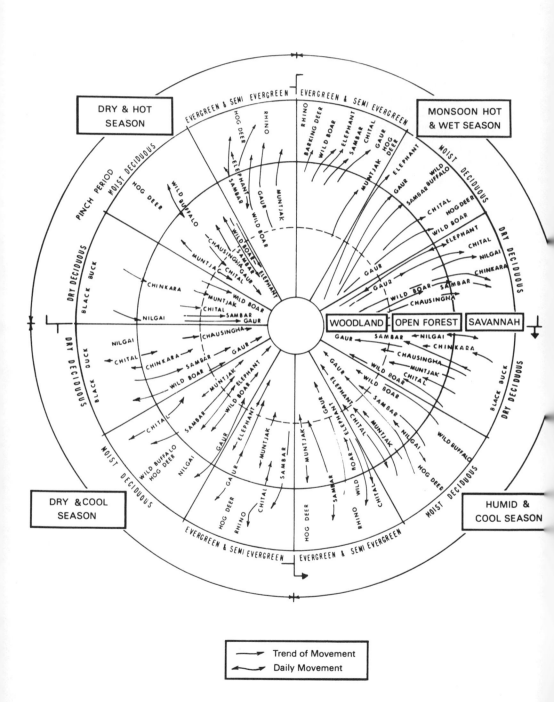

attracts all wild ungulates to the savannas in all habitat types. Elephants, gaur and sambar, which are animals of the woodland, also come to the savannas to graze along with chital, barking deer, nilgai, buffalo and chinkara. As the savanna does not provide cover for elephant, gaur and sambar they retreat to cover each day to rest. The habitat can stand such heavy pressure of grazing because of the rich growth of vegetation during the monsoon season.

As soon as the rains stop in October the grasses begin to dry and the animals feel the pinch of competition. They start spacing themselves out. The elephant and gaur turn to the bamboo forests inside the thickets to seek cool shade from the October sun. Wild buffalo, nilgai and hog deer continue to graze on dry coarse grass in the savanna; but wild boar, sambar and chital shift back to the open woodlands to feed on the drying grasses which have not yet been used.

From January to March is the season of confusion. After the winter burn, grasses grow again on the open savannas and the animal concentrations return. They also feed in the woodlands on the flowers and fruits of zizyphus, mahuwa and aonla (*Phyllanthus officinalis*) trees. Elephants and gaur still remain in thickets near waterholes.

By the time the hot dry season starts in April the savannas have been over-grazed or burnt and there is no chance of their regrowth during the summer unless there is a good shower of rain, which more often fails. The waterholes dry up, but the thickets escape fires and still have water in the pools of their many streams. Leaf litter may serve as alternative food, and even trees like bel, tendu fruit and legumes produce pods which supplement the shortage of fodder and attract ungulates to the thickets in summer.

Rhesus macaque

My visits to Ranthambhor and Kanha during the first rains were revealing: as the leaf fodder of the thickets gets wet it develops mould and becomes unfit to eat. Mosquitoes and leeches increase their activity in the evergreen forests, and the drip of raindrops falling from the trees, even after the rain stops, troubles the animals. In all three habitat types the hot, humid, closed thickets become no place to stay. Once again the fauna concentrates in the open, breezy, mosquito-free savannas where grasses grow luxuriantly and there are waterholes in plenty.

Tigers of course follow their prey, visiting the savannas during the rains and the thickets and forests in summer. The best tigerland is therefore a combination of all three ecosystems, where it is possible for predator and prey to migrate from one to the other in different seasons to overcome deficiencies. However, since so many routes have been blocked by urbanization, agriculture and denudation, seasonal migrations have become almost impossible except from the dry deciduous to evergreen habitats of the foothill forests of the Himalayas, the Western Ghats and the Eastern Ghats of Orissa. Movements of animals are limited to shifts from savanna to thickets, both seasonally and in the course of a day.

In the absence of a favourable area such as continuous dry deciduous forests, animals adjust to adverse conditions by slowing down their life activity. They change their coat and utilize their stored fat to get through the "pinch period". The sambar and wild boars in Sariska and Ranthambhor look particularly ugly and gaunt at these times, but with the first flush of foliage they look healthy immediately. Surprisingly both blue bulls and chinkara look healthier. They seem to like the heat, and are untroubled by the lack of water. In the case of the tiger his pinch period is during the rains when stalking becomes difficult due to the thick vegetation, and the drenching rain also limits his preying hours.

The tiger is not doomed. He is at home in all the habitat types, in temperatures as high as 47°C in the shade in Ranthambhor or below zero in the sub-montane region of the Himalayas. The bone-dry hot winds of Rajasthan do not bother the tiger any more than the moisture-laden air of Assam where the annual rainfall is over 5000 mm (200 inches). He is equally at home in the flat plains of the Terai, the rugged hills of the Siwaliks, the Sundarbans swamps, and the sandy semi-desert country of Jaipur. He drinks the clean, sweet water of mountain streams but also thrives on the muddy, brackish backwaters of the tidal swamps. This tremendous capacity to adjust explains why he has survived in spite of what man has inflicted on him.

We have also seen that the tiger belongs to a biologically fertile species. He matures at the age of about four years, retains the power to reproduce for about ten years, and disappears soon after he has discharged his biological function. The sex ratio in a natural population we have seen is about 48:52, or 10% more females. Although the average number of cubs born in a litter is 2·9 the survival

*After the mating season blue bulls group
into parties of up to 50*

rate is only 1·9, and by the time the cubs have passed through the hazards of their early life this figure is reduced to only 1 per litter. Since the cubs remain with their mother until they are nearly two years old, tigresses deliver only once in two years. Armed with this biological information we can attempt to calculate the reproductive rate.

Assuming that in a population of 100 there are 52 tigresses, if they are distributed uniformly in all age groups then there are 26 capable of reproduction at any one time. Of these, 13 tigresses produce a litter each year. With the estimated rate of survival, we find that only 13 tigers or less are added to a population of 100 in any one year.

We have the well-documented history of the pair of tigers, one white and one normal, caught in the forests of Rewa in 1950. Their progeny amounted to 64 before the effects of inbreeding appeared. There was normal infant mortality, the mature individuals passed through their reproductive period, the old ones died. The reproductive rate works out at 17·06%, but since the data comes from Delhi Zoo it cannot be compared to natural conditions, though in ideal natural conditions breeding is far more successful in the wild than in a zoo; even so, we may consider it to represent maximum productivity. In nature where there are so many unknown variables it would be safer to consider the reproduction rate to be half this figure, that is about 6–8%.

In a special report (1976) Professor Leyhausen underrates the success of Project Tiger when he considered the reproductive rate to be not more than 2%. How he arrived at this figure is not known, for he gives no explanation and quoted no figures in support of it. At the Third Cat Symposium in 1974 Professor Leyhausen remarked that Project Tiger was largely a dream; but the dream has come true.

A reproductive rate of 6–8% is about the same as that of the lion, as estimated by Schaller in Serengeti, and the lion is in no danger of extinction. For a major predator like the tiger such a rate is quite satisfactory.

Since the life-style of tigers causes them to be spaced over a large territory with a wide range of environmental conditions, at any given time there are always some which are not exposed to adverse conditions or natural calamities. This ensures the survival of at least some members of the species, and should always be sufficient to revive the race in adverse conditions. If tigers lived in prides like lions they would by now have been wiped out by trophy hunters and fur traders; their solitary way of life has saved them. Nor has the species developed any specialization which could be detrimental. A tiger's feeding habits are non-ceremonial: he will eat a live animal or one killed by others, and he does not turn up his nose at diseased carcasses or crabs and fish when necessary. The mother-cub relationship is intense and tigresses see that their cubs go through a thorough and elaborate training. Above all, tigers do not hold territories and waste their energies or even their lives in territorial fights, nor do they indulge in cannibalism.

Psychologically the tiger is not a nervous type who would abandon a habitat because of human disturbance unless he was actually driven out. He tolerates man, adjusting his ways if necessary to achieve a peaceful coexistence, and even lives in the vicinity of villages without waging war on man or his cattle. This is amply demonstrated by the tigers living in Sariska where human disturbance by woodcutters, cattle-keepers and visitors is at a maximum. They use the same road at night that has been used by hundreds of men during the day; they visit the same waterhole that has been used by man an hour earlier. The tiger waits for the passing of the last bus, or the ringing of the last temple bell confirming nightfall, to begin his hunting prowl. He is by no means a doomed species in the grand process of evolution; on the contrary, he is ideally suited to live as the dominant predator in his natural environment.

It is a truism to say that the more we learn the more we realize how little we know, and none of us would claim that we know the last word about the tiger. We are still learning, not only the things we should do to promote his welfare but also the things we should *not* do. For example, I suggest that the idea that tigers bred in captivity can be released in the wild is unsound. An individual who has to operate on his own, to be able to search for food and defend himself, has to learn how to do so by rigorous training: learning by trial and error is a long process unsuitable for species with a relatively short life span. It is even more risky in the case of a predator who has to kill quick-footed animals often bigger than himself. If zoo-born or hand-reared cubs are released at too early an age they are sure to die of starvation; and if they are released later their familiarity with man may result in their becoming man-eaters. When we were planning Project Tiger we heard that John Aspinall had 32 tigers on his estate near Canterbury, Kent, and was keen to send us some to help restock the depleted areas of India, but we turned down his kind offer.

Some form of Safari Park with the provision of live baits to enable growing tigers to be trained through easy stages might work, but it is still doubtful how such animals would fare in the jungle when confronted with wild ungulates and man. Obviously the provision of live baits could not be continued indefinitely, quite apart from the fact that this cruel practice does not fit in with the philosophy of India.

We have seen that the tiger is an index of environmental quality. He does not stay to eat the last deer, but leaves the area before the final stages of deterioration take place. Unless we are sure that a habitat is suitable it is unwise to introduce the tiger to it on shikari-type information or out of eagerness to grab the headlines. The whole operation is a most complex process. To trap a tiger and move it to a similar type of home needs experimentation; it may work, provided food is ensured for the first few days, and such a calculated risk need not necessarily be abandoned. But we must thoroughly understand what we are doing.

The latest craze for Safari Parks or the creation of zoos is not the answer for saving a species. I have begun to feel that these institutions change their philosophy faster than the weathercock. In Roman times animal collections were made to keep a stock for entertainment in the amphitheatres. Later they called them zoos; as fashion changed they became "Zoological Gardens", later still "Zoological Parks". Now that ecology, environment and the biosphere are all the rage they are suddenly changing their signboards to become "Ecological Centres" or "Biological Parks".

The new zoos are designed on an environmental concept, as indeed we designed the zoo at Delhi. But even with the best designing we have not come

Confrontation between two male bulls

anywhere near this concept. Before they are brought to the zoo the animals are caught – involving an inevitable degree of cruelty – and then shifted from their natural homes. Birds have their wings pinioned – so depriving them of their life's essence, free flight. Why? Purely for our benefit, to see them in "as natural an environment as possible". The whole idea of bringing a free-living animal into captivity is revolting, and simply because they eat well and reproduce in captivity does not mean that a zoo is a proper environment for them.

Zoos boast that wildlife education is an aid to a better understanding of nature. In practice it is no better than the Children's Corner which I abolished. Specimens exhibited in drab enclosures certainly do not convey the sense of what the stripes or the tusks mean to the animal. Museum techniques are now so far advanced that they are quite capable of creating dioramas that can convey the real meaning of the land and those that live in it. Dioramas together with films on wildlife are far more educational than the sight of an animal walking up and down in a cage all his life. If it is not necessary to bring the Grand Canyon or the Taj Mahal, the desert or the rain forests to your city except in pictures why should there be any justification for netting and snaring animals for educational purposes at a zoo? The marvels of nature must be seen where they are, not where they are planted by human hand. With supersonic travel the world has shrunk to be a small place, and it is within the reach of many to appreciate nature's creations in their natural homes. A visit to one natural area to see a few animals is far more satisfying than gaping at a whole collection in a zoo. One should be selective, enjoying a few rather than becoming bored by many.

Someone will say that zoos serve as research laboratories. They do, but that does not entitle them to keep such large collections, particularly those animals not needed for research. Let us not be wasteful in our experiments.

I have seen zoos from Delhi to Dallas, Hyderabad to Honolulu, London to Lucknow, San Diego to Srinagar. I am sure that many zoo directors will agree with me that a zoo is for the most part a confused institution unsure of its objectives. Although it seeks justification in education it is really more of a carnival for entertainment. Except for a few zoos which do a real job of contributing to knowledge their objectives are pure hypocrisy.

After I left Delhi Zoo and spent two years in the wilds I could not become reconciled to the idea of such animal prisons. The idea of starting a zoo in Singapore was proposed to me; the proposal had a lot of money behind it, but my choice had to be for the animals to be free. I was also called to help in designing a zoo at Chandigarh and Bhopal in India; I attended the first meeting and went to select the site, but my conscience did not permit me to proceed any further. I had to request to be excused. I am becoming more and more convinced that zoos with multi-purpose objectives should be abandoned.

So what is the answer? I would suggest we concentrate on creating reserves where man's interference – or what he arrogantly calls "scientific management" – is minimal. I do not like the term "national parks", for it has been too loosely used. The initial meaning of "the untouched glory of God" has been so diluted that it has lost its significance. The term "park" conveys artificiality and the word "national" limits its universal appeal. The pleasure of a visit to a natural area has been destroyed by the influx of tourists with their transistors and trailers. I would condemn even the camera, except in the case of professionals who employ their skill to interpret nature for the benefit of those millions who never get the chance to visit these gardens of Eden. The casual visitor is always in a hurry, and if he takes pictures he fails to see anything around him: his mind is preoccupied with shutter speeds, lens openings and focusing. The uncertainty of the results haunts him for hours after and instead of enjoying a relaxed holiday he is tensed. Many a wildlife photographer does not hesitate to disturb, sometimes even kill an animal, pluck a flower or destroy a tree to suit his picture. The visitor to a reserve should bring with him nothing but a receptive mind, and take away nothing but the understanding that he is only a small part of the whole complex pattern of nature's ecology.

When I close my eyes I see the nests of half a million flamingos in the Rann of Kutch, the carpet of a million flowers in the Himalayan meadows, the deciduous forests in late February with their extravagant reds, the lushness of the evergreen rain forests. I see shaded brooks banked with ferns, with frolicking deer coming down to drink or a tiger sleeping half-submerged in a pool unaware of my presence. In spite of some inevitable moments of sadness or frustration, when I look back over the past half-century I feel I have lived one glorious day after the other, watching the splash of colour of the setting sun, hearing the alarm calls of chital and sambar warning of the presence of a predator prowling in the night.

There is something for everyone in India. In spite of its having had one of the oldest civilizations for over 6500 years there are still untrodden lands and uncharted river courses. There are inexhaustible opportunities to study nature's master-plan and many fields of research still unexploited. Little is known about the rain forests, for example. The 21 species of mammals which are exclusive to India have not been studied at all thoroughly, yet some of them are threatened with extinction. A naturalist may specialize in cats or deer, birds or reptiles – or in my case the tiger – with no fear that the last word has been said. No one has yet documented tigers in all the ecosystems of India. My success is limited to only four reserves and 43 tigers; I wish I could score a century.

The battle to save India's wildlife may not yet have been fully won, but it has certainly not been in vain. More "encounters" and "frequently seen" pug marks in areas where tigers were quite unknown to the present generation are sure signs of rehabilitation. But we must not relax; cracks are appearing even now, as in the incident when a police squad was called to kill an innocent cub which had strayed from a sanctuary into a village. Such incidents, exaggerated to terrify the people and boost the killers as heroes, can become the beginning of the end if the right climate for the tiger is not maintained. I would like to devote the rest of my life to consolidating the gains before they are lost again through ignorance, and the way to do it is through better educational programmes and good public relations. For one thing, I would like to see the shikar books which have distorted the tiger's image removed from the bookshelves – though I admit that at present I do not know how to do it!

I am greatly encouraged by the response of the habitat, the tigers and their prey in the Tiger Reserves. It may be too early to predict the outcome of this effort, but it is surely not too much to hope that ultimately the tiger will be restored to a less precarious position than he is in at present. If I have made myself unpopular with some people in championing the tiger and not allowing them to exploit him for business ends, that is unimportant to me. I have the satisfaction of knowing that I have played a part in maintaining his dignity and not allowing him to be degraded to the status of a trophy, a guinea pig or a frog in a biology class. Some at least of the world's few remaining tigers are being neither hunted nor confined behind bars – they are free. As we become ever more aware of his value we may be sure that the tiger, his associate animals, and the tigerlands of India will continue to delight and inspire generations as yet unborn.

References

ABRAMOV, K. G. 1961. Method of censusing tigers. Symposium on Organization and Methods of Censusing Terrestrial Vertebrate Faunal Resources: Summaries of Reports (Moscow) 4–8 March, 1961, pp. 53–4.

ABRAMOV, V. 1961. A contribution to the biology of the Amur tiger *Panthera tigris longipilis* (Fitzner 1868). *Vestnik Cesklovenske Spolecnosti Zoologicke* 26: 189–203.

ALI, S. 1927. The Moghul Emperors of India as naturalists and sportsmen. *J. Bombay Nat. Hist. Soc.* 31 (4): 833–61.

1938. The wild animals of India and the problem of their conservation. *J. Bombay Nat. Hist. Soc.* 38 (2): 231–40.

1972. *Handbook of common birds of India.* Bombay.

ALVI, M. A. & RAHMAN, A. 1968. *Jahangir the Naturalist.* Nat. Inst. of Scis. of India, New Delhi.

ANDERSON, K. 1957. *Man-eaters and jungle killers.* London.

ANON. The man-eating tiger problem. *Oryx,* 11 (4): 231.

BAIKOV, N. 1925. *The Manchurian Tiger.* Manchurian Research Soc., Harbin.

BAKER, E. 1887. *Sports in Bengal.* London.

BALDWIN, J. 1883. *The large and small game in Bengal and the North-western Provinces of India.* London.

BAZE, W. 1957. *Tiger! Tiger!* London.

BERRIFF, A. 1932. Number of cubs in a tiger's litter. *J. Bombay Nat. Hist. Soc.* 35 (3): 670.

BOURLIERE, F. 1955. *The Natural History of Mammals.* London.

BRANDER, A. D. 1923. *Wild animals in Central India.* London.

1929. Tiger tracks. *J. Bombay Nat. Hist. Soc.* 33 (4): 972.

BURTON, R. G. 1920. A sporting diary of H. H. Bikaner. *J. Bombay Nat. Hist. Soc.* 27 (2): 386.

1933. *The book of the tiger.* London.

BURTON, R. W. 1929. The tiger's method of making a kill. *J. Bombay Nat. Hist. Soc.* 33 (4): 974–6.

1948. Wildlife preservation in India—India's vanishing asset. *J. Bombay Nat. Hist. Soc.* 47: 602–22.

1952. History of Shikar in India. *J. Bombay Nat. Hist. Soc.* 50 (4): 845–69.

1953. *The preservation of wildlife in India. A compilation.* Bangalore.

BUTT, K. S. J. 1963. *Shikar.* London.

CAMPBELL, T. 1894. A tiger eating a bear. *J. Bombay Nat. Hist. Soc.* 9 (1): 101.

CAPPER, Lt. Col. S. 1920. Measurements of tigers. *J. Bombay Nat. Hist. Soc.* 27 (4): 936.

CHAMPION, F. 1927. *With a camera in tiger land.* London.

1929. Tiger tracks. *J. Bombay Nat. Hist. Soc.* 33 (2): 284–7.

CHAMPION, H. G. & SETH S. K. 1968. *Forest types of India.* Delhi.

CHANDRA, HARISH. 1969. Pugmarks of the tiger. A study in movement. *The Cheetal,* Dehra Dun, 12 (1): 73–7.

CHATURVEDI, M. D. 1955. Future of the tiger. *Indian Forester* Dehra Dun, 81 (II): 7334.

CHOUDHARI, A. B. & CHAKRABARTI, K. 1972. Wildlife biology of the Sundarbans Forests. Observations on tigers. *The Cheetal,* Dehra Dun, 15 (1): 11–30.

CHRISTOPHER, S. A. 1937. Tiger-lore in Burma. *J. Bombay Nat. Hist. Soc.* 29: 276–7.

COOCH BEHAR, Maharajah of. 1908. *Big game hunting.* London.

COOPER, G. E. R. 1923. Tiger climbing a tree. *J. Bombay Nat. Hist. Soc.* 29: 276–7.

CORBETT, J. 1944. *The man-eaters of Kumaon.* London.

    1953. *Jungle lore.* London.

CRANDALL, L. 1964. *The management of wild mammals in captivity.* Chicago.

ECKSTEIN, P. & ZUCKERMAN, S. 1956. The oestrus cycle in the mammals. In Marshall, F.H.A. *Physiology of reproduction.* London. pp. 226–396.

ELLERMAN, J. R. & MORRISON-SCOTT, T. C. S. 1966. *Check list of Palaearctic and Indian Mammals.* 2nd ed. London.

ELLISON, B. 1925. *H.R.H. The Prince of Wales's sport in India.* London.

ETON, R. L. 1974. *The Cheetah. The biology, ecology and behaviour of an endangered species.* New York.

FAWCUS, L. 1943. *Report of the Game and Fishes Preservation Committee on the existing species of game in Bengal.* Bengal Government, Calcutta.

FEND, W. 1972. *Die Tiger von Abutschmar.* Wien.

FLETCHER, F. W. F. 1911. *Sport on the Nilgiris and in Wynaad.* London.

FORSYTH, J. 1872. *The highlands of Central India.* London.

GEE, E. P. 1964. *The wildlife of India.* London.

GLASFORD, A. 1903. *Leaves from an Indian jungle.* Bombay.

    1928. *Musing of an old shikari.* London.

GORDON-CUMMING, Col. R. G. 1812. *Wild men and wild beasts.* London.

HAKIM-UDDIN, H. 1960. *Big game adventure.* Agra.

HAMILTON, D. 1892. *Records of Sports in Southern India.* London.

HARRISON, H. Can wildlife survive in India? *International Wildlife.* 5 (5): 41–9.

HENRICH, H. 1972. *A Report on Sunderban Tigers.* IUCN, Morges.

HICKS, F. 1910. *Forty years among the wild animals of India.* Allahabad.

HIGGINS, J. C. 1934. The game animals and birds of Manipur State with notes on their numbers, migration and habits. *J. Bombay Nat. Hist. Soc.* 37 (2): 307–8.

HORN, H. 1966. Measurement of overlap in ecological studies. *Amer. Nat.* 100: 611–17.

IMAM, A. 1970. J'accuse. *The Cheetal,* Dehra Dun, 13 (1): 51–4.

INGLIS, J. 1888. *Tent life in tiger land.* London.

IUCN 1969. *Red Data Book* vol. 1, Mammalia. Morges, Switzerland.

JOHNSON, D. 1827. *Sketches of Indian field sports with observations on the animals.* London.

KHAN, ABDUL SHAKUR. 1935. *Shikar events.* Tonk.

    1963. *Some narrow escapes.* London.

KHAN, I. 1936. Association between a leopard and a tigress. *J. Bombay Nat. Hist. Soc.* 39: 155–6.

KITCHENER, H. J. 1961. The importance of protecting the Malayan tiger. *Malay. Nat. J.,* Kuala Lumpur, 21st Anniv. Spec. Issue pp. 202–6.

KRISHNAN, M. 1975. *India's Wildlife in 1959–70.* Bombay.

LOCKE, A. 1954. *The Tigress of Trengganu.* London.

LOUKASHKIN, A. S. 1938. The Manchurian Tiger. *The China Journal*, Shanghai 28: 127–33.

LYDEKKER, R. 1907. *The game animals of India, Burma and Tibet*. London.

MACKEYS, E. 1931. *Further excavations of Mohenjodaro and the Indus Civilization*. London.

MARSHALL, J. 1931. *Mohenjodaro and the Indus Civilization*. London.

MARTIN, C. 1975. Status and ecology of Barasinga in Kanha National Park. Unpubl. MS.

MAZAK, V. 1965. *Der Tiger, Panthera tigris Linnaeus 1758*. Wittenberg Lutherstadt.
1968. Nouvelle sous-éspèce de tigre provenant de l'Asie du sud-est. *Mammalia* 32: 104–12.

MEDWAY, Lord. 1969. *The wild mammals of Malaya and offshore islands including Singapore*. Kuala Lumpur.

MORRIS, R. 1927. A tigress with five cubs. *J. Bombay Nat. Hist. Soc.* 31 (3): 810–11.

NATH, B. 1966. Animals of prehistoric India and their affinities with those of the western Asiatic countries. *Records of the Indian Museum* 59 (4): 335–67.

ORIENTAL SPORTING MAGAZINE 1828–1833. 1873. London.

PEACOCK, E. H. 1933. *A game book for Burma and adjoining territories*. London.

PERRY, R. 1964. *The world of the tiger*. London.

PETZSCH, H. 1969. *Die Katzen*. Basel.

PILGRIM, G. E. 1913. Correlation of the Siwaliks with mammal horizons of Europe. *Rec. Geol. Surv. India* 34: 264–326.
1932. Fossil Carnivora of India. *Pal. Indica* N.S. 18: 1–232.

POCOCK, R. 1929. Tigers. *J. Bombay Nat. Hist. Soc.* 33: 505–41.

POLLOCK, F. 1896. *Fifty years of reminiscences of India*. London.

POLLOCK, F. T. & THOM, W. S. 1900. *Wild sports of Burma and Assam*. London.

PRATER, H. 1929. On the occurrence of tigers on the islands of Bombay and Salsette. *J. Bombay Nat. Hist. Soc.* 33 (4): 973.
1940. The number of tigers shot in reserved forests in India and Burma during the year 1937–8. *J. Bombay Nat. Hist. Soc.* 41 (4): 881–9.
1965. *The book of Indian animals*. Bombay.

PROJECT TIGER—A Report. 1972. Govt. of India Publ., New Delhi.

RICE, W. 1857. *Hunting experiences on foot in Rajpootana*. London.

RUSSELL, C. E. M. 1900. *Bullet and Sport in Indian Forests, Plains and Hills*. London.

SADLEIR, R. M. F. S. 1966. Notes on production in the larger Felidae. *Int. Zoo Year Book* (ed. C. Jarvis), London 6: 184–7.

SANDERSON, G. 1912. *Thirteen years among the wild beasts of India*. Edinburgh.

SANKHALA, K. S. 1967. Breeding behaviour of the tiger in Rajasthan. *Int. Zoo Year Book*, London 7: 133–47.
1970. The vanishing Indian tiger. *Proc. IUCN 11th Technical Meeting* II: 34–5.
1976. Pugmark tracer. *The Cheetal*, Dehra Dun, 17 (1): 25–33.

SCHALLER, G. 1967. *The deer and the tiger*. Chicago.
1972. *The Serengeti Lion*. Chicago.

SHAHI, S. P. 1977. *Back to the wall*. New Delhi.

SHILLINGFORD, J. L. 1920. On methods of measuring tigers. *J. Bombay Nat. Hist. Soc.* 27 (2): 391.

SINGH, ARJAN. 1973. *Tiger Haven*. London.

SINGH, GIRAJ. 1972. The ban on tiger hunting. An evaluation. *The Cheetal*, Dehra Dun, 15 (1): 31–3.

SINGH, K. 1959. *The tiger of Rajasthan*. London.

SINGH, R. I. 1971. *Geography of India*. Varanasi.

SINHA, J. P. 1976. Mating seasons in tigers in Palamau Tiger Reserve. *The Cheetal*, Dehra Dun, 18 (1 & 2): 46–55.

SMITH, T. E. H. 1947. Sense of smell in tigers. *J. Bombay Nat. Hist. Soc.* 46 (4): 713.

SMYTHIES, E. 1942. *Big game shooting in Nepal*. London.

SMYTHIES, O. 1953. *Tiger Lady*. London.

SOMERVILLE, A. 1924. *Shikar near Calcutta*. London.

THORNTON, I. W. B., YEUNG, K. K. & SANKHALA, K. S. 1967. The genetics of the white tigers of Rewa. *J. Zool.* London. 152: 127–35.

TINKER, J. 1974. Will India save the tiger? *New Scientist* 61: 802–5.

TOD, J. 1832. *Annals and antiquities of Rajasthan*. London.

TROUP, R. S. 1921. *Silviculture of Indian trees*. Oxford.

VATS, M. S. 1940. *Excavations at Harrapa*. Calcutta.

WARD, R. 1922. *Records of big game*. 8th ed. London.

WARDROP, A. E. 1923. *Indian big game*. London.

WILDLIFE CONSERVATION IN INDIA—A Report. 1970. Govt. of India Publ., New Delhi.

WORLD'S CATS. *Proc. III Int. Symposium on the World's Cats, April 26-8, 1976*, p. 92. Ed. Eaton, R. University of Washington, Seattle.

ZUCKERMAN, S. 1953. The breeding season of mammals in captivity. *Proc. Zool. Soc. London*, 122 (1): 827–50.

Index